INTRODUCTION
TO
THE HISTORY
OF RELIGIONS

INTRODUCTION TO THE HISTORY OF RELIGIONS

Joachim Wach

*Edited by Joseph M. Kitagawa
and Gregory D. Alles
With the collaboration of
Karl W. Luckert*

MACMILLAN PUBLISHING COMPANY
NEW YORK
Collier Macmillan Publishers
LONDON

Macmillan Publishing Company
866 Third Avenue, New York, NY 10022

Collier Macmillan Canada, Inc.

Library of Congress Catalog Card No.: 87-17186

Printed in the United States of America

printing number
1   2   3   4   5   6   7   8   9   10

Library of Congress Cataloging in Publication Data:

Wach, Joachim, 1898–1955.
     Introduction to the history of religions / Joachim Wach ; edited by Joseph
M. Kitagawa and Gregory D. Alles, with the collaboration of Karl W.
Luckert.
        p.   cm.
     Bibliography: p.
     Includes index.
     ISBN 0–02–933530–2
     1. Religion—Study and teaching.   I. Kitagawa, Joseph Mitsuo.
1915–   .   II. Alles, Gregory D.   III. Luckert, Karl W., 1934–
IV. Title.
BL41.W335   1987
291'.09—dc19   87–17186
                                                                                      CIP

Part I was originally published in Leipzig in 1924 as *Religionswissenschaft:
Prolegomena zu ihrer wissenschaftstheoretischen Grundlegung.*

The articles in Part II originally appeared in the 1930 edition of *Die Religion in
Geschichte und Gegenwart.* Reprinted by permission of J.C.B. Mohr (Paul Siebeck),
Tübingen.

The Introduction *"Verstehen* and *Erlösung"* originally appeared in *History of
Religions,* Vol. 11, pp. 31–55. Reprinted by permission of The University of
Chicago Press.

To Susi

Contents

INTRODUCTION: *Verstehen* and *Erlösung*

I HAVE ALREADY said something about Joachim Wach's life in my introductions to two volumes of his essays, both of which appeared in print after Wach's death in 1955—*The Comparative Study of Religions* (1958) and *Understanding and Believing* (1968)— and in an article in *The Encyclopedia of Religion,* edited by Mircea Eliade (1987).[1] There is no point in repeating any but the most essential details of Wach's life here. He was born in Germany in 1898 and received a Ph.D. in 1922 from Leipzig with a thesis on "The Foundations of a Philosophy of the Concept of Salvation," published under the title *Der Erlösungsgedanke und Seine Deutung.* His academic career in Germany ended abruptly in April 1935 when the government of Saxony, under pressure from the Nazis, terminated Wach's university appointment on the grounds that he was descended from Moses Mendelssohn, even though Wach's family had been Christian for four generations. Fortunately, friends were able to secure for him an invitation to teach at Brown University in Providence, Rhode Island. In 1945 he moved one last time, to the Divinity School of the University of Chicago.

When Wach started teaching at Leipzig in 1924, the mission and disciplinary boundaries of the history of religions

(*Religionswissenschaft*) were still unclear to scholars and students of religion. Some of those with a theological orientation insisted that whoever knows one religion (that is, Christianity) knows everything worth knowing about all religions. Others, embracing the nascent social-scientific approaches to the study of religion, tended to reduce religion to its causes, chiefly psychological or social. In the present work, which was his *Habilitation* thesis of 1924, Wach insists on the integrity and autonomy of a history of religions liberated from theology, philosophy of religion, and social-scientific methods reductively applied.

Since Wach's death I have used *Religionswissenschaft* as a classroom text for courses I have taught in the history of religions. Karl Luckert, a former student of mine and a native of Germany, translated the book into English during his stay at the Divinity School of the University of Chicago, and his rough draft has been in use all these years without ever finding its way into print. Now, thirty-two years after Wach's death, I think it only fitting that an English edition be made available to students of the history of religions everywhere. Many have had a hand along the way in preparing *Religionswissenschaft* for publication in English. Most recently, Gregory Alles, now of Western Maryland College, undertook the task of preparing a final, polished translation.

In addition to *Religionswissenschaft*, Wach wrote a number of articles that discuss in summary fashion the concerns of the earliest phase of his thought: human understanding, the discipline of the history of religions as distinguished from the philosophy of religion, and salvation and the savior. The articles that appear here in Part Two originally appeared in the second edition of the German encyclopedia, *Die Religion in Geschichte und Gegenwart*, whose volumes are relatively inaccessible to students today.

The notes that appear in Part One represent only a small percentage of the notes that originally accompanied Wach's *Religionswissenschaft*. They have been included here whenever they are needed to document citations, fill out Wach's arguments, or situate Wach's thought in its larger contexts. I should also point out that for the better part of his scholarly career, that is, until 1944, Wach thought of *Religionswissenschaft* in the singular, that is, as the "history of religion." After he settled in Chicago, however, he made a quite deliberate switch to the term "history of religions" in the plural, and he even set about to revise his earlier works. We have decided to use the plural form throughout this volume by way of honoring what I feel would have been Wach's wish.

It is my pleasant duty to thank Charles E. Smith, Paul Bernabeo, and Elly Dickason of the Macmillan Publishing Company for their advice and assistance in bringing this translation to print.

Thanks also are due to Dean Franklin I. Gamwell of the Divinity School, the University of Chicago, to my secretary, Martha Morrow-Vojacek, and to Peter Chemery, my research assistant, upon whose care and attention my recent work has depended.

To Joachim Wach, the primary task of the history of religions was the "understanding" of religious experience and its expressions. The outline reproduced on page xii presents, in schematic and extremely simplified form, the basic methodological framework in which Wach pursued this task.[2] Wach maintained this basic framework with amazing consistency throughout his life, but there were shifts in emphasis from his early to his middle phase, and again from the middle to the last phase of his scholarly career. It may be somewhat arbitrary to divide Wach's scholarly work into such stages, but one cannot help feeling that Wach had three successive "models" for the discipline of the history of religions.

During the first phase of his life Wach stressed the hermeneutical basis for the descriptive-historical task of religio-historical study, as illustrated by his publications *Religionswissenschaft* (1924)[3] and *Das Vertehen* (1926–1933).[4] These volumes deal with a large number of scholars and thinkers who had influenced Wach. But there is good reason to assume that he felt most congenial with August Boeckh and that he, uncon-

UNIVERSALS IN RELIGION

In the context of history, culture, and society, man has had and has:

(A) RELIGIOUS EXPERIENCES

that are apprehended and experienced variously in terms of (a) Sacred space and time, (b) *Unio Magica*, and (c) Cosmic order as well as the natural, ritual and social orders and organizations.

The criteria of RELIGIOUS EXPERIENCES are:
(a) objective reference, which means that religious experience is a response to what is experienced as Ultimate Reality (power, power center, manifestations of power in nature and history),
(b) integral nature, which implies a total response of the total being to Ultimate Reality,
(c) intensity, which invariably leads man to
(d) practical commitments and acts.

(B) FORMS OF EXPRESSION

of religious experience in primitive, archaic and historical religions are:

(1) *Theoretical*—symbol, concept, doctrine, "dogma." Themes: God—pluralistic-monistic, personal-impersonal (Theology).
World—its origin, nature and destiny (Cosmology). Man—his origin, nature and destiny (Anthropology, Soteriology, Eschatology).

(2) *Practical*—cultus, worship.
Media: tone (music)
words (liturgy)
gestures and movements (dances and processions).
Components of worship: prayer
sacrifice
divination
special rites (lustrations, processions)
sacraments
sacramental acts (naming, initiation, confession).

(3) Sociological—fellowship, cult association.
Types of grouping: natural cult group—family, clan, tribe, nation, specifically religious group—religious society, brotherhood, "ecclesiastical body," sect.
Structure: egalitarian or hierarchical (in group spirit and ethics).
Leadership: personal
institutional
charismatic

* It is to be noted that spontaniety and standardization of all forms of expressions, individual and corporate, as illustrated for example by creativity and reformation, have taken place in the history of religions of the world.

** Unlike theology, which deals with the normative exposition of faith, Religionswissenschaft (scientific study of religions) aims at (a) descriptive (historical) as well as (b) systematic (phenomenological, sociological, comparative) studies of religions and religious phenomena.

sciously if not consciously, regarded "philology," which was Boeckh's subject, as a viable model for the history of religions during the first "period" of his work.

During his second phase, Wach seemed to be more concerned with articulating the systematic aspects of religio-historical study, especially its relation to sociological and anthropological studies, as evidenced by the publication of his *Einführung in die Religionssoziologie, Typen religiöser Anthropologie,* and *Sociology of Religion.*[5] During this phase of his life, Wach seemed to be under the spell of Wilhelm Dilthey, Max Scheler, Ernst Troeltsch, and Max Weber to the extent that his systematic work in the history of religions showed the decisive imprint of sociology, more especially the tradition of *die verstehende Soziologie.*

Finally, during the third phase of his life, Wach advocated the importance of the mutual influence and cooperation between the history of religions and the normative disciplines, as exemplified by his *Types of Religious Experience: Christian and Non-Christian* and his posthumous work, *The Comparative Study of Religions.*[6] In these works we can detect both the positive and the negative influences of theology. These observations are bound to be oversimplifications, but they at least point to some of the dominant themes in Wach's complex and multidimensional work.

On a different level, Wach, who dedicated his life to the task of "understanding" religion(s), never doubted that the central concern of religion was the problem of salvation *(Erlösung).*[7] Thus, while this introduction is not meant to be a comprehensive study of Wach's work,[8] it attempts to portray both the general development of Wach's notion of the history of religions through the three "models" mentioned above and the persistence of the two main themes of understanding *(Verstehen)* and salvation *(Erlösung)* in the unfolding of his thought.

In Search of a Hermeneutical Base

During the first phase of his career, Wach took it for granted that inquiry into the nature of religious experience per se apart from its expressions, like the study of the truth and value of knowledge, belonged properly to the domain of the philosophy of religion and theology. At that time he was most eager to stress the empirical or "scientific" nature of the history of religions, and took great pains to point out the "errors" of C. P. Tiele, P. D. Chantepie de la Saussaye, and Ernst Troeltsch, who unwittingly had equated the descriptive task of the history of religions with the normative task of the philosophy of religion. Evidently, Wach was inclined to draw a rather sharp line of demarcation between "descriptive" and "normative" tasks in the study of religions. It must be recalled, however, that Wach did not advocate the "descriptive" as the only task of the history of religions. To be sure, he disavowed a speculative purpose in this religiohistorical discipline, but he acknowledged that it must comprehend the meaning (Deutung) of the historical data, and in this respect it must go beyond the purely descriptive and move toward its "systematic" task. Here, Wach realized the peculiar difficulties involved in the kind of religiohistorical inquiry that had to deal with the symbolic meaning of religious phenomena. At this point, according to him, "the great philosophical and metaphysical questions appear, questions to which the history of religions leads, but which it is not permitted to raise itself."[9] Wach was surely aware that he was walking a tightrope, fully cognizant of the fact that the methodology of the history of religions needed a solid foundation, especially in regard to epistemological problems.

Obviously, Wach was determined to maintain the boundary between the normative task of philosophy and the religiohistorical task, which belonged on the side of the human studies (Geisteswissenschaften). At the same time, he was aware that the history of religions was compelled to depend on the resources of philosophy for: (1) the logical articulation of the religiohistorical method; (2) the delineation of the philosophical aspects of religious phenomena; and (3) the systematic ordering of religious phenomena as data for the totality of human knowledge.[10] It was but natural, therefore, that Wach turned to hermeneutics, which according to his mentor, Wilhelm

Dilthey, was a connecting link between philosophy and the human studies. While hermeneutics in religiohistorical study, just as in other disciplines, has to be concerned with external rules and principles of interpretation, Wach was persuaded that "fundamentally it involves the whole understanding and inner grasp of the religion itself."[11]

Wach traces the problem of understanding to the most archaic levels of human society, which could not have survived without some measure of *Verstehen* in its thinking, feeling, intuitions, expressions, signs, and symbols. The divine will, revealed in manifold signs, had to be interpreted, and laws that governed the well-being of society also required rules of interpretation. With the emergence of written documents, exegesis and other precursors of philological and literary interpretation came into existence, as illustrated by the work of Alexandrian scholars. In the modern period, beginning with the seventeenth century, the problem of interpretation gradually became the concern of scholars in the fields of theology, especially in the study of scriptures, Oriental studies, jurisprudence, and classics. It was during the nineteenth century, however, that the combined effects of the classic-romantic movement and the discovery of the Oriental languages and civilizations stimulated the development of *Geisteswissenschaften*—liberal arts or humanistic studies—which revived interest in the problem of understanding, more particularly in reference to antiquity, folklore, and philology. It was in this setting that what Wach called the "two great systems of hermeneutics" were developed by Schleiermacher and Boeckh, respectively.[12]

Understandably, Wach, who held the history of religions to be one of the human studies, was convinced of the supreme importance of its hermeneutical task, which to him was the understanding of the spirit of religion and its expressions. "It seeks to understand the whole from the parts, and then again to understand the parts from the whole."[13] In his attempt to define the hermeneutical basis of the history of religions, Wach examined, and was influenced by, a host of scholars and their exegetical theories. Notwithstanding his own acknowledgment of indebtedness to Schleiermacher, Dilthey, Leopold von Ranke, and others, Wach appeared to be influenced most decisively by Boeckh, a philologist and a scholar of antiquity. Wach leaned heavily on Boeckh's hermeneutical theory and his epistemological assumptions, and he regarded the hermeneutical task of philology as a helpful model for that of the history of religions.

August Boeckh was a disciple of Friedrich August Wolf and Friedrich Schleiermacher and a teacher of Wilhelm Dilthey. According to Boeckh, the two great manifestations of life, nature and mind—as well as history, which to him is the evolution of mind—are the subject matter of cognition (*Erkennen*), and it is the task of science (*Wissenschaft*), together with art, to bring into view the whole or unity of all particulars of everything knowable. In this broad sense, philosophy may be equated with *Wissenschaft*, too. Boeckh was persuaded that different branches of learning, each with its own specific mode of approach to knowledge, must depend on one another in the common task of interpretation. For example, philosophy strives for original insight in the pursuit of grasping the spirit of the Greek people. Accordingly, it must turn to philology, which is conversant with the empirical manifestations of that spirit.[14] Conversely, philology, which aims at understanding, must depend on logic, which is the formal theory of cognition in philosophy.

Let us now turn briefly to Wach's account of Boeckh's philological hermeneutics, which reveals unusually close similarities at a number of points to Wach's own notion of hermeneutics in the history of religions. At times one has only to substitute the term "religion" for Boeckh's term "philology" or "language" to get a fairly adequate picture of the general features of Wach's early history of religions.

Wach was strongly attracted by Boeckh's view that the task of philology is to "re-cognize" that which has been previously "cognized" or "recognized," not in the sense simply to learn about what once was known but rather "to recognize the cognized, to present it in its pristine character, to free it of the accretions of time and of misunderstanding, to re-construct in its totality that which does not appear as a whole."[15] In so stating, Boeckh did not refer only to conceptual and/or scientifically verifiable knowledge but included various kinds of signs and symbols—works of art, poetry, and the productions of history, through all of which the human spirit communicates itself—as items to be "cognized." Yet, Boeckh regarded the philological urge as a specially primal condition of life, rooted in the depths of human nature and in the chain of culture (much as Wach held the soteriological urge to be an irreducible aspect of life); and in this sense the unique task of philology was directed toward language, the universal organ of cognition, without which the profoundest human needs for communication and clarification of meaning would not have been possible.[16]

Wach appreciated Boeckh's view that philology's task of "recognition" or "re-production," far from being a mechanical enterprise, requires creative imagination and reflection. In hermeneutical work, every step in the process of reproduction serves the great task of understanding, its ultimate aim being the totality of cognition and cognition of the totality of ideas, even though what can be achieved practically may be only an approximation of that supreme goal.[17] Wach also affirmed Boeckh's two main guidelines for hermeneutics. First, the goal of re-cognition is not attained as long as the previously cognized remains something foreign. In other words, that which is foreign must progressively be assimilated and re-produced as one's own. Second, when this first project is accomplished, the interpreter must get beyond what he has reproduced. He must be able to observe and appraise what has become his own as an objective something apart from himself.[18] Wach appropriated these two tasks as the guidelines for the hermeneutics of the history of religions.

Boeckh's intellectual background, as portrayed by Wach, explains something of Wach's own heritage. Although Boeckh's writings betray the strong influence of Friedrich Schelling, Wach says: "Boeckh's conception of the evolution of mankind as being an organic unity, his ideas of history as the evolution of the Spirit, of freedom and necessity, link him closely with the philosophy of history of German Idealism as represented by Hegel."[19] We must note, however, that Boeckh, as much as Wach, refrained from systematizing the evolutionary process of history too rigidly. At any rate, being a true heir of Idealism, Boeckh believed that the cultivation of understanding is an aspect of true *humanitas*. He also took it for granted that culture is the totality of the manifestations of the *Volksgeist*, whereby he affirmed that the re-cognition of that which man has cognized is one of the best guides to humanity, for it teaches us to know man, that is, to know the spirit of man as it is expressed in all his cultural creations.[20] Furthermore, Boeckh held that an active understanding of humanity itself is unfolded only in the total process of the sweep of the history of culture.

Even such a brief account of Boeckh's view makes it clear that there are obvious similarities between his notion and Wach's notion of hermeneutics. Significantly, both agreed with Schleiermacher in rejecting the distinction between *hermeneutica sacra* and *profana*.[21] As mentioned earlier, Boeckh regarded the philological urge—communication—as the primary element of our humanity, while Wach held that the religious need for salvation *(Erlösung)* was the essence of human nature. Still, they viewed the history of cultures and the history of religions, respectively, in a similar way. There is even a structural similarity between Boeckh's appraisal of antiquity and Wach's appraisal of Christianity as paradigms of the history of cultures and the history of religions, respectively. According to Boeckh, antiquity embodies the beginnings of all disciplines; the primitive concepts, the totality of all conditions, so to speak, of humanity.[22] He stressed the importance of these primitive beginnings, because he felt that the strongest expression of the world soul or the primal principle is manifested in them. Such an appraisal is based on his hermeneutical principle of measuring the historical life of an era or culture by the standard of the ideal of humanity, which is to be uncovered in the developmental process itself.[23] Likewise, Wach, who aspired to understand the religious history of the human race, was inclined to accept Christianity as a high peak, if not the highest, in the long process of man's search for salvation *(Erlösung)* based on a similar hermeneutical principle.

Be that as it may, Wach during his first phase was not concerned to spell out the implication of the hermeneutical task of the religiohistorical study of the question of soteriology. He pointed this out, and evidently meant it seriously, when he said that "the task of the history of religions is to study and to depict the empirical religions. It is a descriptive and interpretive discipline, not a normative one. In studying concrete religious phenomena historically and systematically, it completes its task."[24]

Systematic Articulation

In considering the second phase of Wach's scholarly life, we must bear in mind that already during the first phase he held that there are two distinct but interrelated types of inquiry within the discipline of the history of religions: (1) the "historical," which studies the growth and development of the concrete religions; and (2) the "systematic," dealing with the structure of religious phenomena.[25] It was during the second phase that Wach attempted to develop the "systematic" dimension of the history of religions following the model of "sociology," or more particularly, the tradition of Weber's *verstehende Soziologie.* Thus, the "sociology of religion," to him, was an important branch of the religiohistorical study, dealing with the sociological expressions of religious experience.

A few words concerning Wach's notion of the "historical" study of religion may be in order. He held that in the philosophy of religion the idea of religion comes first and the phenomenon of religion follows, because philosophy's inquiry concerns the *Wesen* (essential nature) of religion and its place in a system of values and in the process of the spirit. In religiohistorical study, however, the point of departure is the historically given religions. It does not inquire about the *Wesen* and/or origin of religion as such.[26] To be sure, Wach is not advocating the sheer amassing of historical data; what is im-

portant to him is discovering the principle that structures
historical facts and events without which it would be impossible
to find meaning in the configurations of the vast amount of
data available to us. In this connection, Wach reminds us that
religious phenomena as such do not exist apart from total
historic events, so that the historical study of religions, while
it has its own aims and procedures, cannot be divorced from
historical studies of human culture in general. More specifically, Wach divides the historical branch of the history of
religions *(Religionswissenschaft)* into (1) the general historical
study of religions *(allgemeine Religionsgeschichte);* and (2) the
specialized historical study of religions *(spezielle Religionsgeschichte)*. The first investigates the general history of religions,
including the prehistoric ones, throughout the historic experience of the human race, while the latter deals with specific
phases of empirical, historical religious phenomena. It must
be kept in mind, however, that historical study is inseparable
from its systematic counterpart, for historical inquiry is impossible without the categories provided by systematic study.
Conversely, systematic study is impossible without the concrete
data provided by historical study.

At any rate, according to Wach's own hermeneutical canon,
systematic study must begin not from a philosophical or a
priori point of departure but with empirical historical data.[27]
Nevertheless, while historical investigation is concerned with
"what has actually happened" and the actual "becoming" *(das
Werden)* of religions, the systematic inquirer attempts to understand in cross-sections "that which has become *(das Gewordene),*" for example, doctrines, cults, and religious organizations—the theoretical, practical, and sociological expressions
of religious experience.[28] For such a systematic inquiry, Wach
depends on the use of historical and ideal "types"[29] and the
concept of the "classical."[30] These are important tools for the
"comparison" of the similarities and contrasts between religious phenomena.[31] Wach was sensitive to the inherent danger
of the comparative approach and cautioned us not to jump
to concocting facile similarities and analogies before the unique
nature of the particular phenomena has been fully grasped

historically and/or psychologically.[32] The aim of systematic study is inquiry concerning the "formation" and "structure" of religions—the factors involved in the formation of a religion, the relationship among the various factors, those instances that brought about the structure of religions as well as the relationship, and the modifications among their various forms.[33]

As the foregoing makes clear, Wach held that the most important task for the history of religions is not historical but systematic study, interpretation, and presentation.[34] In this respect, while Wach was aware of the psychological, theological, philosophical, economic, legal, and other factors involved, he himself was chiefly concerned with the "sociological" aspect of systematic study. In fact, "sociology of religion" was for him the systematic dimension of the history of religions— following the model of sociology. It might be added that to Wach the distinction between the sociological study of Christian and non-Christian religions is one of organization of materials, not of method or principle.

More important, perhaps, is the place Wach assigned to the sociology of religion among the *Wissenschaften*. For instance, in his view, while the sociology of religion is one, albeit an important, aspect of the systematic side of the history of religions, it is also related to sociology in general, and is related to it in the same way as are the sociologies of law, the state, art, and so on. Also, it is related to political science insofar as the state, which is not only a legal but also a sociologically significant phenomenon, should be the object of inquiry by the sociology of religion. Moreover, there are affinities between the sociological study of religion and of law, or between sociology of religion and ethnology. Among other *Wissenschaften* that are related to the sociological study of religion, Wach takes special note of psychology and economics. While he appreciated the sociopsychological dimension of religiohistorical study, he was highly critical, following the example of Max Scheler, of the fallacy of psychologism.[35] Regarding economics, Wach's comments are more tempered, partly because "eminent scholars in this field," notably Max

Weber, had already provided an important stimulus to the advancement of sociology of religion, but also because the sociology of religion must face the fact that social stratification and organization are significantly conditioned by economic factors. Nevertheless, he vehemently rejected the Marxists' one-sided interpretation of history. Thus, he asserted that "in the interest of methodological clarity it is important to work out the most strict separation and exact posing of the problems theoretically in methodology and practically in research," and he also lamented the often repeated confusion of "social" and "sociological," which results in the false notion that sociology is a normative science of the social life.[36]

In his own account of the development of the sociology of religion in Germany, Wach mentions with appreciation a number of pioneers in this field, such as Ernst Troeltsch, who "presented his comprehensive studies of Christian groups and the social and moral concepts"; Werner Sombart, who contributed an "extensive treatment of the development of the forms of economical and correlative social and religious concepts"; and Georg Simmel, who presented "the first consistent attempt at a purely formal sociology."[37] However, the two scholars who exerted the most decisive impact on Wach's own formulation of the sociology of religion were Wilhem Dilthey and Max Weber. Ironically, Dilthey was averse to establishing an independent sociological discipline, but his philosophical and historical work provided both Weber and Wach with systematic and epistemological foundations for the human studies. "Following Hegel," says Wach, "Dilthey clearly demonstrated the interrelationship that exists among the various *objective systems of culture* such as law, art, science, and—according to him—religion and the corresponding *organizations of society* such as tribes, states, nations, and churches, thus obviating the metaphysical construction of Hegel and of Lazarus and Steinthal's 'folk psychology' *(Völkerpsychologie)*."[38] Max Weber was unquestionably Wach's own mentor even though Wach did not follow Weber's method completely. In Wach's view, Weber's significance lies in the fact that not only did he introduce and give currency to the term "sociology of religion" but he tried for the first time "to describe the field and the tasks of the sociology of religion and through the treatment of a vast and varied material he undertook the study of the higher non-Christian religions and developed at the same time the necessary categories in a systematic outline."[39]

Despite his rhapsodic praise of Weber, Wach is critical of him on two accounts. First, Weber neglected primitive religions, Islam, and other important religious phenomena. Second, and more crucial to Wach, Weber's understanding of religion was itself inadequate. In his words: "The categories under which [Weber] classified religious phenomena are not entirely satisfactory, because not enough attention is paid to their original meaning."[40] These, be it noted, are Wach's fundamental criticisms of Weber as much as of Dilthey, who had influenced both Weber and Wach himself. Indeed, Wach follows Dilthey's scheme and holds all products of cultural activity, such as technical achievements, economic systems, works of art, law, and systems of thought, as "objective systems of culture" as distinguished from all "organizations of society," such as marriage, friendship, kinship groups, associations, and the state. It is important to remind ourselves that according to Dilthey "religion" was included in the category of "objective systems of culture," and this scheme was accepted by Weber as well as by the mainline tradition of the sociology of religion. But to Wach, as indicated earlier, religion—man's yearning for *Erlösung*—is a primal condition of life itself, not a cultural product. Yet, to the extent that he appropriated the overall scheme of Dilthey and of Weber, he was inclined to formulate his approach to the sociology of religion on this model, although he was not altogether happy about it. Thus he included the expression of religious experience under the category of "objective systems of culture," "*realizing full well that the core and substance of this experience defies adequate objectification,*" and he adds: "that makes its interpretation often more a perplexing than an enlightening task."[41]

Because of this basic ambiguity in his framework, Wach's approach to the sociology of religion was received enthusiastically by some while being severely criticized by others. No one questioned his erudition, his careful phenomenological analysis, and his historical insights. Even the most critical acknowledged the contribution of Wach's delineation of the reciprocal influences that exist between empirical religions and various forms of social groups. For example, while every religion arises out of a certain sociological milieu, Wach demonstrates that in many situations religion exerts a significant influence on the shaping of social structure even though he does not touch on the important roles religion plays in social control and in social change. More astute critics, however, questioned the adequacy of Wach's basic assumptions and methodology, or rather, the way in which Wach attempted to modify the models provided by Dilthey and Weber. For example, H. Richard Niebuhr observed that while Weber examined the relations of specific religious convictions to economic ethics and Troeltsch dealt with the relation of Christian faith and experience to Christian as well as secular social organizations, Wach attempted to deal with the relation of social groups and a vague thing called "religion." Niebuhr questioned the validity of Wach's two assumptions: "first, that a common type of qualitatively definable psychological experience is the source of all so-called religions," and "secondly, that in any particular culture the religious beliefs, rites, and organizations stem from a common religious source, 'a central religious experience.' "[42]

Admittedly, some of the criticisms mentioned above were legitimate and stimulated Wach to reflect further on the questions that were ambiguous in his scheme. In another sense, however, we might point out that Wach's critics did not realize that he was not writing a sociology of religion per se, even though he explicitly stated his aim as follows: "The author, a student not of the social sciences but of religion, is convinced of the desirability of bridging the gulf which still exists between the study of religion and the social sciences. . . . He considers his contribution more as a modest attempt at a synthesis than an inventory with any claim to completeness."[43] We might even say that it was misleading for him to call such an inquiry a "sociology of religion." What he attempted was a systematic study within the framework of the history of religions with special emphasis on the "sociological" dimension, following the model of "sociology." In this respect, the following statement clearly depicts Wach's concern during the second phase of his scholarly career: "Through this approach [the sociological study of religion] we hope not only to illustrate the cultural significance of religion but also to gain new insight into the relations between the various forms of expression of religious experience and eventually to understand better the various aspects of religious experience itself."[44]

Integral Understanding and Collaboration

As we move from the second to the third phase of Wach's career, the "spiral character" of his lifelong scholarship becomes more evident. That is to say, in each stage he seems to go over the same ground, and yet each stage moves upward toward a greater, higher, and more comprehensive "understanding" *(Verstehen)* of the "soteriological character" of religion *(Erlösung)*. During the third phase, which coincides with his ten years of teaching at the University of Chicago, Wach wrote a number of articles and reviews. (I might add, incidentally, that in reviewing other scholar's works, Wach felt freer to express his views more sharply than in his own articles or books.) Some of his articles are included in *Types of Religious Experience: Christian and Non-Christian* and *Understanding and Believing* (published posthumously in 1968).[45] In addition, his lecture notes, delivered in India in 1952 under the auspices of the Barrows Lectureship of the University of Chicago and in America as the 1954–1955 Lectures on the History of Religions sponsored by the American Council of Learned Societies, were edited and published posthumously under the title, *The Comparative Study of Religions* (1958).

In *The Comparative Study of Religions,* Wach surveys the development of the history of religions as follows. The first period of this discipline, heralded by Friedrich Max Müller and others, stressed mythology as the most important form of expression of religious experience. The new method of inquiry, denoting the emancipation of the new discipline from the philosophy of religion and theology, was greatly inspired by philosophy and history, looking for "parallels" among different religions. The transition from the first to the second period, marked by C. P. Tiele's Gifford Lectures (1896–1898), brought about "historicism," which was characterized by a "positivistic temper." The descriptive task, which stressed "objectivity" at the expense of evaluations, was colored by the view of evolution, which was also fashionable in folklore, sociology, and psychology. This was reflected in the works of E. B. Tylor, Emile Durkheim, Wilhelm Wundt, and others. The earlier concern with "parallels" was taken over by a new concern with the "origins" of religion(s). With World War I the age of "historicism" ended, and was followed by the third period of the discipline which was characterized by three things: "the desire to overcome the disadvantages of exaggerated specialization and departmentalization by means of an integrated outlook, the desire to penetrate deeper *[sic]* into the nature of religious experience, and the exploration of questions of an epistemological and ultimately metaphysical character."[46] Wach considers Rudolf Otto as the most important figure during the third period of the discipline, which now stresses "comparative" studies with the recognition of the "objective character of ultimate reality," "the non-rational element in religion without neglecting the value of rational investigation," and the "dissimilar, specific, and individual" character of various religions rather than any superficial identification and parallelism.[47]

After thus surveying the three periods of the development of the history of religions, Wach goes on to say: "in the present era of the comparative study of religions a new synthesis is being worked out."[48] This is both Wach's assessment of the contemporary trend within the history of religions and the declaration of his own intention and concern during the last phase of his career. His concern is succinctly stated in the following statement:

There is good reason to oppose an unqualified pluralism or even a dualism in matters of method and knowledge. Truth is one; the cosmos is one; hence knowledge also must be one. This insight is all important. Although we will not agree with the positivistic interpretation of this principle, we must incorporate it into our methodology, which will be based on a dual demand. The first demand is that the method be unified. . . . All idealism and all naturalism—including materialism—stand or fall with methodological monism. Yet to conceive of one truth is one thing and to possess or comprehend it is another. We should be realistic enough to see the profound wisdom in the apostle's words that here we know only in part, which is to say that only God himself can be aware of the whole. The second demand is that the method be adequate for the subject matter. This qualifies the first principle, that of a unified method.[49]

He takes these two demands seriously, and during the last decade of his life he attempts to "synthesize" various facets of his lifelong concerns regarding the two main themes, that is, understanding and salvation.

As stated before, early in his life Wach came to be influenced by a hermeneutical tradition that sharply divided the descriptive and normative disciplines. Thus he attempted to establish an objective, epistemological basis for all the human studies, more particularly for the history of religions, and he tried to articulate its nature, limitations, forms, and possibilities. Convinced of the circular nature of the process of understanding, Wach affirmed in principle that every phenomenon has to be related to its total context. At the same time he felt the necessity of articulating the relative-objective standpoint of an inquirer that is imperative for any hermeneutical task. In this respect, it is worth recalling that just as Boeckh was convinced that the philological urge was a primal aspect of life, Wach was convinced of the primacy of the soteriological urge in human existence. Even as a young scholar, he wrote:

As varied in details as awareness of the depth and significance of the need for salvation may be, the earliest stirrings of this sentiment among primitive peoples—and these stirrings appear quite often—lead in a straight line to the deeper and universal conceptions found among the most highly developed cultures. In the growing intensification of this awareness and in the progressive development of the idea of salvation we find one of the most important regions for the evolution of the spirit *(Geist)*. . . . Apart from this universally human, deeply rooted need for salvation, it would not be possible to understand the massive amount of thoughts and concepts, hopes and wishes, ideas and doctrines that the human spirit has devoted to the idea of salvation. Religious geniuses have served this idea repeatedly. Countless great and lesser preachers and prophets have proclaimed and altered it. And wherever human beings have separated themselves from positive, historical religions, philosophers have continued the efforts of the *homines religiosi.* Weighty religious systems have arisen whose theoretical bases often include . . . cosmology, anthropology, and eschatology [all] culminat[ing] in soteriology."[50]

He was also persuaded that every person, being basically religious, has the capacity to "understand" religion, even though no two persons have the same capacity in this regard. The act of understanding, however, begins only when one who has at least a minimal life experience, knowledge, and common sense takes an active interest in a certain object. Moreover, true understanding is not possible until an inquirer becomes self-conscious concerning his own standpoint. Once this takes place, he can attain something of an "objective understanding" of the object of his inquiry even if he is not committed to affirm the truth or value of it. For example, in the religious sphere, a non-Christian who is engaged in understanding the nature of Christianity sometimes can comprehend his subject matter more clearly than many Christians or even Christian theologians.[51] Conversely, a historian of religions, who happens to be a Christian, can attain a degree of understanding of other religions often surpassing that of their adherents.

Needless to say, Wach struggled with the question of objectivity in the religio-historical study of a variety of religious phenomena, for an inquirer is compelled to "compare" these data if he tries to make any sense at all. This concern led him to divide the systematic inquiry of the history of religions into the material and the formal areas. The former depends on the empirical inductive method and seeks to compare phenomena by means of their "historical typology." The latter seeks to depict the similarities in the historical manifestation of religious experience and also to articulate the laws of development of religions by means of abstract "ideal-type concepts." In other words, both approaches use comparison, but the former uses it to understand the unique qualities of each individual phenomenon, whereas the latter compares various phenomena in order to derive a comprehensive understanding of religion itself by structuring the universal elements that are embodied in diverse religious phenomena. The concern with systematic inquiry led Wach to develop his "sociology of religion" during the second phase of his career. Such an inquiry, however, represented one level of the "spiral" development of his scholarship. Thus, while Wach acknowledged the fact that his systematic endeavor, that is, "sociology of religion," was limited primarily to a sociological examination of religious groups, he insisted that this fact "need not be interpreted as an implicit admission that the theological, philosophical, and metaphysical problems and questions growing out of such a study have to remain unanswerable. They can and most certainly should be answered."[52] In dealing with this question during his second phase, Wach still resorted to the formula of "cooperation" between various modes of inquiry, each with its own aims and methods as well as limitations—for example, sociology of religion, philosophy of society, and empirical theology—for the common task of "understanding" or the systematic re-cognition and re-production of knowledge concerning various aspects of reality, even if such a "cooperation" of various modes of inquiry should take place within one and the same inquiry.

During the third phase of his life, however, Wach felt the necessity of "inter-penetration" among various modes of inquiry, preferably within each inquirer, in order to achieve "integral understanding." In this respect, his search for "integral understanding" coincided with his quest for an "integrated person." Both led him to reexamine the relationship between *Religionswissenschaft*, which he now preferred to call the "history of religions" or "comparative study of religions," and theology, following the example of Rudolf Otto.

On the scholarly level, Wach finds hopeful signs in a twofold movement of thought, which in his opinion is "similar to that which we discovered in the age of the Enlightenment." First is "a new interest in 'systematic' or constructive thought" in theology, while the second is the trend in the history of religions to view data "structurally and functionally and to understand their religious meaning."[53] On the other hand, in the domain of religion the world over, he recognizes the increasing challenge of the pluralism of religious loyalties and its relationship to the "problem of truth." In this situation, he is persuaded that "if it is the task of theology to investigate, buttress, and teach the faith of a religious community to which it is committed . . . it is the responsibility of a comparative study to guide and purify it." This has immediate personal implications. In his own words:

> That which I value and cherish and hold dear beyond all else, I also want thoroughly to understand in all its implications. It is true that to love truth you must hate untruth, but it is not true that in order to exalt your own faith you must hate and denigrate those of another faith. A comparative study of religions such as the new era made possible enables us to have a fuller vision of what religious experience can mean, what forms its expression may take, and what it might do for man.[54]

In his quest for "integral understanding" of "truth" Wach finds inspiration in a host of thinkers and scholars, above all, in Rudolf Otto. When Wach states that Otto "stood in a philosophical tradition which was devoted to the solution of the great epistemological problem: What constitutes experience?" and that Otto was "convinced of the specific character of religious experience," Wach is really speaking for himself, too. When Wach writes that Otto during the last two decades devoted himself to two different problems—the philosophical question of the relationship between religion and morality, and the theological question, "What think you of Christ?"[55]— Wach is revealing his own twofold struggle during the last decade of his life. Also, according to Otto, says Wach, "if one wants to say what Jesus was, one has to think of the exorcist, the charismatic. Only from his person and its meaning can we derive the meaning of his message concerning the Kingdom," and "as an anticipated eschaton it becomes the foundation of a community which sees itself as the Church of the Nazarene."[56] Here, Wach is affirming his own understanding of Christology. This does not imply, however, that Wach accepted Otto's work completely. He was not altogether happy with Otto's epistemological assumptions and his notion of "schematism" in the analysis of religious experience, and he was critical of Otto's lack of concern with aesthetics in relation to religious experience.[57] Nevertheless, Wach found in Otto a viable model for his own "synthesis" of various modes of inquiry.

Unfortunately, just as Otto's projected work on "Moral Law and the Will of God" was not completed on account of his death, Wach's untimely death prevented him from developing his notion of a more comprehensive scheme of a comparative study of religion. Thus we can get only a few glimpses of his thought based on his articles and classroom lectures. It is clear, however, that all these sources betray his lifelong preoccupation with the adequacy of understanding, or "integral understanding," of the soteriological character of religion as the primal fact of human life. His starting point— and the goal of the history of religions—is, as it was throughout his life, the quest for the meaning of all the expressions of religious experience and the meaning and nature of religious experience itself. In this, he recognized a kind of circularity: "If we desire to focus our investigation on phenomena to be called religious, we have to proceed on the basis of some presuppositions as to their nature, and yet, in order to be able to articulate these presuppositions, we have to study the widest possible range of historical phenomena."[58] Confronted by the impossibility of dealing with the whole range of historical phenomena, he has recourse to the notion of the "classical" and the typological method in order to do justice both to the uniqueness of particulars and to the universals in religion. While he acknowledges that the descriptive task is not a judge of normative value, he insists that the historian of religions can show "the consequences which were drawn from certain premises in speculation, practice and life, and then vindicate them as historical 'possibilities.' "[59] To put it another way, descriptive as well as systematic studies are now seen by Wach as "the indispensable preparation for evaluation," and he adds: "evaluation presupposes standards."[60]

How, then, does the historian of religions go about the task of evaluation? Wach suggests that there are three main alternatives: (1) yield to historicism and relativism; (2) revert to "classical" standards; and (3) attempt a new constructive solution.[61] Obviously, he opts for the third alternative. His constructive solution begins with the examination of the "universal" framework. He says: "If a study of universal features in the expressions of the religious experience of mankind can supply us with a framework within which we find this experience articulated, it must be possible to test the validity of this framework by applying it in the study of primitive cults and of the universal religions."[62] On the other hand, concerning the "particular" manifestations of religion, the historian of religions should deal with them not only as historical "possibilities" but also "to inquire after their truth." In this task, Wach holds that "the historian of religions does not wait for the final quest for help from the theologian."[63] Concretely, Wach urges the historian of religions to familiarize himself with theological works dealing with Christian and other religions—"without pressing his material to conform to a framework and to notions which are alien to it." At the same time, he expects the exegete, the church historian, or the constructive theologian to acquaint himself with the material which the historian of religions is ready to supply. What he urges for the theologian above all is the necessity of existential decision, which involves "an orientation on the truth apprehended in this experience," which in turn provides him with a "criterion for judgment."[64] What Wach envisages is an interpenetration between constructive theology, which is informed and purified by careful studies in the history of religions, and history of religions, itself liberated from the "narrowly defined scientific approach to the study of religion."[65]

Unfortunately, Wach did not live long enough to develop this theme of the interpenetration of theology and the history of religions. *The Comparative Study of Religions* was, at best, no more than the prolegomena in this respect. Yet, we do have helpful hints as to what he had in mind. In the main, he resorts to two approaches. First is the examination of the "stages of understanding," in which "experience" in the broadest sense holds an important place.[66] Second is the recognition of the different orders of reality, such as matter, life, mind, and self-consciousness, by a coherent system of understanding.[67] Clearly, Wach was influenced by the philosophy of emergent evolution in relating the "stages of understanding" and the "different levels of reality." He quotes approvingly Morgan's famous statement that "the emergent entity is not to be accounted for in terms of antecedent stages of the process" or that "emergent evolution urges that the more of any given stage, even the highest, involves the 'less' of the stages which preceded it and continues to co-exist with it."[68] At the same time, Wach shared William Temple's notion that the mind itself emerges in the midst of the process which it apprehends. In Wach's view: "This means that consciousness is not given priority as that which legislates the principle of possible experience. Rather we must look upon a mind as that which arises out of the background of its given world and progressively constructs its own concept according to the kind of connection which it finds or expects to find in its world. It tries to express this connection in symbolic forms."[69]

He goes on to quote Dorothy Emmet's statement: "We come back . . . to the Platonic principle that if any rational understanding is to be possible, the logos in us must be akin to a logos in things."[70] It is this hermeneutical principle that he attempted to apply to the task of understanding religion. While this aspect of Wach's synthetic scheme was not worked out adequately before his death, his goal was clear. That is the integral understanding of the soteriological character of religion as revealed in the various forms of religious experience and expression throughout the history of the human race. In this sense, the following statement by Max Müller, which Wach often quoted, revealed Wach's own conviction: "To my mind the great epochs in the world's history are marked, not by the foundations or the destruction of empires, by the migration of races, or by the French Revolution. All this is outward history. . . . The real history of man is the history of religions: the wonderful ways by which the different families of the human race advanced toward a truer knowledge and a deeper love of God. This is the foundation that underlies all profane history; it is the light, the soul, and the life of history, and without it all history would indeed be profane."[71]

JOSEPH M. KITAGAWA

The History of Religions: Theoretical Prolegomena to Its Foundation as a Scholarly Discipline (1924)

FOREWORD

More than twenty-five years ago, my much honored friend, the renowned Oxford professor F. Max Müller, gave four lectures at the Royal Institute of London that were published several years later under the title *Introduction to the Science of Religion.* Max Müller's lectures were more an introduction of the science of religion to his hearers and readers—an apology for the young discipline—than an introduction to the discipline itself. Today we can go considerably farther. The past twenty-five years have been especially fruitful for the scientific study of religion, and this discipline has now achieved a permanent position among the various sciences *(Wissenschaften)* of the human spirit.

Almost twenty-five more years have elapsed since C.P. Tiele began his *Einleitung in die Religionswissenschaft* (1899) with these words. In the intervening period, we have once again made considerable progress, and as a result, Tiele's introduction, which for a long time rightly played a leading role, is no longer sufficient. Not only have studies of greater scope made Tiele's work out of date in many respects. The profound depth of today's problems poses questions that were necessarily

unknown in Tiele's time. Among these questions are a number
of problems that relate to the discipline's presuppositions.
These questions must be answered before we can begin to
present the basic issues of the history of religions as an introduction to problems that relate to its content. In this
"Prolegomena," I will discuss a number of these questions
and problems. There is widespread confusion about the methodological foundations of the history of religions. Therefore,
in a theoretical and logical sense, it is important to come first
of all to a clear understanding of this discipline's questions
and limitations. The solution to these problems will require
the cooperation of many.

My first concern here is to stress the empirical character
of the history of religions *(Religionswissenschaft)*. I do so in order
to ensure that the general history of religions *(allgemeine Religionswissenschaft)* is kept separate from the philosophy of religion and to secure for it an equal place among the other
empirical humanistic studies *(Geisteswissenschaften)*. Next, I am
concerned to lay the foundations for a distinction between
the historical study of religions *(Religionsgeschichte)* and the
systematic study of religion *(systematische Religionswissenschaft)*.
These two must be distinguished in both methodological self-
consciousness and practical research. Finally, I draw basic
guidelines for a systematic study of religion, but my guidelines
should be regarded as only preliminary. Further investigations
should extend and deepen them as soon as possible.

In addressing these concerns, I am not proposing programs
or plans for a new discipline. Rather, I am trying to clarify
and bring to methodological consciousness directions, aims,
and tendencies that have been emerging within the history of
religions for a long time. I believe that my efforts will meet
with far-reaching agreement both inside and outside the history
of religions, but I also expect to hear objections from several
quarters. The presentation of a definite point of view cannot
and should not satisfy everyone, even if it seeks to pass judgment from no other vantage point than that demanded by
the discipline itself.

For example, some will be dissatisfied with the way I separate the history of religions from theology. Others will reject, either in whole or in part, my contention that bracketing (*Einklammerung*) is an important methodological presupposition for work in the history of religions. Not everyone will agree with the principles of human understanding that I develop, although they are very important for our cognitive tasks. Still, I will discuss these questions just the same, for in doing so I will be able to advance and clarify many points.

Some may find my style and procedure too formal and abstract. I hope they will recognize that, by proceeding as I do, I am able to formulate decisive questions, hint at solutions, point to connections, and point out new ways of furthering concrete research. While my study should contribute to the history of thought, I also continue to spin threads that have already been begun.

I will pay considerable attention to research in other related fields. Instead of assembling these discussions into a single, concentrated section, I will make my comments whenever the occasion arises, that is, whenever the discussion of certain problems and positions requires me to do so. In addition, I will be attempting throughout this study to elucidate certain important principles and to lend them further support. Because the various problems that I discuss are interconnected in content, I feel that this somewhat repetitive procedure is justified.

Any attempt to consider fundamental principles, as I am doing here, must grow out of the experience of actual research. Philosophy cannot perform the task of methodological reflection for the various disciplines. Nearly all of the basic questions that I raise here were encountered in my earlier study on the idea of salvation and its significance, a study in which I had to work extensively with materials from the history of religions. The present work stems from a desire to answer the basic questions which that study raised.

In closing, I would like to thank all those who have helped make this work possible.

Leipzig
June 1924

JOACHIM WACH

CHAPTER ONE

THE EMANCIPATION OF THE HISTORY OF RELIGIONS

IN GERMANY, the emancipation of the history of religions (*Religionswissenschaft*) from the domination of the other humanistic studies was in progress throughout the nineteenth century. The process of emancipation has still not been completed today.[1] Theologians of the two great branches of Christianity still demand that the history of religions become a part of their field, and there is still no discussion of basic principles that would mark out the boundaries between the philosophy of religion and the history of religions. Theologians, philologists, and historians all engage in the history of religions. Their rich results indicate that in practice such cooperation is very significant. Great stores of data have been assembled, and there has been a great deal of mutual inspiration. But for the inner consolidation of the discipline, for its theoretical foundation and its systematic organization, this development has been somewhat unfortunate. The same conditions that have proved so fruitful for practical work have been less favorable to theoretical reflection. Still today, the systematic foundations of the history of religions are quite unsatisfactory.

In this respect the history of religions lags behind all other
humanistic studies.[2] To be sure, scholars in these other disciplines, too, are far from total agreement on their basic
questions and methods, but at least they have begun to think
about them, and they have some solid preliminary work to
their credit.[3] These other disciplines have not simply relegated
to philosophy reflection that would seem to be of a historical,
methodological, or purely logical nature; instead, they have
engaged in it themselves. In this regard art history (Kunstwissenschaft), philology, and history are exemplary, to say nothing
of the disciplines concerned with law and politics.

The history of religions is not very old yet, but it is
remarkable how long it took before historians of religions
desired to have a clear and systematically ordered discipline.
The early moves in the direction of emancipation were hardly
symptoms of a desire for logical and theoretical enlightenment.
Hardly any of the many scholars who advocated the "secularization" of the history of religions during the nineteenth
century felt a need for that discipline to be founded systematically. It would have taken only a small step for one of the
many critics of nineteenth-century scholarship or for one of
those who proposed an independent discipline to have expressed a desire for a systematically organized discipline.[4] But
only rarely did those within the scholarly establishment voice
such a desire,[5] perhaps because the history of religions was
practiced mainly by theologians, philosophers, philologists, and
historians. These persons had neither the inclination nor the
calling to help liberate this branch of scholarship, whether
they were predisposed by tradition to preserve the status quo
or whether they felt that the nature of the subject itself
required them to oppose the establishment of an independent
discipline. Such attitudes are not hard to find.

Let us look briefly, therefore, at the disciplines from which
the study of religions has descended. We should recall that,
contrary to what might easily be thought, philosophy, not
theology, is the real source of interest in the history of religions. By its very nature, theology, so long as it remained
"pure" theology, was forced to defend itself against a way of

thinking whose thorough relativism could have destroyed the very foundations upon which theology rested. But theology was not able to suppress the destructive tendencies completely. It could only ward off the danger by bringing the entire endeavor under its control. What was more natural than for theology to reject, so long as it could, the questions and research of the history of religions, to suppress and to ignore them, and then later, with equal fervor, to claim them as its own? As the importance of studies in the history of religions increased, a curious but interesting attempt was made to replace the earlier kind of theology with a theology based on the history of religions.[6] It looked as if theology was doomed and the history of religions would take its place. But that was only the appearance. Once again opposition developed to a movement that had been barely tolerated at first but that had then gained the upper hand. Today, this opposition is increasing. We now remind ourselves that the history of religions is far from providing a solid basis for theology; it works and must work under entirely different presuppositions. If theology still resists the emancipation of the history of religions, that resistance must be understood only as an inconsistency, or at most as the result of practical motives. In any case, during the nineteenth century several extremely important changes took place in theology's attitude toward the newly arisen, autonomous study of religions. Later I shall have several opportunities to discuss these changes further.

It is extremely interesting to trace philosophy's relationship to the rising history of religions. At this point I shall mention only that throughout the nineteenth century and up to the present the so-called philosophy of religion, out of which the history of religions grew, took it upon itself to study the specific questions of the history of religions. Only very recently have empirical research and philosophical speculation been strictly separated. It is well known that in the first half of the nineteenth century there was a great deal of interest in the philosophy of religion. In mid-century this interest waned, only to rise once more toward the end of the century. At the beginning of the twentieth century, problems in the philosophy of religion were discussed again, and this time a wider public participated in the discussions. At any rate, the development of the individual humanistic disciplines and their relationship with philosophy prevented nineteenth-century philosophy from providing any impetus to a movement to emancipate and establish the history of religions.

History's service in furthering the history of religions, a service that many think sustains its claim to dominate the younger discipline, has certainly been great. From its inception cultural history has had a special eye for the histories of various religions. The study of religions also received much help from individual historians who were interested in religiohistorical topics. As long as the history of religions was primarily concerned with the historical study of religions (*Religionsgeschichte*), the general discipline of history could maintain its claim to study the history of religions in the same way that it studied other cultural systems such as law, economic systems, and art.

The relations between the history of religions and philology have always been very close. In fact, it was probably philology that was chiefly responsible for the great upsurge in the history of religions during the nineteenth century. When philology is conceived more broadly and not limited to the study of language as such, it is quite possible for it to become interested in at least a historical study of religions. Thus, most of the outstanding classical and Oriental philologists have also studied religions. As with all relations of dependence, the root of this relation—in addition to empirical, traditional, and personal affinities—lies deep in the nature of things. Whenever a historian of religions must study literary sources and interpret physical artifacts in order to explore a historical phenomenon, or more generally, whenever he must investigate language as the most important tool of communication and means of understanding, philology will be very closely associated with at least the historical side of the history of religions. Not only have the great philologists been competent in the practice of the history of religions, as I just mentioned; they have also on occasion formulated theories to defend their religio-historical efforts. Here, too, however, any attempt to consider broader principles has been quite rare.

It is self-evident that the history of religions is and must remain closely related to ethnology. Ethnology seeks to understand a people's entire culture, material and spiritual. Up to the present time, the study of primitive peoples has been left to ethnologists. Unfortunately, students of religion have often succumbed to the mistakes and false hypotheses with which the history of anthropology, ethnology, and the study of myth and folklore is filled.

At present the history of religions is plagued by conceptual confusion and terminological carelessness, as it has been throughout most of its young life. It would be wrong to believe that this confusion and carelessness only affect appearances but do not reflect the unclear and unfinished state of the discipline itself. That people speak indiscriminately of the history of religions *(Religionswissenschaft),* the historical study of religions *(Religionsgeschichte),* and the philosophy of religion[7] is not merely a matter of words. It indicates that the various subjects have not been sufficiently distinguished from one another. This rather embarrassing uncertainty about the place, task, and significance of the history of religions can be seen in externals, too: in the haphazard way in which it is located in various divisions of the university, and in the way it is exploited by dilettantes and obscure speculators. From a cultural-political point of view, too, this discipline needs greater clarity and distinctness.

In recent times the various scholarly disciplines have rightly desired to free themselves from external domination, especially from the domination of politics and dogma, not only to proclaim the principle of free inquiry in theory but to establish it in practice. Only those who have studied the history of the history of religions can appreciate the peculiar difficulties which that discipline has encountered from the very beginning in its struggle to be free from domination. Likewise, it is in this discipline's history that we must look for the first source of its present confused state, and a very important source it is.

There we can see the various motives that have led other disciplines, communities, associations, and even the state to engage in the study of religions. The last few decades have seen significant progress, but even now opposing parties confront each other too harshly to allow both the simple deliberation that the subject demands and the pursuit of the corresponding organizational measures *sine ira ac studio* [free from passion and self-interest]. As odd as it may seem to some, external [that is, institutional] obscurities and uncertainties have obstructed the internal development of the discipline. They are a tremendous burden on the pursuit of scholarship. They prevent a free and unprejudiced consideration of basic questions; they force compromises and concessions; and they hinder agreement among particular branches of study. From both an ethical and an economic point of view, therefore, external encumbrances are lamentable. But we can also see the damage they do to the internal organization and activity of the discipline. Historical and systematic study are not sufficiently distinguished; systematic study in the history of religions has long been neglected and is still terribly undeveloped—these are among the many encumbrances that result in part from external constraints imposed upon would-be historians of religions.

Can it surprise anyone if as a result the history of religions has been forced, as hardly any other discipline has, to support and serve now this, now that establishment, cause, or movement? Certainly we should always welcome any occasion in which a scholarly discipline may be of service to practical life. But if this service is transformed into servitude, the discipline's character as a pure science is threatened. Who would wish to prevent a theologian from immersing himself in the history of religions in order to be able to defend and to propogate his own religion? But the purpose of the history of religions is not to compile an illustrated manual or primer for students of any one doctrine and become their servent. Can we object if a philosopher, no matter how radical his thoughts may appear, immerses himself in the study of religious history in order to provide evidence for his theories and examples for his teaching from that field, as well as from ethnology and philology? But such a philosopher must not expect that from then on the history of religions will simply undertake to demonstrate that his views are correct. We cannot prevent anyone from deriving arguments from the history of art against the propriety or even the possibility of art itself. But would anyone make the history of art responsible if someone else interpreted its results in that manner? I think not. Similarly, we cannot hinder anyone from interpreting the findings of the history of religions in his own way, from forging from them weapons for his own battles against either one religion or all religions. But by the same token, we cannot prevent anyone from drawing from the findings of the history of religions evidence for the beauty, worth, and sempiternality of religion. We may establish only one restriction, but that restriction is absolutely necessary: the history of religions itself has little to do with any of these endeavors.

For all these reasons, one may well say that it could hardly be more interesting to study the history of any other humanistic discipline in the nineteenth century than that of the history of religions. It constitutes a major portion of the history of German thought, rich in conquests, successes, and discoveries, but almost as rich in blind alleys and detours. Throughout all this history there stretches a dramatic thread. Passionate warriors have chosen this field for their struggles, and almost no other humanistic discipline, with the exception of political science, has been so closely connected with currents and movements of contemporary cultural life in general. I shall only note here that from the beginning those who are not themselves scholars have shown great interest in the findings of the history of religions.

The prospect of studying the development of this discipline in relation to philosophy is especially alluring. I have already emphasized that the history of religions has been closely connected with philosophy from the beginning. In fact, it would be enticing to trace in general terms the significance of a given philosophy for the various humanistic studies with which it is contemporary, then to examine how much the latter have given that philosophy in return. This is a systematic question of immense importance, a question whose answers will vary according to the different ways in which those who answer it understand the nature and task of philosophy. Depending upon one's standpoint, one will view such an examination as either gratifying an interest in history or preparing for systematic investigations that might constitute a basis for the humanistic studies. Dilthey, of course, has already pondered all this. Following his lead, others have examined, from a philosophical point of view, the contribution of philosophy to the development of specific humanistic disciplines and its influence on their structures. Curiously enough, such a study has never been undertaken, at least to my knowledge, from the point of view of a specific discipline, unless one counts works on the development of the philosophy of history.

Still, it remains an alluring prospect to explore the nature of the relationships between philosophy and the study of law, the arts, the state, and religion during the different epochs of the nineteenth century. Naturally, such a study would not be limited to the histories of particular disciplines; but these histories would furnish material for examining philosophy's role, both giving and receiving, in relation to the various disciplines. Where we can detect that an idealistic philosophy, such as Hegel's, has directly fertilized and influenced an individual discipline, the task is relatively simple. We would need to analyze only how far that influence extends: did philosophy merely provide general terms, schemes or constructions; did it affect the discipline's methods; to what extent did it create presuppositions as to content, especially presuppositions governed by the philosophy of history? We would also need to consider the extent to which the worldview of a particular generation has penetrated into the process of philosophical systematization itself. At other periods philosophy does not influence the systematic and methodological synthesis and organization of individual disciplines; instead, it contributes certain basic convictions and concepts concerning the content of a study, which may then serve as a background to the particular findings of positive disciplines, or may round out or fill in the gaps in these findings. Among such ideas are above all certain metaphysical concepts, assumptions about the world of values and about the divine, and so on. It is very instructive to discover the source of these conceptions, the reasons that they were borrowed instead of similar conceptions from competing systems, and the extent to which borrowing was determined by internal necessity or by chance, whether of a higher or lower order. On the other side, it is no less enlightening to observe the extent to which particular disciplines influenced the philosophy or philosophies that were contemporary with them. The degree to which a philosophy is "saturated" with data, the breadth of the empirical basis for philosophical construction, and the shape of a philosophy's methodology may all be traced to the influence of a particular discipline or a particular group of disciplines. For example, from the middle to the end of the nineteenth century the natural sciences exerted a powerful impact on philosophy. This influence was for the most part formal (methodological, epistemological); in terms of content it was less significant. To take another example, at the beginning of the nineteenth century philosophy was closely connected with those disciplines that studied the historical world; and the great idealistic systems show just how thoroughly philosophy at that time was saturated by historical data.

It has recently been pointed out, and pointed out correctly, that certain conceptions of life, certain worldviews, often underlie individual scientific disciplines, even where one cannot speak of a philosophy as such. These conceptions and worldviews may be seen in the way scholars choose and treat their materials, in the nature of the methods that they use, and in the entire basis and structure of particular studies. In this manner, scholarly work provides evidence of the attitudes and positions held by individuals and generations, that is, they reveal a scholar's "philosophical vein." However, since particular studies usually renounce, implicitly or explicitly, the claim to express general truths, it is, naturally, most difficult to formulate their products in philosophical terms. In most cases, even their language avoids philosophical clarity and

commitment whenever possible. When one senses this philosophical reticence on the part of scholars, it is incorrect, of
course, to suspect immediately that these studies have been
influenced by the professionalized philosophy of the time; it
happens quite often that philosophical ideas migrate indirectly
and undergo changes through various links and channels.
Decisive impulses have often come even to philosophy itself
from the private and occasional musings of an individual
scholar—and not, I believe, to philosophy's detriment. To
believe that the encounter between the work of individual
disciplines and philosophy should be limited to introductory
and concluding questions is a misconception that is not limited
to any single epoch. This encounter cannot be treated simply
and summarily in introductory and concluding chapters, without even so much as a glance at speculation and methodology
in the chapters that intervene. Of course, professionalized
philosophy is not a little to blame for the popularity of this
misconception. Similarly, the neglect of what the various disciplines have to offer, both formally and materially, will always
be avenged: philosophy, as an isolated system, will be abstract
and alienated from the world, "constructionist" in the bad
sense of the word, and boycotted in turn by the disciplines
which it has itself neglected. In a reply to Eduard Meyer, Max
Weber expressed this very nicely in his characteristic style:
"The most significant accomplishments of professional epistemological theory operate with ideal-typical images of epistemological goals and procedures; they fly so high above the
heads of actual goals and procedures that at times it is difficult
for the theorists to recognize themselves with unprepared eyes
in their own discussions."[8] The same complaint is heard repeatedly from the individual disciplines. The loudest com-
plaints about the one-sided, epistemological concerns of professionalized philosophy have come from history.

Recently, we have begun to pay more attention to similarities in the development of the various humanistic studies.
When we can infer from a crisis in the philosophy of law that
the relation between the philosophy of law and the scientific
study of law is unhealthy, we will without doubt stumble upon

entirely similar sets of problems in regard to the philosophy of religion, art, or language. It would be fascinating to study the changes and fluctuations, the shifting emphases and constellations, within the various branches of professionalized philosophy during different periods, especially in relation to corresponding developments in individual scholarly disciplines.[9] Such investigations would lead to profound considerations of the nature of basic assumptions and worldviews, of psychological, biological, and sociological problems, and problems in the philosophy of history. Naturally, when an epoch is primarily concerned with epistemology, that is just as little a coincidence as when it is inclined to metaphysical speculation or when it prefers induction to deduction.

Such investigations would bring us a little closer to answering a very important question: What factors determine the development of a scholarly discipline? Naturally, these factors are different from those that are decisive for the progress of philosophy. We must consider the extent to which the subject matter of a discipline propels its development (the "immanent logic"), the extent to which the formal example of other scientific disciplines or their actual content exert any influence, the extent to which psychological factors are involved, the effect of the actions of individuals and of generations, and other questions. It would be especially enlightening to study the "becoming" *(das Werden)* of the history of religions from these points of view. Such a study would reveal the continuing dependence of the history of religions on philosophy in its true light.

We may regret that the emancipation of the history of religions has been drawn out for so long, but we must also admit that the long, entangled path of its development has not simply been the product of chance. Whoever realizes the degree to which the history of religions has depended upon other disciplines will not wonder that the tempo and the path of the development of the history of religions have been so irregular. Certainly, we need to cooperate with these disciplines today as much as ever. We will always be dependent, formally, upon the methods and tools of other disciplines and, materially, upon the results of their research. But this dependence is no longer a sufficient reason to halt the process of emancipation. It is no reason to condemn the history of religions to a perpetual minority. No discipline can and should work in isolation. Each will be more or less dependent upon the help and cooperation of others. It is good for "parental disciplines" to oversee and protect a discipline in its youth. But some day the moment must come when a discipline declares itself free and of age.

CHAPTER TWO

THE TASK OF THE HISTORY OF RELIGIONS

THE SUBJECT MATTER of the history of religions is the multiplicity of empirically given religions. Its aims are to study them, to understand them, and to portray them. It does so in two ways: "lengthwise in time" (diachronically) and in "cross-sections" (synchronically), that is, according to their development *(Entwicklung)* and according to their being *(Sein)*.[1] Thus, the task of the general history of religions divides into a historical and a systematic investigation of religions.[2]

Religions are historical phenomena. The discipline that seeks to study them must approach them by using all the methods and tools required by the various humanistic disciplines. To have recognized and repeatedly emphasized this need is especially the achievement of the *religionsgeschichtliche Schule*. That school's only error was to believe that such an undertaking was primarily theological.

The history of religions *(Religionswissenschaft)* is identical neither with the historical study of religions *(Religionsgeschichte)* nor with the psychology of religion (see Chapter 5). It is not a purely historical discipline because, to a very great extent, systematic interests are properly included within it. At the same time, it is not in any way a one-sided investigation of the way religious subjectivity comes to life in the various religions, just as it is not directed exclusively to the objective side of religion. Fundamentally, the history of religions shows no preference either for collective (national, tribal) and communal religiosity (cf. Wilhelm Wundt) or for individual piety (cf. William James). Partisan leanings of this sort always avenge themselves. As a result, the history of religions tries to avoid them. The scholar of religions knows the limits of historical knowledge, and he knows how to give the psychological approach its due. But he also knows that important spheres in the history of religions necessarily escape the notice of these two approaches. The scholar of religions will never base his research and conclusions on material drawn from only a single area of the religious life. Before him is spread all the phenomena that deserve to be called "religion." The whole "world of religion" constitutes his field of research. He conceives of this world as a unique configuration of life, with laws and principles of its own. He seeks to understand life in the particular form of "religious life." Here, as elsewhere, he encounters one of life's archetypal characteristics *(Urphänomen)*: in its living fullness, life displays a restless productivity; it drives toward expression in a never-ending series of forms. These expressions, in some sense isolated from cosmic and biological evolution, undergo an evolution all their own; they experience "history." The historian of religions interprets these expressions and relates them to the life from which they have derived and in which he himself in a quite definite sense also participates. But the circle closes again upon itself. As the inquiring mind discovers the essence of these modalities of life within the experience of life, this experience of life is itself enriched and deepened through the understanding of its modalities, their nature and richness, their multiplicity and laws.

We no longer need to defend the delimitation of an autonomous realm known as religion within human cultural life *(Geistesleben)*. Earlier, it was necessary to maintain the autonomy of religion against the onslaught of English and French positivism and above all against the many shades of materialism. The positivists and materialists argued that humanity was about to leave the religious stage behind—a stage entered upon long ago, but at a time that could still be recognized—and that religion was a historically limited phenomenon which sooner or later would have to yield to science. Whatever view one took of religion—whether it was considered to be a conscious or an unconscious invention, whether it was lamented as mental confusion or acknowledged to be a necessary stage in the evolution of the human spirit—the autonomy and necessity (the "sempiternality" *["Ewigkeit"]*) of religion were denied. The source of this entire current of thought is well known: it derived from deism, which gained such a large following during the enlightenment. This movement reached its climax when the philosophies of Comte and Spencer were predominant. Since the turn of the century, however, its influence has waned. Thinkers who forged their weapons from the tradition of German idealistic philosophy played a significant role in repelling its attacks. Above all, Ernst Troeltsch—a pupil of Albrecht Ritschl and a follower of Rudolf Lotze and Rudolf Eucken who later came under the influence of Henri Bergson and Heinrich Rickert—sought to defend the autonomy of religion with the same means by which it had been attacked, namely, philosophical argumentation.[3] Others followed him, especially Rudolf Otto among Protestant thinkers and Max Scheler among Catholic thinkers. They raised the question of the "specifically religious": What makes religion what it is? In trying to answer this question, certain scholars fell into psychologistic errors, but their failings in no way diminish the significance of the question itself. The counterattack also took a decisive turn toward "objectivity." Today it is recognized that the problem of the specifically religious can be solved only by carefully considering the "objective" (*"gegenständlichen"*) side of religion.[4] At least this turn to objectivity cleared the way so that Protestant and Catholic theology and the philosophy of religion could formulate new arguments in favor of religion's autonomy. In other respects, the problem of autonomy is a question for the history of religions as well as for the philosophy of religion.[5] What is of interest here is that the *conditions* for a science *(Wissenschaft)* of religions that is truly free and unprejudiced were first created in the successful parrying of attacks against the autonomy of religion. It is obvious that a preconceived notion of the (nonautonomous) nature of religion will of necessity endanger the discipline that studies religions. By contrast, accepting the autonomy of religion implies no prejudice. Historians of religions simply take the religious claim, the religious self-expression without debate and explicitly suspend, or bracket, the question of truth. Here they must steer a course between Scylla and Charybdis. On the one hand, they must not become dogmatic; on the other, they must guard against psychologism, whose one-sidedness will never do justice to the phenomena (see Chapter 4). For with its theory of illusion, psychologism destroys the subject being studied and discredits it in the eyes of all outside observers.

Can the question of truth be so easily ignored? Many have answered this question positively, others have answered it negatively, but so far the debate has occurred primarily within the fields of theology and the philosophy of religion. When historians of religions have addressed the question, they have done so most often from a psychologistic point of view. The history of religions must avoid this mistake. The example of Max Scheler, a most ardent opponent of psychologistic views in the philosophy of religion, demonstrates that it is possible to suspend the question of validity and still recognize the intentional character of religious acts. Scheler's notion of a "concrete phenomenology of religious objects and acts" makes sense only if the possibility of suspending the question of validity is presupposed.

But apart from this, the practice of the history of religions shows that "bracketing" (as I will call the suspension of judgment) is quite feasible. Historians of religions have studied and described very different religions, they have disclosed their meanings, and they have still avoided discussing the claims to truth that these religions naturally make. This does not mean, of course, that they deny the truth of a given religion. Bracketing does not in any way support the theory that religion is an illusion. But neither does it support an unlimited relativism. Rather, we must recognize that knowing a religion and "choosing" it—to use Kierkegaard's term—are two different things.[6] I do not need to choose a religion to know it, and in order to choose a religion, I do not need to "know" it in a scholarly sense. It is one thing to study Buddhism to become familiar with it, to study Buddhism as a subject of scholarly research; it is quite another to "choose" Buddhism, which to be sure also happens among us these days. In the first instance I bracket my judgments, but I do not completely surrender a point of view. Rather, the more I get to know this phenomenon, the more I will approve or disapprove of it, necessarily. But that has absolutely nothing to do with my cognitive task. Similarly, if I choose Buddhism, that is in itself no reason to avoid studying it—although one would need to examine whether the basic principles and conditions are present that satisfy the epistemological ideal of the history of religions. But if two researchers have made it their task to know a religion, their results should be the same, whether they have decided for it, against it, or not decided at all. In actual practice, this is seldom the case, and later I will have to discuss the great difficulties associated with understanding foreign religions.

(As is well known, the medieval scholastics speculated rather subtly on the nature of faith. Protestantism, too, has included the significance of faith in its doctrines. In both views, it is possible to *know* the truths of salvation and still not believe them. To know salvation does not mean that one has decided in favor of it. This insight is of enormous significance for the study of religions. It implies that it is possible for someone who chooses negatively, that is, who rejects a religion, to know its doctrine; it also implies that even from a theological standpoint it is possible for someone who does not choose, either because he is unable to or does not wish to, still to know a religion more thoroughly than one who, without knowing the torture and mystery of choice, believes on the basis of authority, desperation, or, as commonly happens, is accepted into the community and guaranteed saving power through an external confession. In this regard, Kierkegaard's philosophy of religion has a significance for the epistemology of the history of religions that has not been sufficiently recognized.)

It is only through the application of bracketing that the subject of the history of religions emerges clearly. Say, for example, that we have before us a theological system created by a particular religion or church, a complete set of statements and assertions about religious "truths." As historians of religions, we separate out all of the meanings of this system and regard them as the expression of a given religion. Or say we observe a certain species of cultic form, perhaps in order to make comparisons. Each representative of the species stands before us with a bracket that contains its specific claims. Similarly, when we come to know a religious community, we discover what binds it together, but we do not ourselves become a part of that community.

When we learn that a prayer has been effective, in whatever community it is spoken and to whatever deity it is addressed— that is, not when we perceive a prayer's effectiveness visibly, but when we hear that it has been effective, as in a report of a healing—when we hear about the experience of being uplifted or strengthened or made joyful as a result of prayer, then, as scholars of religions, we take notice. But we will not build theories of self-hypnosis on the basis of such reports, nor will we regard the "visible effect" as confirming the reality of the deity invoked. We do not discuss such topics, for they lie beyond our competence. If historians of religions discussed such topics, they would infringe upon the precincts of theology and the philosopy of religion. In one sense, historians of religions are only recorders or registrars, even if, as human beings, they are not just scholars. Hegel was entirely correct when he wrote: "If knowledge of religion were only historical, then we would have to regard theologians as servants in a merchant's household. They would keep the books for someone else's wealth, working for another without possessing anything of their own. Their merit would accrue only from serving and recording that which belongs to another." Keeping records is not the task of theologians—they have other work to do—but it is the task of historians of religions. The latter should and will be fully satisfied if they are able to keep accurate records. Their own possessions are not in question; these are booked in separate accounts. On the balance and relation between the two I will have more to say later.

No one will deny that bracketing makes it possible to study the *philosophical* systems of all peoples and times and to value them as expressions of worldviews. It is possible to be concerned with fathoming the intention of each system without raising the question of whether they are true. Those who study the arts are familiar with this procedure. Their discipline attempts to understand a work of art by attempting to draw out its "meaning"; it does not raise the question of "truth." Of course, there is always a second question: How far do such attempts succeed in individual cases? But here we are discussing ideals and principles. Certainly, many of the fine points and profound insights of a philosophical worldview are disclosed only at the end of a long and intimate acquaintance with it. Certainly, a work of art exerts its highest and final effectiveness when one completely surrenders to it. But this only means that one must know thoroughly what one wishes to understand and that not everyone will be able to achieve the same inner closeness with regard to every phenomenon.

In asserting that knowledge in the history of religions is similar, I run the risk of being accused of rationalism. I will probably be told that in the case of religion we are not dealing with theoretical reflections and aesthetic forms but with something deeper and greater. This something cannot be understood by reason, for religion discloses itself only in faith. Knowing the message of salvation always means that one has embraced it; whoever does not embrace it cannot know it; and so on. Along these lines religions have formulated their doctrines of revelation, divine election, and sacred scripture.[7] But the accusation of rationalism is not justified. The history of religions does not posit reason *(ratio)* as its highest norm. Analytic reason is given no control over what is to be understood. The primary task of scholarship—fathoming meaning—

does not fall to reason alone. Whoever understands understands with his whole heart (*mit der "Totalität des Gemütes"*).

Rudolf Otto was entirely justified when he pointed out recently that the duality of rational and nonrational moments is found to varying degrees in all religions. The ambition of the history of religions must be not only to do justice to religious expressions to the extent that they are rational, but also to give the nonrational its due. How pitiful is that study which describes a theological proposition or a cultic performance as nonsensical and devoid of meaning simply because it confronts logic with a riddle.[8] Of course, the rational does dominate many religions; nevertheless, it is certain that our understanding is in error if it merely dissects a religion before the forum of reason. In the case of Christianity, Kierkegaard recognized and demonstrated this impressively in his theory of the paradox. A scholar of the caliber of Max Weber has now and then neglected this principle, and not without regrettable consequences. Consider the totemistic theories advanced primarily by English scholars—each more rationalistic than the last—and the answers that have been given to questions about the religious nature of totemism. The structure (*Gesetzlichkeit*) of religious life—and I must emphasize this point here—is original, and thus in the end it cannot be comprehended from the point of view of philosophy, science, or ethics. I should also emphasize that the history of religions, which, as we have seen, must avoid making value judgments, is not entitled to censure the objects that it studies, whether morally or ethically. Anomy, libertinism, orgy, ecstasy, and others, exist as facts which this discipline must treat as such.

Once more I must struggle against a misconception that threatens to crop up everywhere in this book. My demand for bracketing is not to be understood as a recommendation for "the" psychological method. As important as psychology may be, the history of religions will not succeed with it alone. Showing the limits of psychology is the accomplishment of the phenomenological school, an accomplishment that can scarcely be overestimated. Psychological studies have been extraordinarily important for the history of religions, but in the past a certain kind of psychology of religion eventually came to the point where it saw religion as completely lacking in meaning, where it destroyed the specifically religious phenomenon and thus propounded an extreme and groundless relativism. Both Feuerbach and Nietzsche overstepped the limits of psychological observation in the direction of an often excessive psychologism. Later, two trends of thought carried this one-sidedness to greater extremes: the so-called American psychology of religion and psychoanalysis. The first was marked above all by its naive lack of concern for what is decisive in every religious phenomenon, the intentional content, which it psychologized away completely (cf. Starbuck). The second was marked by one-sidedly favoring questions of origin, which also led to psychologism.

The "bracketing" that I have advocated takes place, in contrast to all psychologistic procedures, in full awareness of and with explicit emphasis on the intentional nature of religiosity. Bracketing applies not only, and not even primarily, to religious acts but to the phenomenon as a whole. It includes act plus "content": the doctrine and its meaning, the cultus and its significance, and piety and the object to which it is directed are all enclosed in brackets.

We must now consider the obstacles that every historian of religions faces. According to one well-known scholar, the history of religions presents three difficulties: (1) the great quantity of material; (2) the nature of the material; and (3) the question of truth.[9] The first two difficulties deserve a closer look. Given what I have said already it is not necessary to consider the third any further.

The history of religions shares the first difficulty, the immense amount of material, with most related disciplines, such as history and ethnology. This difficulty is not insurmountable. But because the history of religions is a young discipline, it has not had enough time to centralize and collect studies; as a result, tracing, gathering, and organizing materials can be rather toilsome. The scholar of religions must gather data from literature and life, from every nook and cranny on the face of the earth. To compound the difficulty, the documents of foreign religions are, naturally, written in foreign languages, and even with the best of intentions a scholar cannot master or even begin to understand all of these languages. Further, source materials are of the most varied kinds, and a religion can never be studied in isolation but must always be seen in close connection with the cultural and social conditions in which it is found (see Chapter 3). All of this presupposes extensive knowledge in many fields. The history of religions is not concerned with examining the principles governing the relations between religion and culture. That is a problem for the philosophy of religion. Nor is it concerned with the conceivable relations between religion and society. That is a theme for sociology. The history of religions is concerned instead with the actual influences which particular cultural systems such as science, art, and law have exerted on the various religions.

What I have just said indicates that the work of the history of religions cannot be done on the side by one or more disciplines. It is absolutely essential for a large number of able, talented individuals to pursue this work within the confines of an independent discipline. Of course, this independent discipline will always be obligated to seek and to preserve the closest possible cooperation with related disciplines.

The second objection that advocates of the history of religions ordinarily confront is somewhat weightier. It concerns the nature of the material. Is it really permissible to study religion from the point of view of a scientific or systematic discipline? When this question is answered affirmatively, another question arises: If so, is it possible to do so? Does not what is best in a religion elude an approach that claims to be "devoid of presuppositions" and that is armed with a scalpel? Since I will address this question more intensely in Chapter 4, I will give only a very general answer here.[10]

First, it should be noted that the same difficulty is found in the other humanistic disciplines. Here let me single out the study of art and literature. Practitioners of both disciplines have had to defend the possibility of using scientific or systematic methods against the objections of both enthusiasts and skeptics, and they have done so successfully. Today there is no doubt that such an approach is justified in studying works of art and creative writing.

Of course, with respect to the study of religion the situation is a degree more serious. Nowhere is there so great a danger of stumbling over externals and missing the path that leads to genuinely profound insights as in the understanding and interpretation of religious life. But this life too has its forms, its "language," in which even mysticism expresses itself, a most internal and individualistic form of piety that appears to get along without any form of objectification. The expression of religious life is a bridge to its understanding. But this bridge would be impassable if there were no certainty that somehow one soul can understand another. I will have more to say about this presupposition and its implications later. But one thing above all may give us courage and hope: the conviction that religion is not dead but alive, that more or less innately, more or less purely actualized, it lives in all of us; that the soul's final attitudes, experiences, and decisions are "eternally human," and that this "eternally human" includes not only the general attitudes toward life that are expressed in particular religions but also the modalities in which they express themselves. In this sense Novalis was correct: "The highest is that which is most understandable."

Scholarly understanding need not be cold and unfeeling. When scholars are animated by a pure desire for knowledge, when no other forces direct them, they will approach great mysteries and secrets respectfully, not to profane or destroy them, but to see them in their glory and their misery, their awesomeness and their power. The great historians are wonderful examples of being moved in this way by their subject matter, high-minded and spiritually powerful men who, animated by a pure striving for knowledge, have been able to show us so richly, so wonderfully, and from so many different angles the lives and destinies of both peoples and the individuals who led them, their characters and wills—in a word, history as it actually happened.

Everything depends on how the task is carried out. The chief and fundamental prerequisite for a scholarly treatment of such phenomena will always be that the investigator possess and nurture an *Organ*, a sensitivity to the nature and peculiarities of the subject he studies. Whoever wishes to understand the pronouncements of law with any sort of profundity must have a feeling for law. The world of musical sound and visual images will only disclose itself to the person who possesses a sense for art. Likewise, there is a prerequisite without which no one will understand religion: a religious sensitivity. This phrase must be understood in a "pregnant" sense. Not long ago a scholar rather new to the study of religions reminded us of Schleiermacher's maxim that "religion must be viewed with religion." To me, this is spoken from the heart. To be sure, historians of religions must leave to the philosophers the task of determining what this religious feeling looks like both potentially and actually—a noble task, although I, too, shall formulate a sort of minimum definition (see Chapter 4). But all false sentimentality should be set aside. The less said about the brittle, incomprehensible, and mysterious nature of the subject being studied, and the more uninhibitedly and straight-forwardly problems are handled, the better—always, of course, within the bounds set by the presuppositions that I have stated. It is precisely from this point of view that the separation of theology and the history of religions which I am about to discuss becomes necessary. Just as not everyone is born to be a theologian, not everyone is born to be a scholar of religions. All human activity has its own presuppositions and conditioning factors; and it may be that characteristics which aid in one endeavor are detrimental to another.

If the task of the history of religious is to study religions empirically, must one not ask at the outset what religion actually is? Above all, must not this question—the question of the nature or essence *(Wesen)* of religion—be asked and answered at the beginning of a discourse that intends to prepare for the establishment of the history of religions?

I am convinced that the unfortunate question about the essence of religion, which in this form derives from Schleiermacher, has been more of a hindrance than a help in developing a free, unprejudiced, empirical history of religions. It is actually a question for the philosophy of religion, but it has not been raised as such. Instead, it has been introduced into the history of religions proper, and there it has confused more than it has clarified. The question should really be examined exclusively from a normative and philosophical point of view. Neither at the beginning nor at the end of our research should we say what the essence of religion is. The findings of the history of religions may confirm or refute the definitions which philosophers of religion give, but of itself the history of religions can never answer this question.

Precisely where the question of the essential nature of religion does belong produces different opinions. Some consider it a problem for theology; others a problem for philosophy and psychology; still others a problem for the history of religions. Georg Wobbermin, for example, declares: "The entire task of theological systematization, according to the method of the psychology of religion, is organized about two main questions: What is the essential nature of religion, and what is the essential nature of Christianity?"[11] In his view, the question of the essence of religion has been from the time of Schleiermacher, and will continue to be, the fundamental problem of the scholarly study of religions. Troeltsch, too, views the major task of the history of religions in terms of "the great question of the essential nature of religion."[12] He distinguishes four subdivisions of this task; he admits that his entire approach is philosophical in nature; and he claims to be linked with the positions of Kant and Schleiermacher. Heinrich Scholz dedicates an entire volume of his *Religionsphilosophie* to this problem. He considers the question of the essence of religion one of the two major classical problems in the philosophy of religion.

More divergent still are the different opinions on how to go about answering this question. The history of religions cannot be totally disinterested in the various approaches that have been taken. Not only is it interested in the specific answers that the philosophy of religion gives to this question; the history of religions can learn quite a lot, positive and negative, from the methodological controversy. Theology faces a similar situation. The question of the essential nature of religion is not itself a theological question, but this question has still been most enlightening in terms of both theological method and content. Therefore, I will examine briefly some typical attempts to define the essence of religion.

Basically, there are two possibilities. Either one seeks to understand the essential nature of religion empirically or one seeks to derive it in a deductive and a priori manner. A third method has attempted to mediate between the two; it tries to overcome the one-sidedness of each method and to combine their good points.

The procedure of the so-called *religionsgeschichtliche Schule* is typical of the first approach. This school holds that one ought to be able to comprehend the essence of religion by comparing the empirically given religions, ignoring their differences, and extracting what they have in common. As we shall see, such a procedure is not only permitted within the framework of the history of religions, it is required. Nevertheless, it will never lead to the desired a priori. To be sure, the "essence" defined by this approach will vary somewhat depending upon whether it is derived from psychological data or from the data of historical documents.[13] But in any event, the key concept in this entire approach is "religious experience" (*Erfahrung*).

My task here is not to criticize the content of this method. Others have correctly pointed out its deficiencies. Defined in this manner, the essential nature of religion must be rather empty and formal; as a result it cannot satisfy the needs of philosophy. Above all, normative and universally valid conclusions may never be drawn from experience.

The second approach begins with a concept of religion that has not been discovered from an examination of experience. In this approach, the empirically given religions do not constitute the material from which a concept of religion is deduced and abstracted; rather, what counts as religion and what does not are determined by the concept. Three methods are typical of this approach: (1) the deductive method (Kant); (2) the a priori method (phenomenologists such as Scheler); and (3) the normative method. Granted, the last method takes its "yardstick" from the empirical realm by absolutizing a religion which it regards as "true." Closer examination reveals, however, that this method does not absolutize a concrete historical religion. Rather, it uses a particular religion's "ideal" as a yardstick to determine the essential nature of religion. This ideal is actually obtained by means of the deductive or a priori method, however much its discovery may be influenced by historical observation. It is self-evident that consensus on the results achieved by a deductive method is even less likely than consensus on results achieved by the empirical-historical method.

Perhaps a third possibility would be to combine the normative and the inductive methods, as Scholz and Wobbermin have tried to do. Thinkers who try this approach expend much effort in attempting to discover the central or constitutive ideas of religion: the idea of "God," the relationship to the "supernatural," the "Holy," and others. Quite a number of such concepts of religion—from extremely general notions to those very rich in content—have been posited. But time and again one can show that this or that religious phenomenon does not fit the proposed definition, that a definition is too broad and therefore meaningless, or to narrow and therefore useless in practice. Not all philosophers of religion can bring themselves to exclude one or another religious phenomenon just because it does not happen to conform to their definition of what religion ought to be. Buddhism is especially troublesome in this regard; as a result, it has become a sort of black sheep in the eyes of the philosophy of religion. Anyone with any historical sensitivity cannot help but protest against such procedures.

To show that the question of the essential nature of religion is not at all a question for the history of religions, and to show that the scholars who have given it the greatest attention have actually treated it as a problem for the philosophy of religion, even if they have not always made this clear, I shall present and criticize the most important of their theories.

Ernst Troeltsch argues his position in greatest detail in his essay on the essence of religion and *Religionswissenschaft*.[14] He thinks that the expression, "the *Wesen* of religion," is multivalent and therefore misleading. It gives the impression that it is possible to solve the various problems that the phrase invokes through one and the same kind of investigation. As I mentioned earlier, Troeltsch divides the problem of the essential nature of religion into four parts. First of all, "the essence of religion" signifies for him "the essential characteristics by which religious phenomena are recognized as phenomena pertaining to the psyche or the soul." Since in saying this Troeltsch is referring to the "real *Wesen*," in contrast with "mere appearance," and to the "truth content" of religion, he must complement psychological investigations with epistemological studies. To these two he then adds investigations from the point of view of the philosophy of history. These investigations test the results of epistemological work against all the empirical material, critically evaluate historical religious forms, and raise the question of the "ideal religion" and the "religion of the future." Finally, Troeltsch adds metaphysical reflection, which confronts the problem of the relationship between religion and our other ways of perceiving the world.

He then goes on to explain that as vigorously as the modern history of religions has led to an understanding of religion from within, this understanding is still always only temporary. The old concerns of the philosophy of religion in a narrower sense—study of the philosophical foundations or classification of religious ideas within the totality of human understanding— must in the end continue, and rightly so. This rather general remark makes it appear as if the philosophy of religion has the last and decisive word even when the history of religions takes up the issue of the essence of religion. Thus, according to Troeltsch, the question of the essence of religion is limited to the "analysis of the spiritual phenomenon, conceived as purely and as factually as possible, that we call religion," in terms of the four points of view mentioned. All this aside, Troeltsch is not inclined to think that this whole problem is very important. He especially dismisses the "scholasticism" that these definitions frequently foster.

A critique of Troeltsch's position must naturally begin with the psychologistic way in which he frames the entire problem. This approach is seen especially clearly in his prescriptions concerning the psychology of religion and epistemology. What is significant for us is to see, given Troeltsch's entire position, how empty the specific task of the history of religions really turns out to be.

Heinrich Scholz makes a new attempt at understanding the essence of religion in his *Religionsphilosophie*. Together with Troeltsch he formally defines the essential nature of religion as:

1. the content of those moments that are of fundamental significance to the empirical aspect of religion;
2. the peculiarity or individuality of religion;
3. the immanent idea or "intentional" character of religion.

According to Scholz, in studying the essential nature of religion, we must seek not the goals of religion but its foundations, not the interests that religion serves but the factual circumstances on which "the religious consciousness rests." His tools for understanding the essence of religion are primarily self-understanding and the "pregnant" instance. There is no need to detail his notions further here.

The methods that Scholz proposes can never achieve his goal. They are one-sidedly psychologistic. The possibility of self-understanding is, of course, a prerequisite for all work in the history of religions, but it can hardly be considered one of the most important methods by which to achieve an understanding of the essence of religion. At the very least, this method must be complemented by another method, history. Here, too, in the final analysis, the essence of religion is not understood inductively but deductively (a priori). No empirical basis is present, and the results are philosophical insights, not conceptions that further the history of religions. The way Scholz extends and applies Troeltsch's position on how to conceive the essential nature of an empirical religion to the question of the essential nature of religion as such cannot be deemed fortunate.

The question of the essential nature of a particular religion, of Christianity, say, or of Islam, is quite different. It is of great practical significance to research in the history of religions. In addition to studying particular facts and their interrelations, the historian of religions will always have to characterize the essential nature of the religion under study. "Each of them, that is, each of the historical religions, has its own unique and particular character, its own inner life-principle, its own peculiar spirit (Geist). This 'spirit' differs greatly and in many ways from the 'spirits' of other religions, and grasping the individual spirits of particular religions is the most difficult and delicate of the tasks undertaken by the psychology and historical study of religion." So wrote Rudolf Otto, one of the most important scholars of religion. Already Herder and, even more magnificently, Hegel, undertook just this task, and by comparison the work of others appears impoverished and pale, despite the fact that these others had access to much more material. With the steady increase in the tendency toward positivism during the nineteenth century, the field of history sought more and more to drop the philosophical and metaphysical presuppositions that gave rise to its entire enterprise. A study of the empiricization of the historical disciplines would be extremely interesting and, so far as I know, has yet to be written. In any event, matters went so far that even today one still finds among many historians a pronounced fear of asking questions about the essential nature of a phenomenon. They are inclined to see in such questions a lapse into metaphysics, or at least an impermissible hypostasization.[15] In the wake of this empiricization, concern for finding essences was limited to the Western investigator's own religion, Christianity; that is to say, the problem was trans-

formed from a problem for the history of religions into a
problem for theology.[16] The theology of the nineteenth century adopted this approach; think only of the attempts of
Feuerbach, Baur, and Harnack to determine the essence of
Christianity. When Harnack's book appeared, a controversy
arose in the course of which the methodological problems and
difficulties surrounding the entire question were finally illuminated. The honor of having clarified the matter belongs
once again to Troeltsch. In his foundational work, "What
Does 'the *Wesen* of Christianity' Mean?," Troeltsch described
historically and systematically the very entangled interconnections implied by this phrase, and he pointed to the presuppositions, the means, the sense, and the goal of the entire
endeavor.

From Troeltsch's essay it becomes clear beyond doubt why
every attempt to seek the essence of Christianity can be oriented only toward historical work and how this approach must
proceed. "*Wesen* can only be discerned from an overview of
all relevant phenomena; to discern it we must exercise historical
abstraction—the art of divining the whole altogether—and at
the same time have at our disposal a full store of precise,
methodically obtained data."[17]

Unfortunately, Troeltsch himself confuses the dogmatic,
normative standpoint with the historical standpoint, especially
in his notion of synthesis, more specifically, through his concern
for the future relevance of the essential nature that is to be
discerned. In this connection, his concept of the "ideal" fur-
thers the confusion. As a result, Troeltsch once again abandons
the empirical standpoint, not so much by sliding off into a
philosophy of history but by introducing a theological and
normative point of view into historical and systematic work.
Still, Troeltsch's work has been and remains the most significant and comprehensive attempt to solve this exceedingly
difficult problem. All future efforts to determine an essence
by historical means will have to reckon with his results, both
positive and negative.

Any historical study of religions that does not wish to limit
itself to superficial appearances and does not see the mere

compilation of facts and data as its goal must seek a unifying
and organizing principle that holds the individual phenomena
together. From such a principle one can then understand the
particulars of the historical process. Systematic study is concerned with the "center," with that which provides the key
for understanding particulars. It must identify the point around
which all particular trends order themselves. Observation tells
us that each particular understood correctly helps us understand the next. As Boeckh says, "Everything understood will
in its turn become a means toward understanding." As a
result, there will always be a circle: the spirit of the whole
can only be comprehended indirectly, by comprehending the
parts, and all particulars can be fully understood only through
that principle which provides internal coherence.

There is one point that I must insist upon: to determine
the essential nature in a strict sense, we must discover the
central point (*Lebensmittelpunkt*) of a phenomenon and its idea.
It is never acceptable to use this expression to refer to the
identification of major historical lines of development or to
the identification of distinctive traits. To preclude this misconception entirely, perhaps it would be advisable, instead of
speaking about the essence of a phenomenon, to think of it
as divided into "spirit" and "idea." (The word "soul" would
only evoke the notion of a metaphysical background, to say
nothing of this word's unpleasant aftertaste. Therefore I shall
exclude it from my discussion.[18]) It would be desirable to
establish a terminological distinction between the actual, life-
giving, organizing principle—the character of the entire phenomenon—that is, the spirit, and the idea, which functions
as a norm. Accordingly, we would distinguish, for example,
between the spirit of Islam, which underlies everything that
is unfolded within the Islamic religion, and its idea. The
potentials contained in the idea will hardly ever be fully
realized. Every factor that influences historical occurrences
drives actual developments in specific directions and cuts off
other possibilities. The particular characteristics, both collective and individual, that inhere in a religion, carry their own
"a priori"; they produce transformations and changes in both

the development and the nature of that religion. In response to actuality, all sorts of concessions, adjustments, and assimilations take place. As a result, the dichotomy that I wish to highlight distinguishes the *idea* of a religion from its *history*. History is the flux of development and becoming, the changes that occur both in the subjective realm and in the realm of expression and its forms. Over against the historical stands another approach, which is also concerned with the totality of expressions but which seeks to fathom not their "becoming" *(Werden)*, that is, not changes in expression but their being *(Sein)*. It attempts to see the unity of what occurs in individual patterns and groups of forms. It seeks to depict the spirit that supports and rules the whole. To this spirit corresponds an inner, subjective state: to continue my previous example, the psychology of the Muslim. The scholar of religions must trace this subjectivity in its basic structure and development. In doing so, he must bear in mind that the piety of the masses is no less important than the religiosity of great personages, who experience many things as representatives of the masses, who anticipate the masses with respect to other things, and who experience still other things as mediators for the many.[19]

Understanding what pertains to the soul or psyche *(das Seelische)* is the task of psychology. But the "spirit" of a phenomenon must be understood and interpreted as the inclusive aggregate of what exists objectively within the phenomenon. I shall have more to say on this later; here let me merely mention in general terms that the decisive task of the history of religions is to penetrate to the center of the phenomenon, from which all particular traits, forms, and manifestations are nourished. Troeltsch articulates this in a phrase that is not completely free from ambiguity; he writes that here we deal with "eine der Historie eigentümliche Abstraktion, vermöge deren der ganze bekannte und im Detail erforschte Umkreis der zusammenhängenden Bildungen aus dem treibenden und sich entwickelnden Grundgedanken verstanden wird."[20] It will not be a simple task to extract this fundamental conception *(Grundgedanke)*, which embraces both spirit and idea. It cannot be done through simple induction. Here again a prior intuitive comprehension of the whole and the understanding of the parts must complement each other. On the one hand the analysis of a religion's becoming, as well as the analysis of the spirit that lies at the heart of all its expressions, must work with what in its individual traits characterizes the religion as "idea." On the other hand, the idea can only be pointed out in something that is empirical. But one question will always remain: What provides the yardstick for our knowledge about the content of the idea? For example, shall I take the teachings of the Qur'ān as the idea of Islam, or shall I begin with the Sunnah of the companions? Muslims, of course, have recognized the Sunnah of the Prophet and his companions as authoritative, next to the Qur'ān. On that view, the Sunnah is a commentary on and exposition of the Qur'ān. It is very interesting, however, to observe the introduction of a third factor, *ijma,* the consensus of believers. As opposed to the static Qur'ān and Sunnah, *ijma* is a dynamic principle that undertakes to mediate between the idea and history. Certainly, in the case of *ijma* the idea has already become "cloudy." In comparison with the Qur'ān and even with the Sunnah of the prophet, historical development has contracted, widened, changed, and transformed many things. Nevertheless, the Sunnah of the companions has become the norm for the others. And although the Sunnah has been conditioned by certain influences, although it has been stylized by a certain exegesis—that is "transformed"—in practical life historical development has been measured by it. One must then begin to think about the nature of this "transformation."

If a scholar believes in an objective dialectic of things, as in Hegel's idealistic philosophy, then historical movements become for him necessities. He will be convinced, for example, that developments within Islam follow a definite, fixed order. So far as his grounds permit, he must regard historical development as closed. Or else he must read the basic conception out of the totality of individual empirical phenomena, and he must grasp the idea from history and its unfolding. If he does not believe in such a "logical consequence," then instead of a teleological order he will have to reckon with a full range of one-sidedness, error, malformations, and accidents. These will emerge for him no matter how or where he seeks and finds the norm.[21] Most frequently he will seek the norm in the original proclamation; but he must not forget the great modifications that can occur in the course of later developments. The idea of Mahāyāna Buddhism, for example, cannot be derived entirely from the teachings of the Buddha; one has to consider the transformations these teachings have undergone in the emergence of the Greater Vehicle. In practice such a scholar will need to distinguish between a religion's self-expression (the authenticity of an interpretation referred to tradition passed down from the time of the beginning— Hadith, Halacha; the same is also true for the classical religions of India, Persia, and China) and what is proven to be a factually valid idea by historical investigation (this, of course, is different again from practice.) The consequence is that our impartial, synthesizing approach, based on empirical data, must work in three directions: first, it must work out the course of historical development; second, it must understand the spirit of the totality of expressions in conjunction with the psychological exploration of the internal as its subjective correlate; and third, it must understand the idea as the driving force of the whole. Here again, on the next higher level, there will be a mutual understanding of one by the other and from the other. A slogan for this approach might read (to continue my example still further): "What Islam was, what Islam is, and what Islam wants to be."

In a scholarly study, the question of the essence, and above all, the idea of a religion, must not be confused with the practical question, "What must we do?," as frequently happens. It does not matter how we stand personally with respect to the ideal. We must identify the essence and idea without regard for any attachments or syntheses (Troeltsch), and we may not avoid doing so just because this task has no immediate application or utility.

As I said already, in gathering data, discerning particular traits, and penetrating to the center of a phenomenon from its characteristics, our goal cannot be comprehensiveness. It is an old truth that one may know everything about something and still not understand it. One must identify characteristic traits and combine them. Traits that are conspicuous and significant as far as externals are concerned are not always the most important. I may know many of a person's particular deeds and characteristics and still not find the focal point that ties his life together. But at some point the opportunity might come for me to look more deeply into his nature. Suddenly all the separate traits combine and supplement one another and form a complete picture. The experience of the scholar of religions is not exactly the same, but it is very similar. He works for a long time, perhaps in philological studies; he compiles data without perceiving completely their inner connections or organization. Then, whether slowly or by a sort of sudden intuition, the depths of the phenomenon's essential nature open into view, and he understands how the various traits are connected.

It will not always be easy to combine and fix in a simple verbal expression what one has come to recognize as the organizing principle, idea, or essential nature of a phenomenon. As Troeltsch has said, it will probably never be possible to encompass the formative spirit of a religion in a simple concept. Such a concept must be quite broad, for it must embrace and contain within itself even the strongest of tensions. The unessential will repeatedly impose itself upon our attention, and one may despair of ever finding an enduring process in the flux of historical development or a common ground in a series of independent phenomena. The scholar will repeatedly be forced to examine whether his assumptions are correct, with regard both to their own truth and to the context in which he places them. He will continuously have the opportunity to learn new things, and he will constantly have to refine his basic concepts. And as I have said, these tasks will be impossible without hypothetical constructions. In the end, one must be consoled by the hope that successive hypotheses will complement preceding ones, improve on them, or make them unnecessary.

Certainly, in such a procedure the limits of empirical research strictly speaking are transgressed, but this transgression is necessary. Moreover, the scholar will continuously test and correct his results against experience. The trick here is to avoid the extremes of historicism and completely unhistorical speculation and to arrive at a "synthesis" of methods, just as the highest task of every discipline is to achieve a methodological synthesis of the empirical and the philosophical. The historical study of details will always be the starting point and foundation, but of course it will not be possible to attempt to comprehend an essential nature without a certain hiatus. On the other hand, there is something in empirical research that points and drives beyond itself.

One more point must be considered. Some have pointed out, and they are right to do so, that the determination of essences in this sense still bears obvious marks of the subjective standpoint from which it has been undertaken. But we ought not overestimate the importance of this fact. The broader the historical base from which we start, and the truer our devotion to the subject we are studying, the less the danger of subjectivism. Nevertheless, it is exactly at this point that it becomes clearly necessary to separate historical research from critical, "political" research. In the end, Herder's words are still valid: "Only by the spirit that we bring to history and draw from it will the histories of persons and peoples be of any use to us. Facts compiled without spirit yield no profit; even the unfolding of historic occasions can serve no other purpose than to be evidence, truth."[22]

The subject that the history of religions studies must, therefore, be considered a given. The discipline will have to work with a concept of religion that is very general and hypothetical and that cannot be directly justified, at least in the beginning. The ultimate clarification and working out of this concept remains the task of the philosophy of religion. Of course, the history of religions will not proceed arbitrarily. It will have to orient itself about the empirical. For example, in order to delimit its field—and delimitation is the primary issue here—the history of religions will have to consider both scholarly and general linguistic usage. If in the process one or another aspect of a proven view is erroneously excluded, or if some aspect of an unproven view is included, the error will be able to be corrected easily, especially if historians of religions cooperate as closely as possible with neighboring disciplines. Finally, however—and this is decisive—the history of religions will repeatedly be able to make improvements on the basis of the certain results of the philosophy of religion.

The history of religions also does not ask about the essential nature of religion in the sense of seeking its origin. Whether religion is rooted in feeling, in reason, or in the imagination; whether religion is a theoretical or a practical affair of the human spirit; whether it grows out of the totality of human nature—these problems concern the history of religions as little as the endless controversies about them. Finally, the history of religions also does not ask about the purpose of religion—whether it be concern for happiness, longing for salvation, or the fulfillment of some other need.[23] Questions of essence, origin, and purpose are in themselves of no concern to the history of religions. Until now a preoccupation with these questions has constantly hindered work in the discipline, so that knowledge of this fact should help free it for positive work.

After all that has preceded, we may simply say that the totality of the phenomena to which we assign the general designation "religion" forms the subject of an independent scholarly discipline which we call the history of religions. That would seem to be self-evident and apparent. And yet, several difficulties with and objections to this contention arise immediately.

The history of religions is not the only discipline to claim the world of religions as its field. Supported by its age and its tradition, theology—or perhaps it would be better to say theologies—stake the same claim.

First of all, theology claims a more or less exclusive right to treat its own religion normatively, historically, and systematically. In doing so, it removes a specific group of phenomena (the Christian religion, Protestantism) from the competence of the history of religions—provided, of course, one has already granted that the subject matter of the history of religions is the totality of all empirical religions without exception. It seems obvious that theologians need to justify the exclusion of Christianity from the history of religions, but instead they go much farther. We saw in Chapter 1 how theology has ambitiously taken hold of the impulses to do research in the history of religions and has attempted to enclose this entire approach within the confines of its own system. It should not surprise us, then, when theologians declare that theology is itself the history of religions (*Religionswissenschaft:* the scholarly discipline devoted to the study of religions) and then claim for themselves the right to study foreign religions. They either completely deny or narrowly circumscribe the possibility and right of a nontheological discipline to study religions.

In general, however, theologians would rather surrender foreign religious phenomena to the history of religions than surrender its own religion to that discipline for either partial or complete examination. When the latter takes place, a dualism results: the same religion is studied in both theology and the history of religions. There is no question that even when theology is most generous toward the history of religions, it retains the right to use the results of religiohistorical investigations for its own purposes (comparison, measurement, the constructions of grades or stages of religion) and perhaps to revise these results from the "immanent" point of view. I will have more to say about the normative tasks of theology shortly.

In the confrontation with theology, one must first distinguish between a theoretical treatment of principles and practical and organizational concerns. In theoretical terms, there can be no doubt that the independence of theology is justified. When scholars of religions express the opinion that theology should become a part of the history of religions, we must oppose them. Such a view seems self-evident to thinkers who treat religion as something that is or ought to be overthrown. For them, to include theology in the history of religions is the first step toward abolishing it. But once we admit that there will always be theology because there will always be religion, we soon realize that the task, the object, and the method of the theologian are so different from those of the historian of religions that including theology in the history of religions would undermine the fundamental principles of the latter. Consequently, the scholar of religions, just as much as the theologian, must reject the demand that theology be included within the history of religions.

There is no normative history of religions. The only normative disciplines that pertain to religion are the philosophy of religion and theology.

Although we must reject the far-reaching demand that the history of religions annex theology, we must still investigate the task of theology and its relationship to the history of religions from the point of view of the history of religions.

It is clear that a dogmatic formulation of faith—the core of theology—is required for the systematic and normative formulation, presentation, and teaching of a religion. It seems impossible that this task could ever be taken on by the history of religions. Certainly, presenting the Christian religion from the point of view of the history of religions is not only possible but is absolutely necessary. But the history of religions proceeds specifically by bracketing, and dogmatics can never "bracket." As a theological discipline, Christian dogmatics must remain Christian. I explicitly oppose the view, recently reasserted even by some theologians, that the theological study of the Christian faith need not be Christian, just as criminology need not be criminal.

I need not discuss here the question of how far such a dogmatics can or should be considered a scholarly discipline (*Wissenschaft*). Behind the claim that it is lies the assertion that a particular religion is true, which will always be the first and last assertion of every dogmatics. A characteristic circle results: dogmatics must demonstrate the truth of its religion, but it must first establish itself on the basis of that same truth. It will never be able to do so by taking a detour through the history of religions, as the *religionsgeschichtliche Schule* (Troeltsch,

Wobbermin) held. The Protestant theologians who stand further to the "right" have seen this impossibility correctly. The teachings of a faith do not constitute a historical discipline but a normative or "norming" discipline. They state what ought to be. That is the decisive difference that distinguishes theology from the history of religions, which is concerned solely with knowing what is. For the same reason, dogmatics does not have to be on a collision course with philosophy and other disciplines, although it frequently happens that such a collision is the major emphasis of dogmatics today. For dogmatics, such confrontations, however important, are still secondary problems. Its primary emphasis must be on providing a foundation for its own point of view.

Closely allied with theoretical dogmatics are the practical theological disciplines. Naturally, my purpose here is not to present the tasks of theology, and as concerns the practical disciplines there is little room for misunderstanding: practical theology will never come within the realm of the history of religions' competence. After considering the fundamental principles of the two disciplines, it is necessary to acknowledge that theology and the history of religions are independent. This distance will always be perceptible from the practical point of view, but the situation is different for those theological disciplines that do not enjoy the special status of the theological disciplines discussed so far: the biblical disciplines, such as exegesis, criticism, and the theologies of the Old and New Testament, and historical disciplines. There can be no doubt that in principle these disciplines must operate by the same rules and with the same methods as the corresponding "profane" disciplines, philology and history. As a result, their independence from the history of religions is much more difficult to establish. As a matter of fact, we can say very little *against* including them within the history of religions. Questions of origin and historical development aside, it seems obvious that theologians must be very interested in establishing the closest possible links between auxiliary disciplines and the historical side of theology.

Once the history of religions has acknowledged the independence of theology, how should it study and portray the
Christian religion? There can, of course, be no talk of neglecting Christianity. It would be improper on several accounts
to deprive the history of religions of the right to treat the
religion that pertains to us [in the West] the most. It is possible
to collaborate in studying Christianity historically without much
difficulty. Of course, it will be difficult to draw boundaries.
The scholar of religions may certainly avail himself of the
results of theological work, but he will be able to do so most
freely when the biblical-critical and historical disciplines proceed entirely by general historical and philological methods.
Especially in dealing with systematic religious conclusions and
insights, the scholar of religions must establish controls and
possible tests that he may apply to theological findings—
counterparts of the theological controls mentioned above. Obviously, histories of the church and of dogma would look quite
different if written by theologians for theologians than if
written by scholars of religions in general. This is not a
lamentable shortcoming of theological work, as, interestingly,
many theologians feel. It is both necessary and good.

We have no choice but to be satisfied with a dualism. The
Christian religion is a subject that theology and the history
of religions both study. There is no need to fear differences
and quarrels so long as both sides proceed strictly according
to their own principles. The viewpoints of these undertakings
are so basically different that it is not necessary for conflicts
to arise.

The result is that theology and the history of religions
work side by side in relative separation. Not only does this
separation correspond to historical development and practical
necessity; it is grounded in the subject matter itself.[24]

There is another question: What may theology and the
history of religions contribute to one another? Theology's
significance for the history of religions consists primarily in
the immense amount of material which the latter receives from
theological work. The thorough, penetrating, and extensive
work that theological systematics, exegesis, and history have

produced present the history of religions with quite a unique set of materials, and the more a theology is convinced of the uniqueness, truth, and beauty of its religion, the more significant will its results be as data for the history of religions. It is possible to incorporate directly—with certain corrections—the results of systematic-biblical and historical work, but the propositions of systematic theology (dogmatics) must be used indirectly. The benefit which the history of religions has derived and still derives from the historical study of the Old and New Testaments and of the Christian church can never be overestimated.

On the other hand, as many have emphasized, at times perhaps too strongly, theology can expect to receive much from the history of religions. This is not the occasion to present what, in my opinion, the history of religions can contribute to the construction of theology. The extent of this contribution depends upon one's understanding of the nature and task of theology. In the view I have adopted here, the history of religions promises theology a large increase in materials, an expanding horizon, and a new appreciation for one's own religion. Nevertheless, it is decisive that no one can derive the absolute value and truth of his own religion from the history of religions. The history of religions can only point to "eminence"; it can show "uniqueness" in the sense of extraordinariness, but never in the sense of absoluteness. Consequently, I reject both the view that the history of religions is to be seen as an enemy or rival of theology from which nothing but evil can be expected, and the view that theology can expect to receive from the history of religions everything that is good.

To summarize: the task of the history of religions is to study and to describe the empirical religions. It is a descriptive and interpretive discipline, not a normative one. When it has studied concrete religious phenomena historically and systematically, it has fulfilled its task. To expect it to demonstrate somehow, whether through induction or deduction, the truth of "the" religion in an ideal sense, is just as misguided as to expect it to provide practical instruction. Philosophy and theology have a normative, prophetic character, but the history of religions lacks this character entirely. As a scholarly discipline it must proceed without presuppositions; that is, it must limit itself to studying the concrete. So far as possible, it must work apart from subjective evaluations and philosophical speculation; it must refrain from all explicit evaluation in a sense that I shall discuss later. None of this prejudices the personal convictions of the scholar of religions. It is certainly possible for a scholar who practices an empirical religion to do work in the history of religions in the more exact sense, that is, without presuppositions. There would be only one requirement: that he believe himself capable of possessing—and actually possess—a sufficient measure of objectivity. The extent to which this undertaking would harmonize with his personal religious commitment is of no concern here, for I am exploring the qualifications for undertaking work in the history of religions only from the point of view of that discipline. On the nature and limits of objectivity I will have more to say later.

It is astounding that there can be any doubt at all that the history of religions is a purely empirical discipline. If a person studies this discipline in order to discover "the" true religion, that makes sense only as long as that person is seeking from the history of religions the relative valuation of *a* religion.

No one should be forbidden to take a stand about the results of the history of religions. On the contrary, the more strongly a person ascribes to a particular point of view, the more fruitful and lively will be that person's confrontation with the discipline's results. Such evaluations do not, however, belong within the discipline itself; at best they can only serve preparatory purposes. Just as we must resist the demand that the history of religions award prizes and pass judgment as the culmination of its work, so too we must reject the other extreme, the view that a total absence of a point of view is a prerequisite for doing work in the history of religions. Later I will examine what the prerequisites are for doing scholarly work in the history of religions. There we will see that indifference, skepticism, and the lack of a point of view do not enable a person to do such work. But a historian of religions must know how to separate research and preaching, scholarship and prophecy, scholarly discipline and philosophy. In order to achieve the greatest possible objectivity, the historian of religions must demand a strict adherence to the facts, as is done in all the procedures and methods of the human studies and especially in historical scholarship. We shall see later the extent to which personality, individuality, and point of view are implicated in one's choice of subject matter. We shall also learn the degree to which these positive factors have a rightful place in the presentation of one's results. In between these two extremes, however, there is the realm of scholarly discipline strictly speaking, the realm of research.

I need to mention one more point. To accomplish the task of the history of religions—and as a result to assure the discipline recognition and equal status among the humanities—there must be a proper relationship between the scholar of religions and the subject he studies. I have already discussed this relationship to some extent, and I will have much more to add later. For the moment, let us recall only that so long as some so-called scholars of religions see their task as proving that religious expressions are meaningless nonsense and that scientific and philosophical thought is superior to religious thought, the history of religions will rightly be mistrusted. The odium of polemical and destructive intentions which the history of religions still possesses in the minds of many must be dispelled.

As a preparation for work in the history of religions, it will be important to advance the study of "religious language," to develop, by means of individual study and comparison, a kind of "grammar" of religion, which will serve to exclude many misunderstandings. The philosophy of religion will contribute to this undertaking a theory of modes of expression as a complement to empirically based work. Studying religious language is just as difficult as deducing grammars from spoken languages. Every religion, in correspondence to the spirit animating it, develops a larger or smaller number of pictorial, conceptual, and symbolic expressions. (Here I am using the word "expression" in an extended sense to include mythology, ritual, and other classes of phenomena, not in the narrower sense of a "means for making oneself heard" or a "communication"). Comparative study of these expressions will reveal how great the agreement among them really is. The language of mysticism has already received scholarly attention, and its dialects show surprising similarities and analogies. To the study of "language" in a narrower sense historians of religions will add a study of those actions and customs that have religious significance and symbolic value. It is easy to see that such a study would have great significance for understanding and assessing religious life that strikes us as foreign. The interpretation of such religious life is and will remain the task of the history of religions.

We will not be able to specify the precise range over which the concrete tasks of this discipline extend until the history of religions has been established on solid foundations.

CHAPTER THREE
THE BRANCHES OF THE HISTORY
OF RELIGIONS

As we have seen, the task of the general history of religions is to study the religions of all times and places systematically and historically. In the preceding chapter, I clarified to some extent the themes of this discipline and rejected several approaches to its problems as false and dangerous. Now I shall proceed to show how the discipline structures itself upon closer examination.

First, there must be a clean methodological distinction between historical and systematic studies. In Chapter 5 I shall present the basis for this distinction and elaborate on it in detail. For the moment, I simply state it as a requirement.

Because of this distinction, the general history of religions is divided into two major branches, the historical study of religions and the systematic study of religions (*systematische Religionswissenschaft*).

Let us first look at how the historical study of religions is structured. Its theme is the becoming (*das Werden*) of religions; its task is to study and present their development. This task must be discerned distinctly and clearly. The idea of a purely historical study of religions has not attained its true significance because as usually practiced it also pursues systematic tasks. Today scholars often speak of a general historical study of religions (allgemeine Religionsgeschichte). Such an expression implies one of two things: either that completeness is the scholar's goal, that he wants to include all empirical religions in his studies, or that he is attempting to "construct" a schema of religious history that establishes its unity. To the first—which would emphasize the comparison of one religion with another, for example, Indian with Greek—I have no objection. Here "the general historical study of religions" corresponds to designations in parallel scholarly disciplines, where one also speaks of a general history of law, of art, or of the economy.

But what about the second implication? Is such a "constructive" treatment of religious history still conceivable, and if so, is it possible within the parameters of the history of religions, or does it perhaps belong to the philosophy of religion? It is well known that such constructions were very much in vogue earlier, and they supplied a fairly coherent "history" of religion. The beginning of this approach dates back to the early period of Christianity. Occasionally such constructions have been found in historiography and the philosophy of history as such. For a long time, historiography was historia sacra; and the "history" of religion, the history of salvation. All history was viewed from a theological point of view, and this point of view was preserved even after the secularization of the historical study of religions. The eighteenth century, with its vigorous interest in Religionswissenschaft and the philosophy of religion, cultivated a general interest in the historical study of religion. Philosophers have commonly preferred a constructive approach to the historical, but today there has arisen, especially with the blossoming of church history, a quite "positive" history of religions.[1] Forerunners prepared its way, especially David Hume. Both approaches crossed and united in Herder, the genius who, if anyone at all, was the man at the crossroads of this discipline. After Herder, the constructive view of the historical study of religions reached its zenith in the superb system of Hegel. He, as no other, exhibits both the advantages and the disadvantages of the speculative approach. Universal constructions down to the present day have relied upon ideas in Hegel's speculative philosophy of religion. Some of the more original thinkers in this line were Ed. v. Hartmann, Dorner, and Pfleiderer, while in F. Chr. Baur the speculative method was applied to church history with particular success. But in the actual historical study of religions, which has increasingly developed into an independent discipline through the efforts of Max Müller and which has emancipated itself more and more from the philosophy of religion, no one has made any significant speculative attempts.[2] Instead, the task of combining findings about particular religions and understanding them from a teleological point of view has been taken on by the philosophy of religion. Church history and the history of dogma have parted with speculation even more emphatically. As the great works of Harnack, Loofs, Seeberg, and Schubert typify, they have abstained almost entirely from universal constructions. More recently, however, a call has gone up for a philosophy of church history, most notably from Köhler. In the history of religions proper, we see today a strong dislike of everything extensive and of all constructions. Scholars limit themselves to studying specific religions, specific areas, and specific problems (cf. the "philology of religion" among classical scholars). Attempts to "construct" a general religious history *(Religionsgeschichte)* come only from outside this discipline.[3] At any rate, we must distinguish the approach that sets out to construct universal syntheses from attempts to identify leading ideas and principles. In an empirical and historical approach, the latter is not only possible; it is, as I will show later, necessary. But a universal construction, even in a specific area of human thought, will never be possible on an empirical basis It can be undertaken only on the basis of philosophical convictions about history.[4] Proving this was one of the great accomplishments of Troeltsch's work on historicism. It follows, then, that the construction of a universal religious history must proceed speculatively, and that as a result this cannot be a task of the history of religions, for the history of religions is an empirical discipline.[5] It is not necessary for the empirical history of religions to question the right of such constructions to exist. At most, it may point out what the possibilities are; it may never decide about these possibilities for itself, whether for them or against them, nor may it allow itself to be tempted by speculations of one kind or another.

The history of religions must, however, study the *development* of religion. By "development" I do not mean the beginnings or origin of religion in a philosophical sense.[6] I mean the reconstruction of the historical course and development of religions. It is not the evolution of relig*ion* that interests the student of religions the most; it is the "becoming" of relig*ions*.[7] Confusion between these two has its source in Schleiermacher's thought. An outstanding exponent of both *Religionswissenschaft* and the philosophy of religion, Schleiermacher merges and confuses the two in theory as well as in practice. Whenever he begins to talk about "relig*ion*," the empirical religions, their development and their differences, fade from view, despite his great interest in them. His successors, down to Troeltsch and Wobbermin, have repeatedly given the history of religions the task of identifying this "religion." The historical study of religions is only of use to them to the extent that it pursues this goal. In his *Einleitung in die Religionswissenschaft* (in the chapter on "The Concept of the Evolution of Religion"), C. P. Tiele expressly states: "By (the evolution of religion), I do not mean that religion develops now in this, then in that form, but that religion, in distinction from its manifestations, evolves continuously with humankind." "The evolution of religion"—here the difference becomes quite clear—"may better be described as the evolution of religious man, or of humanity to the extent that it is religious by nature." Such a view does not allow us to say that religious conceptions or doctrines, activities or cults, evolve. They are renewed and modified. Their growth is not unconscious. "It proceeds intentionally and with full consciousness." Consequently, these changes, occurring in complete consciousness, are not evolution per se; they are its results.[8]

In opposing Tiele's view, let us first remind ourselves that changes in an objective religion do not result in any way from the intent and consciousness of the founder (see Chapter 5 and appendix). Such a thoroughly rationalistic explanation cannot help but appear strange in the context of the history of religions. It is in the realm of religion, if anywhere at all, that hidden forces play their role in the depths of an individual soul or in the soul of a people. The saying, "What he weaves no weaver knows," is valid in the realm of religious forms, if it is valid anywhere. According to their own testimonies, great personalities are tools. Hardly ever do they reflect on or know what they have done. The historian of religions who desires to study more than mere changes in form must study forms in connection with their center points. Despite Tiele's remarks, the ongoing development of objective religion is also a subject matter of fundamental importance to the historical study of religions. The historical study of religions has the wonderful task of bridging the gap that now more than ever separates two approaches: on the one hand, the one-sided study of the history of forms and ideas; on the other, the exclusive study of changing attitudes, the concern for psychological and philosophical questions. Other disciplines, too, must overcome the same one-sided oversimplifications. In any case, the major task for the historian of religions is not to study or reconstruct the history of the soul of religious man; it is to study the development of particular religions and religious forms.

To understand the development of religions, a person must be able to do more than record internal or external changes. To understand the development of religions, he must be able to trace, with the fine *Organ* of a born historian, the coming into being of particular phenomena, of individuals, of objective forms, or of a people. He must sense the laws by which the dialectic of becoming proceeds, by which it subjugates itself to a universal order and still follows a law of its own. Certainly, the historical study of religions deals only with concrete historical foundations. But the rise and fall of these particular phenomena can be understood only by one who has, through previous experience, attained a general knowledge of the rise and fall of other spiritual realities. It does not follow, as Tiele thinks, that historical study must be interested only in the evolution of "religion," as if religion were something that evolved beneath a surface of features that are less important. It is precisely the rise and fall, the blossoming and fading away of temporal, empirical appearances that is most important for the historical study of religions.

Thus, the historical study of religions studies the "becoming" of religions. But is this still possible after the idea of a universal, constructive historical study of religions has been rejected? In the sequential compilation of data, in the assembling of a mosaic, must there not be a unity and a focal point from which the presentation is ordered and proceeds? Earlier, when "construction" was in vogue, the focal point had been "religion." "Religion" was thought to develop or to evolve and reach its zenith in the past or in the future; at any rate, the point at which it reached its zenith could be determined. The development or evolution of religion was supposed to aim toward this point, the absolute religion, and consequently, presentations of religious history (Religionsgeschichte) were oriented toward this absolute.[9] Today the situation is different. Hegel's vast construction can no longer be maintained, even with the alterations made by his successors. The materials have grown unceasingly, and the horizon of the scholar of religions has continually broadened. Today it seems impossible to capture the wealth of phenomena within the few and often schematic categories of the great philosopher. But in addition, the attempt, especially by ethnologists, to sketch a scheme of religious evolution more empirically—following Comte and Spencer—has been doomed to fail from the beginning, in spite of the progress that recent corrections have made possible.[10] Recall the fate of the grandest of these undertakings, Wundt's evolutionistic construction. First, its basic assumption, the theory of animism, recognized to be unfounded and false, was dropped. Scholars of various persuasions—Söderblom, Otto, Schmidt, and Beth—pointed out Wundt's mistakes. Meanwhile, Lang had renounced Tylor and his predecessors. Today we are completely without a generally accepted construction of religious history. It may be noticed how well-guarded Otto's hints are about the evolution of religion in his book, *Das Heilige* [Eng. trans., *The Idea of the Holy*]. It would be wrong to believe that the theories developed so far have merely been deficient and that in time they may be replaced by more complete theories. It is time, I think, to realize that the history of religions has little or nothing to gain from such attempts. They cannot lead it to its goal.

To construct a series of stages for the evolution of religion from the standpoint of a single empirical religion taken as the absolute is also out of the question for the history of religions. The works of the *religionsgeschichtliche Schule* have taught us that. For the scholar of religions, a religion's highest point can only be a result of scholarship, not one of its presuppositions, as Troeltsch emphasized repeatedly. For the theologian, of course, the situation is different. It must be regarded as of no consequence, then, when scholars imitate attempts at reconstruction in the Hegelian sense and proceed by a strictly historical method to introduce the idea of progress into the study of religions. The question of progress is not an issue for the history of religions. In pursuing its own apologetic tendency, theology may group religious data historically to indicate progress; the philosopher of religion may be interested in proving that progress has taken place in the direction that his systematic reflections on the development of the world spirit and other topics demand; within the framework of a total philosophy the question of whether and to what extent religious development manifests progress may be discussed. But the history of religions cannot discuss this question. Tiele wanted to adopt the idea of progress as a working hypothesis, and he tried to derive "progress" in religions from the "law of the unity of the human mind *(Geist)*." But the history of religions is not even permitted to adopt the idea of progress as a working hypothesis.

Research on individual religions and groups of religions centers on the focal point, on the unity of lines and spheres of development, and nothing more.[11] This cannot be expressed more beautifully than in the words of Herder: each religion contains "within itself the central point of its happiness." Thus, each religion is unique and incomparable and must be understood in its own terms. Once this has been recognized, the temptation to rank religions artificially and to turn individual formations into transitory stages of a more basic reality will be overcome.[12] The question of how to understand the principles of particular religions—whether it is possible to postulate that they are internally connected—must be considered by the philosophy of religion in conjunction with the general philosophy of history.

Therefore, the most important task of the historical study of religions must remain that of understanding the "Becoming" of particular religions, of understanding their development as unfolding the principles inherent in them. Spengler saw this quite clearly; but long before him, so too did scholars of the German historical school, whom Troeltsch called *Organologen*. In a certain sense the history of religions must continue where Herder left off. Only now we must proceed more strictly, more exactly, and more empirically.[13] When I refer to Herder, I intend to invoke only his basic attitude.

I need to mention one more point that seems to speak against the way I conceive the historical study of religions. One might object that my procedure will lead to a complete "isolation of individual totalities"—to use Troeltsch's words— to an atomization of history. One might also point to connections between individual phenomena and remind us that, like individuals and cultures, religions too are dependent upon the past and upon their predecessors, that history must always be understood as a whole. Religions, too, live on the basis of what has preceded them.

All this is correct; but I fail to see how it speaks against the plan that I have outlined. Certainly, one religion influences another; certainly, there is also continuity, and more perhaps than continuity, as Spengler would like there to be. Still, a historical study of religions (*Religionshistorie*) must understand the development of a religion first of all from that religion's own principle. Here again we encounter a great danger to which many historians of religions succumb: preoccupied with the history of forms, they forget the essence. Regardless of whether conceptions and customs, dogmas, myths, and cultic forms travel from one religion to another or whether they are inherited, they never remain what they were. The principle that brought them forth, and from which they live, sustains them as long as it possesses a "creative force." When that force is extinguished, the forms die. They may well be claimed by others, but then they mean something different. They occupy a place within another total context. They stand in a different relationship to the organizing principle of the new religion. Perhaps their new content changes them and gives them new life; then they themselves have become something other than what they were. Or they may remain as vestigial features in a new body and be recognizable as such.

This much we have already established: the historian of religions cannot simply study the history of forms, just as he cannot simply study the history of attitudes *(Gesinnungen)*. He must see both together, the change in inwardness and changes of form.

It is a mistake to begin the history of a religion with its appearance in the world, with the coming of a founder or a prophet. A religion begins to come into existence earlier. Every religion has its prehistory. Where prehistory seems to be missing, it is simply not known; one has not yet looked for it carefully enough. From this angle every religion is a syncretism. But there comes a moment when it becomes more than a bundle of already existing elements, when it becomes a formation that follows its own laws. The point in time of the "manifest" beginning can perhaps be determined only negatively. Often it will seem to coincide with the time when the religion appears in the world. A feeling for individualities is needed here to discern what is correct, a feeling for the uniqueness of historical formations that all the great and true historians have had. The final and finest philosophical truth of this feeling is contained in the skeptical confession, *individuum est ineffabile*. The final aspect of uniqueness can no longer be comprehended rationally. One can only give way to "divination," which then zeroes in more closely. Today, when the nature and value of historical meanings are often threatened, in spite of, or perhaps because of, the remarkable development in the sense for the historical, we need again to emphasize strongly their significance.

In outlining the structure of the historical study of religions, we must proceed accordingly.

What confronts us first is the immense quantity of historical data that we must process by historical methods. Naturally, this processing will have to be modified in accordance with the nature of the subject under study. In the end, the method has to match the subject of study. But even given the greatest agreement on the basics of procedure, there will still remain particular differences among the various historical disciplines. This is true of purely technical procedures, but it is even more true of the higher functions of comprehension, exposition, interpretation, and so on. A methodology of the historical study of religions would have to work out all these points in detail.

If one describes the discipline concerned with the "Becoming" of religions as the "general" historical study of religions in the first of the meanings mentioned above (p. 54), that already implies the presence of a "specialized" historical study of religions. The specialized approach divides up the total endeavor on account of the often difficult nature and immense quantity of material and on account of the trend toward specialization common among scholarly disciplines. To date, specialization has occurred along several quite different lines[14]:

1. Formal and historical-systematic: the history of particular religions, or particular religious communities (churches, sects, schools), of particular objective forms (such as the dogmas of one or more religions, a certain doctrine, the cult), particular personalities (such as religious heroes).
2. Classification according to locality (according to geographical, anthropological, ethnological, and genealog-

ical points of view: by continents, countries, races, peoples, and tribes).

3. Classification according to time: the history of religions within certain epochs and periods.

To these must be added:

4. Classification in regard to value judgments.
5. Descriptive classification (characterization).

It is obvious that these points of view overlap in actual practice. I shall discuss each of them in turn, but first, I must mention yet another point. As I have said already, we are still rather poverty-stricken when it comes to actual genetic studies, historical studies of religions in the strict sense. Systematic problems constantly plague historical investigations; systematic points of view constantly enter into historical descriptions. In general textbooks and compendia, but also in more specialized works that study religions historically, the systematic presentation of doctrines has come to predominate.

As important and as necessary as systematic presentations may be, the historical study of religions requires strictly historical research even more, however more difficult that research may be. Certainly, a historian interested in the historical development of religions will always encounter a lack of source materials and considerable ambiguities in the materials that do exist. But these difficulties will not prevent him from seeing the significance of the historical approach. (For methodological reasons I discuss this approach in isolation from its total context.) The dual nature of spiritual phenomena once again confronts us. On the one hand, we have the history of the internal side of religion; on the other, the history of objective religion, of doctrine, cult, and so on. Is a history of piety even possible? Can we think meaningfully about something like a history of Islamic religiosity? I believe that we can. Consider church history, where such problems are not unknown. Scholars in that field have demonstrated over and over again that, alongside the history of the church and other objective religious elements (doctrine, cult), changes and movements that pertain to the inner religious life may also be studied. Given the present state of knowledge, it is obvious that for a long time to come most efforts in the historical study of religions, too, will be directed to the history of institutional churches and to describing the external fates of religious communities and establishments. This need not, however, be the case forever, and especially a methodological study like mine must point to other tasks. The history of piety (that is, of pieties) cannot consist merely of a series of psychological investigations of famous religious personalities; it will have to direct its attention above all to the development of folk religion. From such studies we gain extremely valuable insights into the nature and significance of factors that operate in the course of religious history in general. One further point: scholarship is to some extent justified in concerning itself with the origin of religions. The time of the origin, in conjunction with the acknowledged originating impulse, is especially important for religious forms as they develop. But historical research must not concentrate exclusively on origins. Its primary goal will always be to understand the total sequence that the evolution of a religious formation has followed. Here the historian may occasionally have to curtail the philologist.

Even in concrete, historical religious formations there is something that may be called their inner form. It pertains to the ways in which the various modes of expression relate to one another (conceptions and cult, prayer and sacrifice, and so on), and this relationship's development and alteration can be traced by history. As we have just seen, it is possible to understand religions only by discovering their characteristic centers, from which particular traits become comprehensible. Now that I am discussing historical becoming, I may add that the historian cannot be satisfied with finding the organizing principle or with analyzing the spirit of an objective totality, as the systematician may. Rather, the historian will constantly search the continuous flux of events, the continuous flow of development, for new centers, in order to resolve the concrete flux into a sequence of particular units of meaning understood in terms of whatever their central ideas happen to be. Church history has employed this procedure with great success. Its classical form is, indeed, a history of the Christian religion, understood and grasped in this broad manner. Over and over again this discipline has also sought at the right moment to advance from an analytic to a synthetic approach, and it has thus counteracted the danger of dissolution and fragmentation.

It is not difficult to understand why the development of no single, non-Christian religion has been studied as precisely and as consistently as that of the Christian religion. Theology has long approved of the distinction I am advocating between historical and systematic study, and this distinction has proven very fruitful. As a result, we really do have a *historical* study of the religions of the Old and New Testaments.

By contrast, the historical study of Buddhism or of Islam— to say nothing of other religions—is only in its initial stages. The poor state of these studies is not entirely due to the newness of the approach or to the difficulties of the material. The historical study of law, art, the economy, and literature are in this respect far ahead of the historical study of religions. It may be true that law shows more changes than religions do; the latter are in the habit of becoming rigid when their initial impulses weaken. But then, it is very intructive to study the processes of dogmatization, scholasticization, regeneration, and reformation. Even apart from their effects, these processes are very interesting historically. To date, concrete sequences of events have received more attention than the analysis of the intertwined factors that function in these developments. But it is certain that when the latter have been studied more thoroughly, the greatest imaginable benefits and advantages will result for the concrete study of particulars.

I shall now use a few well-known works in the history of religions and the historical study of religions to illustrate what I mean by a necessary and distinct methodological separation of the historical-genetic and the systematic. Consider, for example, Ignacz Goldziher's fine *Vorlesungen über den Islam*, a book most useful to anyone interested in this religion, whether general reader or scholar. In this book, Goldziher has two intentions: first, to describe Islam's "Becoming," its development (history); then to present the Islamic religious system in cross-sections. In the actual presentation, these two are not kept separate. The chapter titles show this failing clearly: (1) Muhammad and Islam; (2) The Development of Law; (3) The Development of Dogma; (4) Asceticism and Sufism; (5) Sects; and (6) Later Developments. As these titles reveal, the historical approach dominates. The writer seeks to portray historical becoming. (This is especially obvious in chapters 2 and 6, but basically every chapter is historically oriented.) The description of Being is structurally submerged. This example is very instructive. Naturally, scholarship on Islam has produced works concerned solely with historical development. Wellhausen, Nöldeke, Lammens, and above all, Goldziher himself were all interested in Islam's origin. The well-known descriptions by Robertson Smith and Curtiss are arranged systematically. Grimme's *Muhammad* separates the two points of view more distinctly. Part One treats the life and the development of Islam; Part Two treats the theological system of the Qur'ān. Horten's approach to the philosophy of Islam, with his detailed analysis of the Islamic worldview, is arranged entirely systematically, and it is especially helpful for illuminating the systematic approach. Often, however, the two tendencies are out of balance; they struggle continuously with each other and preclude harmony. Quite apart from aesthetic considerations, which are secondary, it can be rather dangerous to confuse these two approaches. The great, of course, are justified; they have their own ways of looking at things. And certainly it is the highest goal of scholarship to integrate these two in research and writing. But when we are concerned not with a few great individual performances but with the continuity, progress, and deepening of historical research on a more modest scale, a clearer distinction in both methodological consciousness and actual research would be desirable for the specialized historical study of religions.

Let me return now to the question of classification: the simplest and most popular kind of classification is classification by location and geography. It is not possible to say that all the deeper implications of geographical classification have been sufficiently expounded. The primary insight that spiritual phenomena and the physical environment are interconnected—an insight that we owe to the eighteenth century and that today is the mode of classification most favored in dealing with the material of religious history—has not been cultivated at all satisfactorily. How promising were Herder's first beginnings! He attempted to apply Montesquieu's ingenious ideas to the history of religions, which Herder himself had actually founded; that is, he had attempted to trace the influence of climate and landscape on religions, their rise, and their development. Have we gone very far beyond these beginnings? Have the magnificent works of Karl Ritter, of Ratzel and his successors, been fruitful for the historical study of religions? Historical studies of the religions of the ancient Israelites and of the New Testament are much more advanced. These studies have given geographical factors due consideration, without feeling any need to formulate universal propositions from their results. In most handbooks of religious history classification by location dominates, frequently with an anthropological and ethnological orientation. The difficulties of classifying religions according to races have been pointed out especially well by Jeremias.

A chronological classification yields the historian of religions very little. Of course, he can take the history of the religions of classical antiquity, the ancient world, the ancient Near East, or the history of the cults of the Roman Empire as his special object of study. But dividing the entire historical study of religions by this principle will yield nothing. It is more or less arbitrarily forced on the subject matter from the outside. Such periodization does not result from the things themselves but is imposed upon them for some practical reason, such as analogy. A possible exception might be a consideration of the actual beginnings and early periods of various religions. It would also be useful to delimit a specific field known as "the religion of prehistoric times." The study of this religion involves special difficulties that invite hypotheses and constructions. Methodological deliberation, however, may prevent many erroneous conclusions in this field too.

The key idea for distinguishing religions according to their value systems is *Klassification*. From the beginning evaluative classification has played a large role in the historical study of religions as well as in the history of religions. When it did not serve explicit theological and apologetic interests, it most often presupposed some philosophical theory that it sought to illustrate. As long as the speculative construction of the evolution of religion underlay this pursuit, it was justified. But as these presuppositions fell by the wayside and as the so-called historicism became increasingly influential, attempts at evaluative classification appeared more and more barren and groundless. They were no longer a matter of logical classification but of evaluative grouping. I need only mention a few such classifications to show how impossible it would be to use them in the history of religions today. The distinctions between "true" and "false" religions and between "natural" and "revealed" religions are theological and dogmatic. Likewise, the distinction between a religion that "has arisen" and one that was "founded" is of little use; we can never be sufficiently certain about a religion's rise to apply this distinction, mainly because we always have a distorted view of the role of the founder.

The list of different types of evaluative classification also includes the distinction between "natural" and "ethical" religions. This distinction, until recently a favorite with philosophers of religion, has been strongly promoted by C. P. Tiele. It is especially questionable because it confuses description and evaluation. One can hardly assume that the history of religions will be helped much by such evaluative classifications. It is not necessary to decide here how useful they might be in the philosophy of religion.

Much more important is descriptive classification; its distinctions rest on a principle grounded more deeply than every other kind of classification that I have mentioned. I distinguish four kinds of descriptive classification: (1) formally objective; (2) formally subjective; (3) objective with regard to content; and (4) subjective with regard to content. To the first group belong such distinctions as those between mythological and dogmatic, national and global, and scriptural and oral religions. The distinguishing principle has been taken from the sphere of objective phenomena, and these phenomena are structured according to "formal" points of view. By contrast, I would call a distinction "formally subjective" if it is based on the predominance of a psychological function, for example, religions of feeling and religions of the will. This distinction hearkens back to the psychological origin from which a religion is nourished. Describing religions as ascetic-soteriological or prophetic-revealed would characterize them objectively with regard to content. Such a characterization aims at the spirit of the doctrine, cult, and institutions. Finally, a distinction among types of piety (joyful, melancholic) would be subjective with regard to content. Many classifications involve a mixture of several of these principles.

None of the above distinctions is better than the others in an absolute sense. One must inquire into the purpose for which classification is made and toward which it is oriented. In any case one must insist that classificatory schemes are consequent and derived. This derivative character is not clear, for example, in a scheme that has been used frequently lately, the distinction between religions of law and religions of salvation. The expression "religion of salvation" is to be understood only as an example of the third, or perhaps of the fourth, type of descriptive classification; the term "religion of the law" belongs to the first, or at best to the third, type. Therefore, only if both expressions are understood as describing the spirit of objective religion may they stand as components of a consistently applied developmental principle. The prototype for mixed classifications is, by the way, Tiele's system.[15]

We have not yet gone far enough to be able to undertake a truly satisfactory classification. Such a classification would require not only that we understand the historical phenomena from their centers, not only that we penetrate as deeply as possible into their "spirit," but also that we know more about the structure of objective religion and its interconnections than we know today. Only then will we be able to arrive at the structure that "emerges from the object of study itself." Finally, we must keep in mind that a grouping for didactic, methodological purposes is one thing but a philosophical classification from a speculative point of view, quite another.

There can be no question that one religion is just as worthy of study as any other. The history of religions must neither underestimate and despise the so-called lower religions nor overvalue "primitive" religions. Of course, a historian of religions may prefer one religion over another because data about it are more readily accessible; in principle, however, the history of religions, like all disciplines, strives for the greatest possible comprehensiveness. Since the history of religions must refrain from every evaluation, it cannot join philosophy in its preference for the "high religions." On the contrary, it must be fervent in its treatment of ethnographic materials. These materials need to be multiplied and to be studied thoroughly. In this regard we can learn much from non-German scholarship. The studies of Frazer, Lang, Marett, and others—to set aside for the moment the questionable hypotheses that they advance—are of value and importance to the history of religions because of the wealth of material that they contain. The situation is similar with German scholarship. What scholar of religions has not learned something bearing on his historical and systematic studies from the works of Bastian, Ratzel, Schurtz, and Frobenius, no matter what he might think of their opinions and theories?

Especially in the last few decades we can detect among many scholars a one-sided preference for the high religions, for "religion's summits," and for "great religious personalities." Experimental psychology errs, perhaps, in the other extreme by preferring the "average" (cf. Starbuck's statistical method), which it takes delight in flaunting before those who are more humanistically inclined. In any case, the issue plays a great role in problems associated with the psychology of religion. James, Troeltsch, and others have already tended to move in this direction. Today especially Scholz advocates such views very sharply and one-sidedly. Partiality of this sort is very dangerous for the history of religions; it avenges itself severely. The danger is especially great when the scholar focuses more emphatically on systematic work. It is in such work that the extent of the discipline's historical base is decisive. On the other hand, the history of the history of religions shows that the danger of erring on the other side is no less great. During the past few decades, scholarship has moved away from the old conviction that the religion of primitives deserves privileged attention. That religion was supposed to reveal to us the primeval type *(Urtypus)* of religion; its study and knowledge were supposed to be of special pedagogical value. These notions are no longer as prevalent as they once were, but here and there the idea still lurks that the history of religions must give preferential treatment to primitive religions, that in primitive religion the sources flow purer and, above all, interpretation is easier.

Another error that more recent scholars, especially Max Scheler, have been right to criticize is the overvaluation of deviant religious phenomena, especially in studies influenced by American and French psychology of religion, for example, James's principle of the extreme typical instance. To be sure, the study of the symptoms of illness has a rightful place in the history of religions, but that place is limited by the actual significance and role of these phenomena in empirical religions. We must especially reject that approach which would attempt to interpret normal phenomena in terms of basic principles, opinions, and methods borrowed from a pathology of religion. Such an approach transgresses our basic principle that every spiritual phenomenon must first be understood and interpreted on its own terms as an "individual totality"; an atomizing analysis can never dissect such a totality into its elements without dissolving or destroying it.

Over against specialization in the historical study of religions stands the expansion of its proper field of study, which I shall discuss in the context of the question just raised. Granted, this discussion is important not only for the historical study of religions but also for the history of religions as a whole. But it seems advantageous to raise this issue in connection with the classification of tasks.

In order to carry out a historical or systematic investigation, it is possible to isolate one or several religions from the total context in which they stand. But just as the life and experience of an individual soul is embedded within the larger context of internal events, which condition and are conditioned in many ways, and in a lively interchange with other phenomena of the material world and the world of the spirit, so also religions are embedded within the totality of events that constitute their historical contexts. Their external fate and their internal development, their rise and their decline are conditioned by a thousand factors. At the same time, they also exercise a very strong influence on the development of the peoples and cultures with which they are associated. As I said, for the sake of specialized study, all these interrelations can be omitted. But naturally, this is possible only for very specialized studies and only on a temporary basis. In this work, a scholar of religions will always be forced to pay attention to the wider context.

Historians of religions have always been very attentive to the dependence of religion on culture. They have attempted to understand religions in connection with the contexts out of which they grew and on which they thrive. These relationships, however, have seldom received theoretical consideration.[16] In this area, the systematic branch of the history of religions still has virgin territory to explore. Here, too, the historical study of the religions of the Old and New Testaments has always been a step ahead. We know the historical, cultural, and social background of no other religion so completely as we know the background of Judaism and Christianity. For the magnificent results of which this approach is capable, merely recall the works of Cumont, Reitzenstein, Seeck, Wendland, and Norden on Hellenistic religions and their reciprocal interaction with culture; Kremer's history of the dominant ideas of Islam; the far-reaching investigations of Islamic culture by Becker and Mez; Jeremias's studies of the spiritual culture of the ancient Near East; Meissner's treatment of the religions of Babylonia and Assyria and Erman's study of Egyptian religion within the framework of their respective cultures; certain accounts of the Indo-Europeans (those of Hirt, Schrader, and others); and Oldenberg's and von Glasenapp's investigations of the religions of India—to say nothing of the various works on the religious history of the Greeks and the Romans, which have progressed farthest in this respect. From the other side, the study of profane history moves toward the historical study of religions. Naturally, historians such as Ranke and Eduard Meyer, who are especially interested in the histories of various religions, have illuminated these relationships considerably.

Since the days of Schleiermacher and Hegel, philosophers of religion have considered in ideal terms the relationships between religion and culture. In doing so, they have not always clearly distinguished between ideal and actual relationships. A religio-philosophical approach always tends to become normative; it always tends to blur the distinction between recording and evaluating. For example, some have presupposed that a positive relationship between religion and culture is the ideal and have then paid homage to particular religions on the basis of this philosophical view.

Between these two approaches a third has appeared, an approach that I consider appropriate for the history of religions. In this approach one studies, on the basis of historical research, the relationship of empirical religions to culture, first in regard to spirit, then in regard to practice. The historian of religions needs to avoid both premature generalizations and a persuasive but axiomatic judgment that the best relationship between a religion and a culture is positive, negative, or indifferent. The history of religions is not concerned with whether a given religion has been useful or harmful to a people's entire culture. It simply records recognizable effects and draws its conclusions from them, interpreting the effects as far as possible within a wider context. Recall here Burckhardt's fine reflections on the interrelations of "forces" *(Potenzen)* in his *Weltgeschichtliche Betrachtungen* or Max Weber's theory of the stages of asceticism.

What is true for culture as a whole is also true for particular cultural systems, for the dynamic interconnections of effects (*Wirkungszusammenhänge*), to use Dilthey's term. Every religion is closely related to the law, the art, and the economic order with which it is contemporaneous. The historical study of religions must unravel these relationships, on the basis of historical studies and the systematic approach will have to formulate its conclusions. Again I must warn against confusion: the philosophy of religion also investigates the interrelations of religion and law, religion and art, religion and the economy, but its questions are different from those of the history of religions. The philosophy of religion investigates what ought to be, in this case, the ideal relationship between these various realms. At any rate, a number of admirable investigations in different fields have demonstrated the fruitfulness of the empirical approach: the works of Max Weber, Werner Sombart, and Ernst Troeltsch, about which I will say more later; recent studies in Babylonian law; Kohler's far-reaching studies in the history of law and religion; Sachau's attempts to study Syriac and Islamic law; Snouck Hurgronje's studies on the history of Islamic law; learned theological and legal studies of later Judaism; and so on. Moreover, works on medieval art can hardly ignore the connection between art and religion: Thode's studies of the Franciscans; Strzygowsky's extensive research on Near Eastern art and religion; Herzfeld and Sarre's discussion of Persian art; Diez's treatment of Islamic art; the works of Grünwedel and Le Coq on Buddhism and art; and many others.

The same principles apply also to studies of the relations between religion and social forces (Dilthey's *"Organisationen der Gesellschaft"* [organizations of society]). This field, too, consists of historical and systematic investigations of the relations between religion, on the one hand, and state, society, classes, and communities on the other. Again, it is not the theoretical questions of religion and state or religion and society that interest us; we leave these questions to the philosophers. Historians of religions must investigate the reciprocal interactions among various forces. Only recently have scholars directed their attention toward these questions, and as a result not even the basic categories and methods have been developed yet. The embryonic state of these investigations is related, of course, to the fact that political science and sociology are still in their infancy, and political scientists and sociologists disagree on the basic questions concerning the delimitation of these fields, their branches, and their methods.[17]

The sociology of religion in a strict sense has been established by the works of Sombart, Troelstch, Scheler, and above all, Max Weber. We do not yet have a detailed program or presentation of its tasks and methods. Many are pleased to find that this field of study has jumped immediately *mediam in rem* [into the midst of things] instead of raising methodological questions in the manner of general sociology. Consequently, sociologists of religion have achieved some very fine results, and they have written a number of admirable works. But because methodology has remained uncertain, this endeavor has had no plan from the beginning. Even Max Weber's religio-sociological studies are characterized by this lack of planning. Be that as it may, the sociology of religion will have to come to terms with several different approaches. First, the sociology of religion will have to consider the various forms of religiously determined societies, a task that has only scarcely been undertaken as a whole. That is, it must identify such categories as church, sect, school, order, and association, and it must illustrate these categories with empirical materials from the historical study of religions. Next, the sociology of religion will have to study the significance of social forces, powers, and relations for various religions (as, for instance, in Max Weber's systematic sociology of religion), and it will have to consider in turn the influence of religions on social activity and on the organization of society (see Troeltsch's *Social Teachings* and his many ethnographical works). It would be best to reserve the name "sociology of religion" for these tasks alone and not broaden it to include studies of the relations between religion and economics. Unfortunately, the boundary between sociology and economics is not maintained strictly enough, but within the history of religions, which borders on them both, these two tasks can be distinguished.[18] As yet we have no name for the approach that studies the relations of religions to their surrounding cultures or to the individual cultural systems mentioned above, but a study of the relations between religion and economics would belong to that general approach. Typical of these studies is Sombart's work on capitalism, which develops its questions in conjunction with those of the sociology of religion in a stricter sense. Similarly, Max Weber's treatment of the economic ethics of world religions combines both approaches.

But studying the relations of religions and culture, religions and the state, and religions and society does not exhaust the possible relations in which religions may find themselves. Long ago, the history of religions and its neighboring disciplines discovered religion's relation to race and to nationality. Here, too, researchers have approached the question from two sides: scholars of religions have observed characteristic similarities and differences among the religions of associated groups, tribes, nations, and races; anthropologists and ethnologists have always been interested in the effects of the tendencies that they observe on spiritual, cultural, and especially religious realms.

The division of the general history of religions—of *Religionswissenschaft*—into historical and systematic study is sufficient. Apart from these two, there are no other branches of the history of religions.

Many will be surprised by this claim. "What about the psychology of religion?" they will ask. "Surely it is an independent branch of the discipline *(Wissenschaft)* concerned with religions, if it is not an entirely separate discipline altogether." To these views I must now reply.

The psychology of religion arose from two sources. It owes its first flowering to the philosophy of religion. Later it was vigorously nurtured by a theological movement that tried to expand dogmatics in a psychological direction. Thus, the psychology of religion has not arisen from the history of religions or from the historical study of religions. It is understandable, then, that a number of scholars wish to make the psychology of religion a branch of psychology proper. Others, however, link the psychology of religion with theology, and within theology they make the psychology of religion neither a method nor an independent subdiscipline. The place of the psychology of religion in the history of religions is similar to this second approach.

There is no doubt that a historical study of religions devoid of psychological questions is as unthinkable as a systematic study of religions that does not address psychological questions. In these studies it is primarily a matter of applying psychological knowledge and insights, concepts and methods, questions and explanations, in practice. None of the human studies may do without these psychological elements; the savant, the historical genius, the systematician, and the creative thinker have always used them. Furthermore, there is no doubt that the history of religions, and above all the historical study of religions, must make greater use of the psychological in this sense than it has in the past. Psychological questions always lead to the deeper sides of phenomena; consequently, they free the historian from merely collecting, compiling, and arranging materials. They prepare for understanding and they make it possible to discover the relationships by which the particular phenomena may be grasped more fully. Wherever we encounter individual personalities in the historical study of religions, psychological questions will not be fruitless. Wherever systematic study is concerned with characteristic types, psychological questions must be raised. But historians of religions must not limit psychological investigation to subjective and personal processes. Objectivized expressions must be investigated and subjected to (psychological) interpretation, too.[19]

In addition, it will always be necessary to inventory the "religious consciousness" systematically on the basis of an analysis of religious "experience"; that is, it will always be necessary to investigate and examine subjective religious processes thoroughly and comprehensively. The intentional character of the psychological must not be overlooked. For some purposes abstractions are permitted, but for a total understanding of a subjective or objective religious phenomenon, a treatment according to the psychology of religion is never sufficient. The intentional character is not something added to the psychological act; as Brentano and Husserl have shown, it is immanent in its essential nature *(Wesen)*. Still, abstraction is possible; it is not necessary to investigate its boundaries and limits here.

The psychologism that often dominates the psychology of religion—historically understandable but unnecessary—is responsible for the contempt that many have for psychological questions. The sharpest contemporary critic of the psychology of religion, Max Scheler, directs his chief arguments against the psychologism of which so many proponents of this discipline are guilty.

Inasmuch as I have already mentioned the various branches of the psychology of religion, I can be rather brief in discussing its tasks.

Scholars interested in the psychology of religion will ask about the psychological source of religion, its "Becoming" *(Werden)* and its place *(Ort)*; about the psychological characteristics that define religious phenomena as manifestations of the internal; especially about religious feeling but no less about religious concepts, to the extent that they are available to psychology; and about the development of the psychological realm and the laws that govern it. Finally, they will investigate the religious personality and religious community from a psychological point of view.

All this will probably not justify making the psychology of religion a separate subdiscipline within the history of religions. Rather, the historical and systematic studies of religion will use questions from the psychology of religion, just as theology does.[20] The psychology of religion proper will remain within the philosophy of religion, where its themes show that it belongs. Finally, to the extent that precise methods can be brought to bear on the tasks of the psychology of religion, psychology proper will be their source.

The overemphasis on religio-psychological investigations, which were considered for a time the source of every possible good, has finally begun to subside. Even scholars who prefer a psychological approach now expressly acknowledge its limits.

CHAPTER FOUR

THE METHOD OF THE HISTORY OF RELIGIONS

IN WHAT FOLLOWS I will undertake to discuss a few important methodological questions. I do not mean to present a complete methodology of the history of religions; that would fill an entire volume in itself. Moreover, it is not possible to write such a methodology until the discipline has received a firm foundation. Such a volume would have to discuss the study of sources, their criticism, and their interpretation especially with regard to the method of the historical study of religions. It would have to contain a thorough study of the method-ological problems inherent in the systematic study of religion, comparison, and so on. Furthermore, it would have to discuss forms of religious expression with regard to their value as sources for religio-historical understanding. These forms must be understood with the help of a preliminary theory about the process of objectification in religion that is formulated by the philosophy of religion. The literature contains many initial attempts at such a theory, but at present there are not enough comprehensive studies.

I am content, therefore, to discuss systematically a few basic problems. We must first be unambiguously clear about the nature *(Charakter)* of the history of religions. Two guidelines should help here. First, the history of religions is an empirical, not a philosophical, discipline. It follows that the history of religions can never be a part of the philosophy of religion, even less can it be identical with it. Thus, one task before us is to delimit research in the history of religions from the concerns of the philosophy of religion. Second, it is nonetheless incumbent that we ask about the philosophical presuppositions underlying empirical work in the history of religions. There can be no doubt that even an individual researcher's simplest attempts are conditioned by certain basic philosophical convictions, methods, and points of view.

The problem is basically the same in the older humanistic disciplines. It is the question of the relation between empirical study *(empirische Wissenschaft)* and philosophical theory *(philosophische Disziplin)*, for example, the relation between the science of law and the philosophy of law, between the history of art and aesthetics, between linguistics and the philosophy of language.[1] In all these studies, scholars have fought vehemently about the tasks and limits of philosophy. As is well known, attempts have at times been made to ban all philosophical questions from the various sciences *(Einzelwissenschaften)*, to proclaim that the scientific study of law has put an end to the philosophy of law, that linguistics has put an end to the philosophy of language, and so on. These attempts were all related to the development of the humanistic studies in the nineteenth century and to their confrontation with professionalized philosophy *(Fachphilosophie)*.

In Hegel's day, speculation reigned supreme, even to the point of being accepted within scientific disciplines; since that time, however, speculation has fallen out of fashion. Philosophical positivism has helped ban metaphysics and philosophy from the various scientific disciplines. Today, we wonder instead whether we ought to introduce once again the philosophical spirit into scientific fields.[2] We can best study the way in which this question has developed and its present state by examining the relationship between the scientific study of history *(Geschichtswissenschaft)* and philosophy.

Issues in the philosophy of history have always occupied a significant position in methodological debate. It is in the history of historiography that historians of the human studies have always found the nicest and clearest examples of distinctive points of view. The tasks of the philosophy of history are always being redefined. The strictest views of history have always rejected the philosophy of history, refusing to grant asylum to a "centaur." The reason is clear: particular empirical studies are at odds with the introduction of speculative views and of subjectivism into empirical research. As for the philosophy of history, some now distinguish between a material philosophy of history and a formal philosophy or logic of history *(Geschichtslogik)*. Some of the objections to the philosophy of history in general are no longer valid against this formal philosophy of history, which stands close to the intent of actual research. But enough "philosophy" still remains— one would not like to get along without philosophy altogether.

The method and outlook of the newly arisen history of religions was shaped by this general development of thought. Other factors also influenced its formation. At present this young branch of study has barely freed itself from the umbrella of philosophy and theology, as I briefly mentioned earlier, and as a result, the relationship between the history and the philosophy of religion has remained undefined to the present day.

There is no need for me to survey current tendencies in the philosophy of religion, nor do I intend to sketch its history. Many surveys and histories have already been written from the point of view of the philosophy of religion itself. My concern is what the history of religions may expect from the philosophy of religion. Others have emphasized repeatedly that the best nourishment for the philosophy of religion is material from the history of religions, and this statement requires no explicit justification. Of course, some philosophers of religion still float sovereignly above all that the history of religions has produced. It is hard to know whether these philosophers regard the history of religions as having no value, or whether they are simply unfamiliar with it. In either case, this type of philosophy of religion is of no concern to us: it accepts nothing from the history of religions, and historians of religions should not expect anything from it in return. But before I ask the other philosophers of religion what the history of religions may expect from their discipline, let us listen to what scholars of religions have said about the relationship between the history of religions and the philosophy of religion. Some of them have very unclear conceptions of both enterprises. For example, C. P. Tiele, himself a respected scholar, writes as follows:

> The history of religions is a specialized discipline, a *Fachwissenschaft*. It does not belong, therefore, to general philosophy, but it constitutes the philosophical portion of the investigation of religious phenomena. Students of these phenomena make it their goal to penetrate to their ground. The history of religions is not a philosophical dogmatics, a dogmatic system of what is commonly called "natural theology"; it is not a religiously colored philosophy, still less a philosophy about God (theosophy). All these lie outside its realm. The history of religions leaves them to theology proper and to metaphysics. Actually that discipline is nothing but the philosophy of religion in a literal sense that is now, and properly, establishing itself more and more; that is, the philosophy of religion as it must be reformed, at its present level of evolution, in accord with the demands of scientific understanding.[3]

It is pointless to object when the same scholar distinguishes between "a general and historical study of religion *(Religionskunde)*"—a study that perceives, collects, associates, compares, and arranges the facts and traces their development—and the science of religion *(Religionswissenschaft)*, which employs these findings to try to answer the question of the essence and origin of the religion that reveals itself in these phenomena. But I do object to the purely philosophical nature of the tasks Tiele assigns to the history or science of religions *(Religionswissenschaft)*, and especially to his nomenclature. In addition, the task of Tiele's "study of religion" *(Religionskunde)* remains obscure, and many of the subjects that Tiele assigns to it will undoubtedly lie within the province of the history of religions.

As his actual practice shows, Tiele is convinced that the history of religions is an empirical discipline. But his terminology is extremely vulnerable and almost makes it sound as if he believes the opposite. He writes:

> I think, therefore, that we must not hesitate to recognize the philosophical nature of our discipline and to apply within it the same method that is valid for all philosophical disciplines, the deductive method. We should not employ the onesided empirical method that reaches its climax in positivism and that recognizes and arranges facts but is unable to explain them. Neither should we adopt the genetic-speculative method, for that mixture of history and philosophy is devoid of all unity, nor . . . the onesided speculative method that floats in mid-air with no solid ground under its feet. When I speak of the deductive method, I mean the speculative method least of all. On the contrary, our deductive inferences must begin with what has been established by induction, by the empirical, historical, and comparative method.[4]

This much is certain: for Tiele, the boundaries between the history and the philosophy of religion are blurred. This blurring is best seen in the methodological section of his *Grundzüge der Religionswissenschaft*. Under the heading, "The Philosophy of Religion as the Science of Religion (*Religionswissenschaft*)," he writes:

> The philosophy of religion is neither a philosophical dogma (the creed of a "natural religion" . . . or of a religious thinker) nor that part of general philosophy that concerns itself with the origin of all things. Rather, it is the philosophical investigation of the general human phenomenon that we call religion. As such, it is nothing but the science of religion in the narrower sense of the word, for science (*Wissenschaft*) is the philosophical treatment of knowledge (*Wissen*) collected, arranged, and classified.[5]

For P. D. Chantepie de la Saussaye, too, the history of religions divides into the philosophy of religion and the historical study of religions. According to him, the grouping of the various religious phenomena (religious phenomenology) forms the transition from historical study to the philosophy of religion. The latter "considers religion according to its subjective and its objective sides; it contains a psychological and a metaphysical aspect."[6] Louis Henry Jordan expresses similar views.[7] He distinguishes more or less clearly between the history of religions and the philosophy of religion; but in spite of his lengthy discussion, he actually has very little to say.

It is evident that by following this path no one can achieve any clarity regarding the relationship between the history and the philosophy of religion. Before I myself take a stand on the question of their delimitation, let us listen to what philosophers of religion have said about it. I shall focus on those philosophers who either support in principle an association of philosophy with empirical study *(Wissenschaft)* or who seek in practice to orient their philosophy toward its results. It would not advance our cause to discuss the many projects in the philosophy of religion, from the ancient to the most recent, that deal with the history of religions only to the extent that they need an overview, more or less summarized, of the development of religion or of the major types of religions. I shall simply examine what Ernst Troeltsch, Heinrich Scholz, and Max Scheler understand by the history of religions and the philosophy of religion and how they conceive of their relationship.

The conceptual confusion in the works of one of the most outstanding recent thinkers, Ernst Troeltsch, is most unfortunate. Not only do Troeltsch's writings constantly blur the distinction between the philosophy of religion and the history of religions, he has, in fact, never developed a clear concept of the nature and task of the history of religions. This is all the more amazing in that Troeltsch has repeatedly addressed theoretical questions fundamental to scholarly work. His discussions have proceeded mostly from a philosophical point of view and, insofar as they have concerned the study of religion, they have always been motivated by theological interests. Thus, it is understandable that he provides relatively few grounds for the establishment and foundation of an empirical history of religions. As is well known, Troeltsch himself did hardly any work in the history of religions, and in the historical study of religions in the narrow sense he did no work at all. His studies were concerned primarily with the history of Christianity and specifically with Protestantism. Repeatedly, he attempted to portray, with a broad view unique to himself, and with an ability to synthesize and a knack for presentation, the history of the study of religion since antiquity. In his survey of the philosophy of religion at the beginning of the twentieth century in the *Festschrift* for Kuno Fischer he admitted that the state of affairs in this discipline cannot be considered unified. Similarly, when he depicted and critiqued contemporary philosophies of religion in introducing his own theory of the history of religions, he observed that it was not possible to speak of the history of religions as universally conceived or as possessed in common by all. Here, too, he once again had in mind primarily the philosophy of religion, to which he dedicated by far the greatest portion of his survey in Fischer's *Festschrift*. For Troeltsch, the historical study of religions, too, belongs in the same context; he discussed its position in the third section of the survey.

The confusion of which Troeltsch is repeatedly guilty appears clearly in expressions that are supposed to delimit and define the history of religions. The decisive passage reads:

> The history of religions is limited to analyzing the phenomena of the spirit that we call religion, conceived as purely and as factually as possible. . . . It divides into the psychology, the epistemology, the philosophy of history, and the metaphysics of religion. Synthesizing these four approaches results in whatever scientific understanding of religion is attainable, and it is also responsible for the contribution that such knowledge can make to practical life and to the further development of religion.

The union of these approaches represents what we, "perhaps with too pretentious a name, call the Science of Religion (*Religionswissenschaft*)." Troeltsch counts five main constituents that in his view have shaped this discipline: first, influences carried over from basic philosophical worldviews to the understanding of religion; second, the contribution of theology; third, the comparative historical study of religions that, in contrast to theology, "set aside all practical and normative intentions; fourth, the contribution of epistemology and psychology; and finally, the tradition of the classical, modern philosophy of religion."[8]

We must accustom ourselves to seeing Troeltsch as a philosopher of religion interested in the history of religions only to the extent that it yields general, philosophic points. However much we may agree with him in other respects, we must regret Troeltsch's ambiguity and confused terminology. For example, the terms "philosophy of religion" and "history or science of religions" are used indiscriminately, but not consistently so. Then again, *Religionswissenschaft* blends into the historical study of religions, and so on. In addition, the influence of Troeltsch's own philosophical point of view is visible, especially in his earlier works, and it has strongly affected his understanding of the individual scientific disciplines. He himself once called his critical orientation *(Orientierung am Kritizismus)* an advantage, as it permitted him a certain amount of "simplification."[9] Later, Troeltsch abandoned this point of view, as his works on historicism show. In any case, we should recognize that the Kantian position has been at least helpful for understanding the problems relevant to the history of religions. But neither in historical research nor in the discussion of systematic questions within the individual humanistic studies has it produced much fruit for quite some time.[10]

On the whole, then, I may say that Troeltsch's effect on the history of religions has been hampered from the outset by theological and philosophical obstructions.

Troeltsch claims to see in the history of religions a normative discipline. He has expressed his ideas on this most concisely in his treatise on the nature of religion and the history of religions. There he constantly refuses to distinguish between the history of religions and the philosophy of religion. He writes: "The philosophy of religion has become the history of religions: from a branch of metaphysics has arisen an independent investigation of the factual world of religious con-

sciousness, from the most universal discipline a new discipline."
At another place we read:

> Thus in modern science a science of religion *(Religionswissen-schaft)* has gradually emerged as an independent, distinct discipline, similar to logic, ethics, and aesthetics. It is different from the older kind of philosophy of religion, which was always a philosophical treatment, criticism, interpretation, or even attack upon the religious object. . . . It consists both of an analysis of religious consciousness as an independent and unique form and direction among the creations of human consciousness and of a working out of the hints of truth and meaning that those creations contain, extracted primarily from the phenomenon itself.[11]

On the one hand, according to Troeltsch, the history of religions presupposes the philosophy of religion; on the other, it returns to it. "Between the two poles lies an independent field of investigation, the history of religions in its concrete uniqueness."[12] And again he defines its task in terms of examining the essence of religious phenomena, of the truth and meaning that these phenomena contain, of the value *(Wert)* and meaning *(Deutung)* of the great historical religious forms." These questions are certainly heterogeneous. I argued in the previous chapter that exploring the question of nature or essence *(Wesen)* could be considered the task of the history of religions only in a limited sense. Inquiries into truth-content certainly do not lie within the competence of the history of religions. The question of truth is a problem for theology and the philosophy of religion; about cognitive content *(Erkennt-nisgehalt)*, philosophy and theology must reach their own conclusions. As I have already shown, the problem of value *(Wert)* entirely evades solution by the scholar of religions. Thus, only the meaning *(Bedeutung)* of historical religious formations remains as an actual theme of the history of religions. This term, however, defines the task of the history of religions very unsatisfactorily.

Because Troeltsch is unclear on the boundaries of the history of religions, he is led to attribute to it a task that is entirely foreign. For him, the history of religions also serves a significant *practical* purpose: the "ordering and clarifying of wild growth, the harmonizing and balancing of onesided life-tendencies with the rest of life's content. . . ." The history of religions does not "make and discover" the "true religion," but it does "modify the given religion to the extent that it can be modified." The purpose of scholarly work on religion is explicitly given as to affect religion itself.[13] That purpose is not even philosophy or theology; it is prophecy. Obviously, we must reject such an extension of the tasks of the history of religions as vigorously as possible. Its character as a scientific discipline would surely be endangered by such demands. To confront an empirical religion with its surrounding culture and to determine its direction is perhaps not even a task for the philosopher of religion, but exclusively the concern of the theologian.

Heinrich Scholz distinguishes in his philosophy of religion between a receptive and a constructive approach.[14] This distinction is good; at the least, it helps us sort out the literature of the philosophy of religion from the point of view of its usefulness for the history of religions. Scholz himself rejects the constructive approach, illustrated by Kant, the Marburg philosophers Cohen and Natorp, von Hartmann, and Guyau, and chooses the receptive approach. He then proceeds to draw another distinction between a "pregnant" type of philosophy of religion and that type which is oriented toward cultural history. The criterion for this distinction is "experienceability" (*Erlebbarkeit*),[15] and with this criterion our criticism must already begin. Apart from the fact that this distinction will hardly prove productive in practice, it allows too much room for arbitrary assertions. Scholz himself chooses the pregnant type and pushes the culture-historical or religio-historical approach aside—on very shaky grounds. His studies in the philosophy of religion, then, are exclusively devoted to "experienceable" religion. From the philosophy of religion he excludes questions about the origins of religion and the classification of religions, and he moves the two classical questions of the essential nature and truth of religion into the foreground. Unfortunately, Scholz says nothing about the actual tasks of the history of religions. He mentions this discipline only in passing. Thus, we cannot determine whether for him the history of religions dissolves into the historical study of religions—it almost seems to—or whether in some sense he still thinks that a general history of religions is possible. If the latter is the case, Scholz should have considered the relationship of the history of religions to the philosophy of religion, that is, to that philosophy of religion which he identifies as culture-historical.

Max Scheler is perhaps the only recent philosopher of religion who is clear about the necessity for a strict distinction between the philosophy of religion and the history of religions. In his major work on the philosophy of religion, *Vom Ewigen im Menschen* (Leipzig, 1921), he talks about this necessity in detail. His statements constitute an extraordinarily important contribution to the methodology and foundation of the history of religions. Even though I feel I must disagree with Scheler on decisive questions, I have all the more reason to differ with him because his contribution to them is so great.

Scheler has no philosophical system. On the contrary, he declares that systematic philosophy is erroneous from the start (p. 294). As a result, he has not yet presented a systematic philosophy of religion, a philosophy of religion that defines its tasks, methods, and subjects of study systematically. It is possible, however, to infer his opinions on these matters from the extensive discussion of "Probleme der Religion," where he talks about them more or less explicitly. Still, many important connections are not sufficiently illuminated. For example, it is not clear how the numerous disciplines—in part newly created by Scheler, in part renamed by him—relate to one another. Philosophy of religion, history of religions, psychology of religion—which of these is actually the dominant one *(das Übergeordnete)*? In any case, there is, according to Scheler, a positive systematic study of religion and a historical study of religions (p. 374; cf. Chapter 5 below). To have recognized the independence and significance of systematic study is without question one of Scheler's great accomplishments. In addition to these empirical, historical disciplines,

Scheler recognizes a "concrete phenomenology of objects and acts," an "eidological phenomenology of *Wesen*" (a philosophical understanding of the essential nature of religion), an explanative and a descriptive psychology of religion, and many more (pp. 373ff.). Leaving psychology aside for discussion elsewhere, it is immediately clear that the eidetic phenomenology of the essence of religion is beyond doubt a philosophical discipline, a variety or method of the philosophy of religion. Scheler says so, too, except he adds that it is the foundation not only for every philosophical treatment of religion, but at the same time for each and every scientific (*wissenschaftlich*) study of religion (p. 374). As a result, it is also the basis for the history of religions. Now, of what does this phenomenology of essences consist?

According to Scheler, the phenomenology of essences, insofar as it is directed to religion, has three goals: (1) the ontological constitution of the "divine" (*die Wesensontik des "Göttlichen"*); (2) the study of the forms of revelation; and (3) the study of the religious act (p. 376). There can be no doubt that, as Scheler himself says, the essential investigation of the unique character of objects of faith and of values is a purely philosophical task, a task for the philosophy of religion. The same is true of its correlative discipline, the study of the religious act (noetics *[Noëtik]*), which Scheler properly separates from the so-called psychology of religion. But we must note that in his actual studies, Scheler slides readily and unexpectedly from the philosophy of religion to theological issues. Presenting the results of the philosophy of religion as the credal statements of a certain faith—in Scheler's case, the Catholic faith—will hardly help overcome the widespread suspicion of the philosophy of religion. It is especially Scheler's study of the divine that is open to this criticism. The study of religious acts is undoubtedly a very important and rich field for the philosophy of religion, even apart from its importance for establishing religion's autonomy and the independent significance of religious categories, with which Scheler was particularly concerned. There is no question that this branch of the philosophy of religion, so strongly oriented toward the concrete and empirical, can and must be an extremely valuable ally of the history of religions.

Beside the study of religious objects and acts, the phenomenology of essences also comprises, according to Scheler, the study of the forms of revelation (pp. 376ff.). One immediately feels uncertain about the character of this task. Is it religio-philosophical or religio-historical in character? In my view, a theory of the types of revelation is a task for the history of religions, a task that must be undertaken independently from the philosophical question about the essential nature of revelation. The study of *homines religiosi* and of the structures of religious communities is without doubt a task for the history of religions and must proceed empirically. Certainly, philosophy must also consider the essential nature of the savior, of the genius, and so on, and order all these phenomena into the "system of religion." But the philosophical task must be distinguished from the scientific *(wissenschaftliche)* task. The historical succession of natural and positive modes of divine revelation may be a theme for the philosophy of religion (for the philosophy of religious history) that is also of interest to theology, but the history of religions has no such questions. I have treated this point earlier in my discussion of classification and the idea of perfection in the history of religions.

Between the positive history of religions and the historical study of religions, on the one side, and the phenomenology of religious essences *(Wesensphänomenologie der Religion)*, on the other, Scheler introduces another discipline as a connecting link: the "concrete phenomenology of religious objects and acts" (pp. 373–374) that I have already mentioned. Scheler touches upon this phenomenology only in passing, and as these conceptions are especially important for our purposes and intentions, it is all the more unfortunate that he has failed to discuss them in more detail. Scheler's "concrete phenomenology" is the only instance in all the literature of the philosophy of religion of an attempt to moderate the split between the philosophy of religion and the history of religions by interposing an autonomous strip between them. This "branch of study," the decisive passage reads, "aims at understanding as fully as possible the meaning *[Sinngehalt]* of one or more positive religious forms and further the meaningful repetition of those acts in which this meaning is or has been given" (p. 373). Here, without the slightest doubt, Scheler describes a task of the history of religions, a task that can be performed only with the distinctive methods of the history of religions—bracketing, understanding, and so on—as I am attempting to develop and describe them in this book. Elsewhere I have tried to point out the contrast between such an approach and Scheler's other religio-philosophical presuppositions. Here I must fault him for not distinguishing more sharply and more effectively between the methods, tasks, and aims of the philosophy of religion and the history of religions.

Let me now combine my critique of the theories I have discussed into a brief presentation of my own views.

If the history of religions wishes to become an independent humanistic discipline, it must be clear on how its point of departure differs from that of the philosophy of religion. The history of religions must begin with the historically given religions. Its method must, therefore, be characterized as empirically determined. In this regard it contrasts with the philosophy of religion, which will always depend heavily upon the a priori, deductive method. Certainly, the history of religions, too, cannot proceed without deductions, but it may never begin with them.

Whoever chooses to call the method of the history of religions *(Religionswissenschaft)* "historical" *(historisch)* is free to do so. In that case, the work of all the humanistic studies is historical to the extent that they have no normative tasks to complete. Their object is "historical" *(historisch)*: the objectifications of the spirit *(Geist)*. Their method is research; it begins with interpretation *(Auslegung)* and ends with understanding *(Verstehen)*.[16] Designating the procedures of all the humanistic studies as "historical" only denotes their opposition to everything normative. However, "historical" in this sense does not contrast with "systematic"; rather, systematic treatment is included in the historical. Personally, I do not have much use for such a slogan-like designation. It says nothing, or not enough, about the method and manner of working of scholarship *(Wissenschaft)*. It also fosters the misunderstanding that the task of the history of religions should be limited to genetic analysis.

The history of religions has no speculative tasks. Of course, there is no need for it to remain purely descriptive, even if description is a significant and fundamental result of work in this discipline. The efforts of scholars of religion must always be directed beyond description to the interpretation *("Deutung")* of phenomena.

Interpretation is perhaps this discipline's finest task; it is certainly its most difficult. Granted, the most significant achievement of the student of art is, likewise, the interpretation of works of art. And granted, the art historian, too, will encounter difficulties often enough. Still, his task is not so difficult as that of the historian of religions. The objectification that occurs in the process of artistic creation is more radical than that underlying religious expressions; an art object is more autonomous than a religious expression. Consequently, it is more likely that interpretation will grasp clearly the true, full, and complete meaning of works of art than the expressions of religious life. This is true of both the lower order of "interpretation" that seeks to define the meaning *(Bedeutung)* of an expression and the higher "understanding" *(Verstehen)*, which seeks to locate the phenomenon within its own context. It is especially true for all attempts at far-reaching, symbolic interpretation of religious phenomena.[17] In such an interpretation, the bounds of strictly (historical) "empirical" research *must* be transgressed, for it raises the great philosophical and metaphysical questions, questions to which the history of religions leads, but which it is not permitted to address.

Concrete religions cannot be deduced from the idea of religion. But it is the idea of religion that interests the philosopher of religion. His problem is to fathom the essential nature and meaning of religion, to determine its place within the system of values and the activity the spirit. The extent to which the philosophy of religion can compromise with the empirical and historical, how much it can accept from the empirical realm, will always be a difficult problem. But even where the philosophy of religion allows the empirical to be considered extensively, it will still always have to apply a particular philosophy to religious data. An approach from above necessarily "violates" the results of research that starts from below; at the very least, the application of philosophical principles to religious facts violates the procedures of an empirical discipline. Of course, from the standpoint of history even systematic study is a "violation" of sorts; but as we shall see, it still lives off the empirical material with which it works. The philosophy of religion is different. No matter how much a philosophy is oriented toward "reality," it always sees the historical as accidental. For philosophy, the idea is primary and the phenomenon secondary.

The task of the history of religions is to observe, treat, and interpret the "historical" data. All of the methods and procedures that the discipline has developed contribute to this enterprise. Historical and systematic endeavors unite in approaching the discipline's goal: the understanding of religions. I will say more about this understanding later. The *philosopher* of religion is interested in such understanding in two ways: he is interested in the process of understanding, and he is interested in its results. In some sense he goes to work with the threads which the student of religions has spun.

From my point of view then, no one can deny that the philosophy of religion has a right to exist. To do so would be to imitate the errors of the historical school in its fight against Hegel or the exaggerations of the positivists. In its work, the history of religions must stear clear of all religiophilosophical issues. It must be aware of this restriction even if at certain points—points that must be defined precisely—it is forced to violate it. But the history of religions never can and never will doubt the necessity and the right of the philosophy of religion to exist.

Earlier I emphasized that the concern (*Interesse*) of the history of religions is not practical in the same way that theology's concern is. The history of religions also differs from philosophy on this point. Even if one thinks that philosophy's task is limited to a knowledge of worldviews and rejects all "prophetic" philosophy, that is, even if one tolerates, to use Scholz's terms, only a contemplative philosophy of religion, it will still not be possible to deny a certain practical interest, an interest that, hidden or openly, directs all religio-philosophical thinking, if such thinking is to have any value at all. The theologian and the philosopher of religion may recruit followers. They support, defend, and propagate a certain teaching. Only with this in mind is it possible to understand how a philosopher of religion can pass judgment on certain historical religious phenomena: "We are extremely interested in these phenomena theoretically," but "in practice they are completely meaningless to us"; these phenomena are "religion in an ethnological and historical sense"; the religion that we encounter in ourselves is, by contrast, "a phenomenon in and of itself *(für sich)*." The history of religions never can and never should make such a distinction. If it speaks of historical, or even of dead religions, it uses the term in a different sense. It is never a value judgment, for in principle the history of religions treats the living elements of a historical religion no differently than it treats those that are completely extinct. Historians of religions consider practical significance just as unimportant as any considerations of a propagandistic sort (in contrast, for example, to the place of missions in theological work). We see, therefore, that in the subject that historians of religions study and in the methods by which they try to understand it, there are moments that point beyond a purely empirical treatment. In terms of subject matter, work in the history of religions requires a supplement; it recognizes that it is not qualified to address the ultimate questions that the subject raises, that it cannot answer such questions with the means at its disposal. There are primarily two groups of such questions. The first comprises questions concerned with problems of content: the essential nature, meaning, and significance—in a specifically philosophical sense—of the phenomena that empirical research investigates, and the evaluation and classification of religious phenomena in the context of the life of the spirit. To solve these problems, metaphysics and the philosophy of history must cooperate with the philosophy of religion. The second group consists of methodological problems, questions that result from reflection upon the methods of the history of religions, its tasks and procedures. Answering these questions requires the help of the philosophy of religion, logic, and epistemology.[18] Especially with regard to the second group of questions, the cooperation will have to be very close. The basic philosophical, material questions of the first group can be excluded and treated in isolation more easily than the epistemological issues that accompany the history of religions every step of the way. Basically, the same situation has been observed in the other humanistic studies. Historians especially have clarified the matter by distinguishing between a material and a formal philosophy of history. Recently, Troeltsch has applied this distinction to historical research, and he was quite correct to do so.

But does not all the above contradict my demand that work in the history of religions and the philosophy of religion be distinct? Does it not point to the impossibility of executing such a divorce? I do not think so. I wish to introduce as much methodological clarity into the history of religions as possible, to consider questions of principle from a theoretical point of view. For "strategic" reasons it may be necessary at times to emphasize differences and distance more strongly than the facts appear to demand and than practice seems to allow. I am, however, still convinced that the present clarification can exert a positive influence on "practice," too.[19]

If, somewhat in the manner of Troeltsch, I have pointed out and emphasized the close connection between empirical research and philosophical thought, then in opposition to Troeltsch and to his opponents as well (among others, Bernheim and Strzygowski) I must emphasize that it is not good to mix philosophical questions with the study of particulars. On the contrary, I take this opportunity to point out once again that it is precisely because these subjects (Sachen) are so closely connected and intertwined that the most stringent methodological awareness and clarity are required.

Let me introduce a brief thought here. So far I have been concerned with the relationship between the history of religions and the philosophy of religion, that is, with the connections between these two that derive from their common subject matter. But such connections exist on the "subjective" side, too. Not only does the logic inherent in the various religions themselves impel the inquisitive scholar to the boundaries of philosophy; "philosophy" already inheres to the presuppositions by which the scholar proceeds. Speculation and subjectivism are dangers that threaten work within any discipline that is unclear about its own nature and about how it differs from philosophical reflection. Speculation, in the sense of arbitrary construction, is a threat whenever a field of research and a branch of philosophy consider the same "object" or subject matter. Subjectivism threatens whenever the conditions that the subject [the researcher] must meet, and as a result the relationship between research and presupposed philosophical worldviews, are not made clear. In both cases, methodological reflection is required to provide clarity. Later in this chapter, I will discuss more explicitly what the history of religions requires in its practitioners. We shall find a situation very similar to what we have just seen in regard to common subject matter: methodological reflection reveals that the interconnections between scholarly research and philosophy are actually of great positive significance, and such reflection also overcomes the dangers that threaten every uncritical approach.

Thus, the history of religions may expect three services from the philosophy of religion. The philosophy of religion examines and prepares the methods of the history of religions (logic); it searches for the essential in the object of study and defines that object philosophically (the philosophy of religion proper); and it integrates the phenomenon into the whole *(das Ganze)* of human understanding (the philosophy of history and the metaphysics of religion). In a few words, this formulation joins together the religio-philosophical elements that we must always exclude from the problems and tasks of the history of religions, services for which the individual scholar of religions must turn to the philosophers.

This formulation also offers me the welcome opportunity of pointing out what distinguishes my conception from a number of other prevailing opinions and trends. I advocate a conscious separation of empirical scholarship, both historical and systematic, from philosophy. Unlike most philosophers of religion, I am convinced that it is obstructive and harmful to confuse empirical and philosophical investigations. I differ from the historicists in that I know that by empirical means it is neither possible to attain norms nor to formulate universally valid propositions. I differ from the positivists in that I acknowledge, on the one hand, that the various sciences (*Einzelwissenschaften*) require the insights of philosophy, and on the other that the philosopher can never limit himself to induction. I agree with the positivists that the various sciences must proceed in a strictly empirical manner, but in contrast to them, I assign to philosophy an independent and autonomous realm. Between philosophy and the history of religions there may be nothing less than enmity or tension; but each of them must recognize clearly its own tasks and limitations. To quote a methodologist in the field of history: "The result will be a natural relation of reciprocal improvement between two disciplines so very independent: the one studies particular developments, supported by the universal concepts and ideas that the other provides; and the other studies the universal in the realm of developments, supported by the knowledge of particulars that the first supplies."

Now let us turn to consider the procedure of the history of religions, primarily with an eye to examining its presuppositions. A number of difficulties arise here. The first question is: Is it possible, from a standpoint *outside* a particular religion, to treat and to study that religion? Can its essential nature be disclosed to a person who does not belong to it? Can and may a scholar who is personally a Muslim dare to take Christianity as the subject of his investigation? Does a scholar who is personally a Christian have the right to approach the study of Indian religions with confidence? And if so, to what extent, if any, may that scholar hope to do justice to these alien phenomena? The importance of this question becomes clear when one remembers that if there are no grounds for optimism, the history of religions can never attain the recognition that it needs to be consolidated and established as a discipline. There are other sides to this question, too. Assume, for instance, that we come to the conclusion, for good reasons, that it is indeed possible for someone on the outside to study a religion. Would it not be appropriate, then, to ask whether this external point of view were not merely a possible point of view but in fact the *only* possible point of view, in other words, to ask whether the person who looks from the outside in is the only one who possesses the qualifications that justify research into religion? That is, may we assume that only a certain "distance" from the object of study permits an "objective," true, and unprejudiced encounter and perception, or that the absence of set convictions is among the prerequisites for successful understanding? That would mean that a convinced follower or advocate of a given religion or confession would be excluded from religio-historical work in the proper sense, at least from the study of his own religion, simply on the grounds of his own membership, for he would be predisposed to formulate theological conclusions.

Let us begin to answer these questions by looking at historical understanding in general, which examines the materials that have come down to us in order to fathom what happened in the past.[20] The techniques that produce this sort of understanding have been carefully refined by historians and philologists. Research in the history of religions will have to align itself with the basic principles and methods that historians have worked out, even if questions pertaining to the fundamental principles of the history of religions will require special treatment. The limits of historical understanding are subject to a great deal of debate. Therefore, I must say something more about the extent and the limits of historical understanding, especially with regard to the unique subject matter that the history of religions studies.

The problem, then, is whether, and to what extent, understanding is possible from an external standpoint, specifically, from a historical distance.

First of all, I wish to distinguish between living and dead religions as objects of study, however questionable this distinction may be. Examples of dead religions are the religions of Assyria and Babylon, of Greece, and Manichaeism. I shall speak about these religions and our knowledge of them first.

Parallels from related humanistic disciplines show that it is not too arrogant for a historian to attempt to understand dead religions, and also that the history of religions is not the only discipline at risk. Art history studies Greek art, and it also studies the art of ancient Mexico and the Middle Ages. Likewise, the study of law (Rechtswissenschaft) has successfully investigated the law of Near Eastern peoples, of the Romans, and of the Germanic peoples. The extent to which this study has penetrated the spirit of Roman law, for example, could be enlightening to overly radical skeptics, such as Spengler; it also provides us with an encouraging example. No different is the history of economics, which seeks to elucidate the economic consciousness of the feudal period or the early capitalistic era or the proceedings of the merchants of the ancient Greek states. The achievements of these disciplines speak for the possibility of appreciation by an outsider and, consequently, justify the attempt to do so.[21] But I will still have to say a word or two about the limited capacities of these individual fields of study.

But why stray so far afield? Does not the historical study of religions, too, reveal many successful attempts to study foreign and dead religions, regardless of the framework and context in which such studies are conducted? Thus, the possibility of understanding dead religions from the outside would appear to be guaranteed by corresponding, successful attempts. But who can assure us that we have not misinterpreted these dead religions, that because we lack the possibility of control, we have simply failed to recognize our own mistakes and arbitrary conclusions? Does the persuasiveness of the images we have been given of foreign religions guarantee truth? Does the consistency of everything that we have been taught about them guarantee truth? May not errors appear convincing and true?

Here the skeptics can dump all their arguments on us. Are not we—the members of a later time, another culture, a foreign race—excluded from the start from a true understanding of ancient religions? Are we not doomed to remain sequestered within our own four walls?[22] To be sure, very respectable considerations and observations underlie these objections. Not only does historical study repeatedly come up against what is difficult to explore, in fact, what is incomprehensible, especially when it tries to understand in depth the core and essential nature of the past; research is constantly revealing the errors of our predecessors. But in all this we must distinguish two different problems. On the one hand, we have the fundamental inexhaustibility and incomprehensibility of individuals—both phenomena and personalities—that is, the irrational nature of everything historical and individual, of which I will have to speak later; on the other, we have specific, historical characteristics whose understanding is impeded by our own different standpoint. For the present I shall focus only on the second of these problems.

To recognize these difficulties is already a significant step beyond a dogmatism that proceeds with unjustified certainty. The historical study of religions *(Religionshistorie)* has naturally paid tribute to epistemological optimism; so has theology, which from the beginning approached the past with a normative "yardstick." As a result, human understanding has been limited, often consciously limited. The history of religions must certainly abandon specific norms, but it, too, has occasionally proceeded dogmatically. Simply recall the time of the rationalistic interpretation of myth, a time when, in the absence of a critical, epistemological consciousness, the contemporary mode of thought was transposed to the most ancient past. Of course, it is possible to object that every age must operate on its own terms, that it cannot escape itself. I grant that every generation and every epoch will have its own way of looking at the world and, consequently, its own way of writing history. As a result, after the lapse of a certain amount of time past history must be rewritten, as many have emphasized. But what is decisive is, first, whether an age knows that every age has its own way of looking at the world, and second, whether it knows what its own way of looking at the world is. The historical era has given us this knowledge; we now possess it and, despite all romanticizing attempts, we will never get rid of it. But this knowledge hardly condemns us to a hopeless historicism, to being devoid of a particular point of view. We are simply duty-bound to be clear about ourselves, to become familiar with the standards that we, as children of our age and members of our generation, bring to the world and thus to history, almost unconsciously. This duty we accomplish by examining ourselves and coming to a clear understanding of ourselves, as well as by comparing ourselves with others who are also engaged in conscious, historical study.[23] That such self-knowledge is not a mirage is shown by many successful attempts. After all, no "present" (Gegenwart) is "entirely new"; as a generation, as a historical epoch the present reaches even in its own experience into a portion of the past, from which it must attempt to understand itself. Such insights again distance us from the immediate present (Heute).

The theory of the history of religions, and hermeneutics generally, would benefit greatly from a systematic study of the "relative a priori,"[24] that is, from an investigation of all the differences among those who understand, among objects to be understood, and among both together, to the extent that these differences are relevant to understanding. First of all, this investigation would delineate the categories in which these differences lie: the spheres in which an individual lives and in which it and every objectification appear to be enclosed—time, epoch; culture; race, nationality, status, class; sex, and so on.[25] Then, for the present problem, this investigation would define differences in content, for example, differences between the thought and emotions of Europe as opposed to those of the Far East, or between the Christian conceptions of life and the world as opposed to the Buddhist.

Many different disciplines are already working on these tasks from different angles. In addition to history and philology, psychology, especially ethno- (social) and individual psychology, sociology, and philosophy have given them some attention.

Such a theory would be most generally significant as a corrective, within certain limits, to the often exaggerated claim that human nature is everywhere the same. One methodologist has called this proposition "the fundamental axiom of historical understanding." The decisive question is, how far does this identity extend? One could visualize it, somewhat schematically, in terms of three circles. The innermost circle contains what all have in common: those characteristics that are given simply by being human. In the next circle are those characteristics that change over great spans of time. Here belong the differences between the great ethnic groups. In the third circle are differences that are historically discernible: physiological differences, such as generations and tribes; sociological differences, such as classes and estates; and so on.

The implications of these reflections for epistemology should be immediately apparent. These differences, which underlie regularities that are hinted at but are difficult to clarify, must help us explain the otherwise puzzling feeling of relatedness: the affinity of one time or generation for another, of certain religious movements for others, of individual persons to geniuses (religious heroes) of the past—all topics eminently important for understanding. These differences also provide us with the reason that conceptions of past epochs and historical personalities vary. Recall the different conceptions and evaluations of antiquity or of personalities such as Paul and Socrates, or, more recently, Goethe and Nietzsche. These changes do not simply result from universal progress in intellectual matters or from an increase in human understanding. Even the growth of historical sensitivity (*Sinn*), and above all the development of the historical method, cannot be regarded as decisive here. Certainly, all of these factors play a part. Compare Haas's very informative survey, *Das Bild Muhammeds im Wandel der Zeiten* [Muhammad through the ages](1916), and Schweitzer's *Geschichte der Leben Jesu-Forschung* (2nd ed., 1913; Eng. trans., *The Quest of the Historical Jesus* [1910]). But decisive for these external changes are internal changes, for external changes, such as the growing inclination to historical studies, must be seen as consequences of the latter.

For the historical study of religions this "change of images" *(Wandel der Bilder)* is extremely significant. As a result, it was noticed quite early. We all know that the great founders appear quite different in the different places and periods in which they have been influential. The conception of the gospel varies with the temperaments and personalities of the disciples. The same doctrine takes on different meanings among different peoples, tribes, and races. The contemporary cultural background has influenced the formation of "models," "mythology," and so on.

This important and enlightening investigation of the "relative a priori" must be immune from the polemical tendencies that affect even the study of religions. Some researchers are concerned with emphasizing the identity of human nature; others, for polemical reasons, emphasize human variables (the theory of race, one-sided conceptions of class). In contrast to earlier times, when the identity of human nature was imagined quite concretely, more recent scholarship has preferred to speak of a common structural regularity *(Gleichgesetzigkeit)*. No doubt this approach is more correct, although one still ought to contemplate the possibility that structures might change, at least over great expanses of time. Even the relationship of the most general traits to one another should not be thought of as constant but as varying with races, peoples, and cultural epochs *(Geistesepoche)*. Perhaps changes in the "forms" of the objective spirit point to "internal" changes that we must conceive of as leaps or "mutations," as can be seen most clearly in the succession of generations.

When speaking about the content of universal human nature, one cannot be too cautious. Still, perhaps we may say that the greatest degree of universality is found in feeling and the will, which are likely to be more constant than human understanding and practical activity. I like to think of the inclination to religion as one of the few truly ubiquitous characteristics of human nature. Nevertheless, the finest and best of the "eternally human" is also preserved in the art, poetry, and music of all peoples and all times; these pursuits never cease to honor and depict this "eternal" or to draw upon its never-changing truths. One can learn much from them for the theory of understanding.

There is an important intermediary between the constant, eternal human nature and historical differences: the "type." All humanistic studies proceed by constructing types. Their logical and epistemological status is still under discussion. The first discussions focused on psychological typologies, before they were extended to include typologies of objectification, the so-called historical typologies.[26] The close relation between the formulation of types and hermeneutical theory has not yet been stressed sufficiently. My own notions, which make affinity, interest, and similar ideas the basis for understanding, are very closely connected with the formulation of typologies.

Any further reflection—the interpretation of the identity and particularities of human nature—is the task of philosophy, more precisely, of metaphysics, psychology, and the philosophy of culture.[27]

So far I have concentrated on historical understanding in the strict sense; now let us expand the problems that are under discussion, for, as we have seen, the history of religions is by no means exclusively historical. Certain difficulties and problems of understanding find their solution only through a study of human understanding in a broader sense. What, in general terms, are the prerequisites *(Voraussetzungen)*, nature *(Wesen)*, and limits of understanding in the history of religions?

First I would like to recall once again the radical thesis according to which an "immanent" standpoint would hinder or prevent an "objective" evaluation of a phenomenon, since, in this view, successful understanding requires distance and strangeness. This position more or less reflects the old proverb, "Love is blind." One is often told that mountains can be seen in their full greatness and beauty only from a distance, and there is some truth to that claim. Obviously, every emotion, every passionate involvement with an object threatens to destroy the investigator's ability to make a fair and objective judgment concerning it. At the very least, partisanship raises questions about the purity with which an investigator conceives of the subject he studies. For all these reasons, it is customary to demand that a scholar strive for objectivity. To some degree every period has accepted objectivity as mandatory, but not all periods have understood objectivity in the same way. Even today there is no agreement about what is meant by scholarly objectivity. To some it means setting aside personal prejudices or political, dogmatic, and confessional assumptions; to others it means renouncing every personal point of view, or suppressing personal decisions, or else reducing scholars to allegedly pure humanity, whereby they must attempt to transcend the limitations of individuality and become, so to speak, "pure" knowing subjects.

At the same time, historians and philologists have frequently identified and studied the factors that hinder objectivity, disrupt the process of discovery, and render its results false. Among the lower factors are above all those that specific methods seek to address. Among the higher factors, there is less agreement among methodologists about what needs to be eliminated, but most recognize that critical reflection on perception, integration, and presentation is needed to prevent prejudice (which can even affect the choice of material), an uncritical procedure (above all in the association and interpretation of facts), and a partisan presentation of one's results. The study of history has developed many methods for controlling and correcting subjective errors, and the conscientious scholar will make use of them.

What positive factors contribute to a scholar's objectivity? What is the proper relation to the subject of study, and what distance is demanded of the scholar? It would reveal little experience of life, little knowledge of humanity, and little understanding of the facts if one were actually to insist that scholars completely renounce personal viewpoints and sympathy, or that they obliterate their own personal individuality. On the contrary: without a personal relationship to the subject being studied, a scholar of religions will not achieve any profound understanding and insight. Only where there is reason to believe that an author has worked uncritically, are we justified in approaching his writings with the greatest possible suspicion.

A personal relationship can only exist, however, where there is a certain "affinity" between the scholar and the subject that he studies, an "innerrelatedness" *(innere Verwandtschaft)*, so to speak.[28] All real understanding presupposes interest. For the study of religion, this "interest" is a *conditio sine qua non*. Where an inner indifference toward the subject prevails, the drive and motivation, zeal, ambition, and endurance that make it possible to penetrate that subject cannot develop. Moreover, an internal interest is required to overcome the distance of all foreign religious phenomena, which justifies their study in the first place.[29] There must be an impulse *(ein Beflügelndes)* that first produces contact and drives on the scholar's efforts. This condition explains why it is not possible to understand everything. A person will actually understand only a limited number of phenomena and persons, namely, those with whom that person has an affinity, with whom he can communicate. We may aspire to more, but our best work will always be performed within these limits.[30]

Interest in a phenomenon or problem will always be either positive or negative, and, in extreme cases, love or hate. Very often, however—and this point is decisive but is often over-looked—the specific shade of the interest cannot be defined; it is neutral, not in the sense that it lacks all determination, but in the sense that it has both positive and negative dimensions or a mixture of both, and the positive and negative tendencies neutralize one another. Frequently, and not un-characteristically, the eye of an enemy sees quite clearly; in fact, an enemy sees his enemy much better than he sees a person who lives nearby but who is of no concern to him. This fact can be explained by the presence of interest, in this case, interest with a negative sign.[31]

This kind of participation—the ability to allow oneself to be touched deeply by phenomena and problems—requires human and spiritual individuality or character. It requires, therefore, the opposite of a radical extinction of individuality. The demand that individuality be extinguished rests on a mistaken psychology; it should therefore be banished once and for all from the scientific literature that it still haunts. Character does not immediately imply a predetermined point of view, as many think. From a partial standpoint, we may say that where such character is present, it must be possible to establish a relationship between the observer (in this case, the scholar of religions) and the object of study. This relationship allows the scholar to understand and to interpret, even when there is no possibility of belonging to a group, community, order, or other organization. Thus, it is quite possible for a thinker to have the deepest interest in a question that he would never dare to answer himself, and certainly would not dare to answer positively. It is also quite possible for him to appreciate an object that originates in a foreign world and that he himself could never have created. Thus, interest and character have nothing to do with whether the relation of the scholar to the subject matter is "objective." A historian who is not a Christian may actually recognize and understand the nature of Christianity better under certain circumstances than a Christian, perhaps even better than a Christian theologian. To appreciate a phenomenon it is not at all necessary to take a positive stance toward it.

But if one wishes to understand, one has to be something. The more deeply and broadly one is a human being, the more deeply and broadly one understands. It is almost unbelievable how great the tensions can be within an individual who is human in the highest sense. Such a person can apparently comprehend primeval times when people served their gods in peculiar ways; such a person sees what had seemed isolated and puzzling as interconnected and intelligible. Here we touch upon a problem that has always troubled hermeneutical theory, a problem often discussed but seldom explained correctly. This question has exercised historians, psychologists, and other students of humanity and it is of interest to all scholarly disciplines: is personal experience *(eigenes Erleben, eigene Erfahrung)* necessary in order to understand a human being, a spiritual or intellectual phenomenon, and if it is, to what extent is it necessary? That is, must one be Caesar in order to understand Caesar? According to Simmel, "A person who has never loved will never understand a lover." Is this true? We all sense that it is not. Can a weakling really not understand a hero? Have not many who have been denied great passion sung of the bliss of lovers? Have the heroes of history always been described by their equals? We shall meet with this well-known theory of "congeniality" again and again. But what does "congenial" mean? Might not "congenial" understanding, too, have its limits? And if it does, what are those limits?

"Interest" is, as we have said, the primary requirement for understanding. There must be interest before there can be an inner relationship between a scholar and a subject of study. But how can a small, weak, wretched man attain an inner relationship with a hero, whose entire being *(Wesen)*, thinking, feeling, and acting must be totally foreign to him? Is it really the case, as the most important theorists think, that he puts himself in the hero's place, that he "empathizes" with the hero's manner of acting?

Under no circumstances is understanding what it is often said to be: sympathy (imitative feeling, *Nachfühlen*) or imitative experience *(Nacherleben)*. It is an entirely spontaneous, productive act. The psychologizing definition also fails completely in the case of understanding that is directed to the comprehension of objects. What experience is imitated in that case? The creative process? Hardly. Factual interpretation must be strictly distinguished from psychological interpretation and need not refer to it. If I want to understand the meaning of a religion or a work of art, I certainly do not need to fall back upon the psychological condition of the person with whom it originated. Dilthey and his followers have taught us that. Even in subjective understanding, imitative experience does not play the role that many ascribe to it. Such an approach would have to ignore the entire realm of the unconscious, for how could one hope to imitate in one's own experience the important events in a hero's unconscious?

How, in fact, is sympathy *(Nachfühlen)* possible at all? That is the first question. Once the inner relationship has been defined, the rest is not so problematic. How is "taking an interest in something"—which brings a person who appears foreign so near to the subject that he studies—how is that to be understood? Let us remind ourselves of the way in which this question bears upon a scholarly discipline devoted to the study of religions. Is it possible to conceive of a study of religions apart from the possibility of an inner relationship with what is foreign? How could we understand the Buddha or Muhammad?

The idea of representation *(Vertretung)* is also of no help when we are concerned, for example, with understanding the inner processes of others, processes for which we may not invoke our own experiences. The idea that when one understands, one's own experiences simply vary is no more satisfactory than Simmel's theory that in understanding latent "legacies" become conscious.

The possibilities of human experience are not exhausted with the sum total of an individual's external experiences *(äussere Lebenserfahrung)*.[32] A person does not need to have actually been in love to understand a lover. He does not need to have waged battles in order to understand a general, nor does he need to grow old to understand the aged. There is an internal experience *(inneres Erleben)* in which external experiences *(Erfahrungen)* can be anticipated. Poets know this. They provide us with the practical proof of this ability, and every now and again they reflect upon it theoretically. Here we must deal with this problem—the problem of imagination *(Phantasie)*, of experience *(Erlebnis)* and poetry—generally and in principle. Certainly, external experience is extremely important for poetic creativity.[33] Recently, a literary historian said, somewhat pedantically: the length of the radius of experience is a certain measure of poetic greatness. With this statement, he had already made a second point: what is decisive is what is made of experience. To external experiences is added the inner power of the imagination. It is by imagination that experiences first bear fruit. To an amazing degree, imagination may supplement experiences and even substitute for them. Dilthey, that most sensitive of psychologists, describes the work of the (poetic) imagination as "creativity born from the fullness of internal powers, independent of ordinary life and its goals, and necessarily following its own laws." A more recent poet, Thomas Mann, has given us a profound view of the workings of these internal powers. He has revealed to us what must be regarded as the ultimate motivating power of the poetic imagination: longing or yearning *(Sehnsucht)*. In this concept, the close relationship between creation and understanding is evident. The question that has been raised so often from the time of Nietzsche to the present—are creation and understanding rooted in abundance or in privation?—is a false alternative. Neither answer is correct. When freed of sentimental connotations, the notion of *Sehnsucht* signifies the soul's inner ability and readiness to transcend itself; it also points to that other life toward which the productive relationship unfolds. That is what is so amazing and mysterious: this yearning may become productive; it can create its own fulfillment. It does so with the help of the imagination. For imagination allows ideas to be grasped, feelings to be felt, and realms of the soul to be traversed that actual experience *(Erfahrung)* could never teach the poet.[34]

Something similar occurs in the case of the scholar. His interest is stimulated by the appearance of a great personality, of significant processes, or of a tragic event.[35] Given the inner affinity discussed above, the person who wishes to understand enters into a mysterious communication with the object of study that allows him to penetrate to its core. One side of his being *(Wesen)* is touched. The anticipation of related life drives him on. The desire to learn more, to penetrate more deeply what is striving for expression, to understand more precisely, rouses itself powerfully and gives imagination its wings. He yearns to develop further those dispositions of the soul that have not yet been realized. Thus, the limits of the empirical personality are expanded. Hidden, immature possibilities slum-

ber within every human being; they are roused by the encounter with related life. But they do not gain reality: the
student does not become Caesar, even if he immerses himself
with the greatest success in the study of Caesar's being *(Wesen)*
and activity *(Werk)*. Rather, these possibilities provide the ground
on which a compliant, talented, and fruitful imagination can
work. In this way, the prerequisites for understanding are
created. Understanding possesses the power needed to penetrate the depths, for it is nourished from within. In this way,
not only do the activity, the feeling, and the thought of human
beings, the character and wills of the great personalities—of
religious heroes—become understandable; so, too, does the
entire world of "expression," the simplest sentence, the smallest utterance, the apparently insignificant fact. For everything
spiritual *(alles Seelische)* and everything cultural *(alles Geistige)*
is the expression of a certain inner attitude *(Haltung)* or spirit
(Geist) that is, to be sure, often very complex and difficult to
interpret or comprehend. It is necessary to "understand" this
spirit, to relate to it even those expressions that are most
objective and appear to be most independent, and to interpret
those expressions from the "spirit." This spirit, however, can
be comprehended only when an interest is present that we
can conceive of as the expression of a mysterious, inner *methexis*
(participation), whose laws we may, perhaps, only anticipate.
The bounds of this understanding reach far beyond the circle
of what is "known," "related," and "similar" in a strict sense.
But they are still restrictive: not everything can, in principle,
be understood, but only that in whose nature *(Wesen)* I can
somehow "take part." Thus it is possible to say: you comprehend only what is like yourself, no more.

Experience significantly increases a person's ability to comprehend. The hermeneutical theorists have repeatedly stressed
this point, and correctly so. Starting from the base that personal
interest provides, an integrating understanding applies the
rules of interpretation that experience has developed, rules
that are continually broadened (see Chapter 5). It is from
these observations that I can formulate conclusions for my
particular theme—work in the history of religions.[36]

I began with the assumption that humanity, by nature, is attuned to religion. Even if the need for religion is stunted and suppressed, it is always present, despite appearances to the contrary. Therefore, every person, to the extent that he or she does not willfully bar the way, is able to understand what religion is. It is a sign of pride, of pharisaical self-righteousness, to deny that other persons have this religious sensitivity and to assert as a result that they are incapable of understanding empirical religiosity and religion. Whoever does not belong to a particular religion or even to a particular confession or domination, is often not only labeled a nonbeliever but also declared to be without religion altogether, "religiously unmusical." The study of music knows that there is no such thing as an unmusical person; such a person often lacks only the training and development of an ear for music. It would be good, too, if historians of religions would realize that a poorly developed religious sense never means that such a sense is lacking altogether.

By nature every person is capable of understanding religion and engaging in the history of religions. It is only natural, however, that this ability should vary in degree, just as the strength, liveliness, and cultivation of the "religious sense" also vary. Apart from this, however, a religiously gifted scholar will not decide to study different aspects of religion and different empirical religions arbitrarily. If the scholar is tactful—an essential requirement for this study—he will carefully delimit from the outset the choices that he makes. Perhaps he will never be able to say why he has chosen one area and not another, despite the fact that the two seem so similar. The first, it is said, interests him, it intrigues him, but he feels no inclination to the second. The arbitrariness that appears in our language and in the situation is actually deep-rooted: in some cases the affinity from which interest—the condition for true understanding—arises is lacking. As paradoxical as it may sound, a scholar decides to study a particular phenomenon because he knows that he can understand it. He sets the other to the side because he knows or feels that he cannot understand it. At least, the wise and honest scholar does so; where such a decision is not made, we see the results. But we are often amazed at how one and the same master in a particular field chooses to study in succession topics that seem unrelated in both theme and content. This impression sometimes remains even after a thorough study of his works. Often, however, we discern the nature of these seemingly unrelated phenomena, and then we discover the *tertium* (the "third") that unites them. This relationship is not always a direct relationship between objects. Not seldom is it extremely complicated. But it is also not necessary to locate the relationship in the psychological traits of the scholar. The person who wishes to look more deeply can always find hints of relationships within the subject matter itself. It would be rewarding to investigate comparatively the relationship between the factual and the psychological in the works of great authors, for until now this task has been left to individual biographers. It is very instructive to observe how a mature scholar can take religious phenomena that had been difficult to explain and religious personalities whose psychological constitutions had been puzzling and cause them to appear in an entirely new light, so that they suddenly become intelligible.

In what has preceded my intention has been to show how the conditions and basic principles of understanding in general apply to the history of religions. At the same time, I wish to leave no doubt that it is of particular interest to work in the history of religions that understanding be well-founded and secure. The scholar of religions will always have to examine very carefully whether and to what extent he fulfills the conditions that make his difficult work possible. It may be that psychological requirements are more important in this discipline than in any other form of understanding; in comparison with them, questions of technique and method almost retreat into the background.

The methodology of the history of religions must direct special attention to these psychological requirements. Once they are clarified, the path to even the most difficult task will become clear—the path to a hermeneutical theory of religious expression. Our reflections here have repeatedly led us to recognize that the world of religious expressions possesses a unique structure that must be identified and understood. Above I rejected the point of view according to which work in the history of religions can touch only upon the "external," the periphery of religious phenomena, and not upon what is decisive. If I were to refute that view here, I would start by insisting that one not look upon external religious expressions as "necessary evils" or adiaphora, as those who are mystically inclined do. Rather, the creation of external expressions is essential to all religion, and thus to every particular religion. The shape of religious expression and the structure of the forms that it produces and sustains characterize a religion and are thus of the utmost significance for anyone trying to understand it. We must concede, however, that particular forms, and various categories or sets of forms, vary in value as expressions of religion. For example, social ethics and ritual are not, so to speak, equidistant from a religion's center; they are of different value in attempting to understand a religion. It is certainly possible to make general statements concerning the interrelations of large sets of religious phenomena (myth, dogma, cultus, congregation, discipline, church), but these relations are not always structured in the same way. They experience shifts and transformations according to the spirit of the religion that nurtures and sustains them. For example, some religions in their basic principles or ideas tend to "nomism," while others are by nature indifferent to all social organization. The formal shape of cultus, dogma, and other forms, the importance attached to the formation of these forms, the mode in which they have come about, and the manner in which they are grounded in the total religious life are all determined by the basic attitude *(Grundhaltung)* of which the entire religion is an expression. But even more, the meaning of expressions is itself determined by the character of the particular forms and groups of forms. How one prays, how one sacrifices, how one conceives God, how initiations are conducted—in these and many other ways the spirit of a religion expresses itself; from these one must attempt to understand it. The value of different expressions also varies. An ordinance governing purification or a particular statement of faith may encapsulate and reveal the "spirit" of a religion in a more profound and concentrated manner than a peripheral expression or even another expression from the same general category. This observation contains a practical hint for the scholar and historian of religions. If I investigate the festivals, the cosmogonic myths, or the purification ceremonies of every people on the face of the globe, I have not thereby laid hold of something equally "typical" of the religions concerned. Economic ethics is more significant as an expression of the religion of ancient Israel than as an expression of Buddhism. Cosmogony, eschatology, and myth in general are most helpful in understanding prehistoric religions and a certain type of religion. Here too, we see, many things change in the course of development. As myth recedes, cult and dogma come to the fore. Certain procedures that once formed the focus of a cultic act give way to others that then assume the greatest significance. The cult of a new god asserts itself; from that time on it determines the shape of the particular religion. Thus, from advances in theological speculation and in the formation of ritual, from the reactions of mystics or enthusiasts (Schwärmer) to certain dominant tendencies and fundamental views (ascetic, libertine, rationalist, irrationalistic, nomistic, ecstatic), one may conclude that a process of change and transformation has occurred.[37]

At this point the problem of re-valuation (Umwertung), which is so significant for understanding religions, presents itself. I acknowledge that the value of any given form as a religious expression depends upon the extent to which it is still alive. Hermeneutical theory must study systematically the degrees to which realization is possible, but for the study of religions, the specific question will always be the extent to which a form may be more or less fully realized. In this way one will arrive at a correct evaluation of the decisive turning points—foundings, reformations, restorations—which are always corrections in the structure of a religion or shifts in emphasis. This observation points to something further, something that is especially important for the study of religions: changes in the expressive value of religious forms, its increase and decrease, must be seen as a subclass of changes in the meaning *(Bedeutung)* of religious forms in general. It is, perhaps, easiest to discern changes in meaning in the realm of theoretical concepts; it is in that realm that such changes have been best studied so far. But shifts and displacements of meaning *(Sinn)* do not take place only in the realm of concepts. It is well-known that the objective sphere of religious activity manifests changes in meaning *(Bedeutung)* that can even lead to the complete dissolution of the original forms. One may venture to say that among religious forms such changes occur especially easily because the content—exceedingly difficult to objectify—always tends to burst its form. But certain religious forms, especially in the realm of cultus, do obstinately endure. We may explain their preservation by means of another important characteristic of religious forms: they are capable of a wide range of meanings, which in turn make a wide range of interpretations available to both the religious practitioner and the scholarly interpreter. To appreciate the various characteristics of religious forms, one must always keep in mind a phenomenon that is visible throughout the realm of the objective spirit, a phenomenon that Simmel has called the transcendence of the ideal[38]: life destroys the forms that it has created and destroys itself in the process. The transient character of all forms of religious objectifications emphatically demonstrates their tragic destiny. The inexplicable that is unexpressed in every religious experience, and felt by every pious person seems to make every possibility of expression illusory. For this reason, the mystics remain silent and renounce every form of religious communality. What is amazing is that even in this experience something pushes beyond itself. Its first "expression" is, to be sure, no more than an eruption, a liberation: "I am saved." Many mystics remain at this point. But there has never been a person who simply has experiences in isolation; a human being always lives among many others. The common "calling" that first brought together those who were willing to form a community binds them together and unites them. The first calling is not only an eruption; it is also an appeal or a proclamation, a search for a companion to share one's experience (and these calls mix and mingle like question and answer). Thus is born what should be seen as the seed of every religious form. I can only hint at all this here. To understand forms in all their multiplicity and rich interconnections, a person must also know their characters and history. This knowledge will allow the interpreter to comprehend the nature and movement of religious forms more precisely and to appreciate them more profoundly.

Hermeneutical theory aims at understanding these structures and forms. To establish and develop hermeneutical theory in relation to the study of religions, with their "language of symbols" *(Symbolsprache)*—I now mention the term that must certainly have occurred to many—is one of the chief tasks of methodology in the history of religions. Eventually something will also have to be said about the degrees, levels, and most profound possibilities for human understanding.

All the various elements that I have been discussing are intertwined. When the scholar has succeeded in creating that inner relationship that is as much an internal, innate disposition as a product of dedication, concentration, and reflection— that inner relationship about which I have said so much here— there will have emerged, almost as if they were gifts of fortune, the methods necessary for understanding the speech of another soul, even if its words have been faint, muddled, and only stammered. To combine all this into a complete theory, into a theory that would, indeed, contribute to the great, universal symbolism of the human spirit, will be a task for the future.

CHAPTER FIVE
THE SYSTEMATIC STUDY
OF RELIGIONS

UNTIL QUITE RECENTLY, it seemed that the times did not favor a clear methodological distinction between the history of religions *(Religionswissenschaft)* and the historical study of religions. Indeed, with only a few exceptions, the major task of the "history" of religions had been historical, and the name *Religionsgeschichte* seemed quite proper as a designation for the whole. Today, however, the situation is different. We now have a number of systematic studies of religion, and they justify considering this continuously growing and increasingly significant field as an independent discipline. To be sure, the designation *Religionsgeschichte* is so well entrenched that most people are unable to sense its inadequacy. But today scholarship, far from tracing only historical developments, is strongly interested in working systematically.

To avoid misunderstandings, let me say that the "systematic study of religions" *(systematische Religionswissenschaft)* does not mean a presentation that summarizes, groups or classifies in the sense that the terms "system" and "systematize" usually carry. There is a difference between presenting the history of

Islam systematically, that is, according to specific, ordered points of view, and investigating Islam or a portion or manifestation of it "systematically," that is, not studying its history, its "Becoming," but reflecting upon the individual phenomena in their "Being," or reflecting upon what is typical in them, their essence, in the sense that I will specify below. This second undertaking will also present its results "systematically" in the first sense of the word. Some historians will claim that this approach, this systematic concern, belongs to history, but that would require a very broad notion of history's tasks. In any case, within the framework of the historical study of religions, what I shall call formal systematic tasks cannot be pursued. For this reason, the narrower definition of (the) historical study (of religions) that I have advanced recommends itself. It would, perhaps, be easier to claim for history the study of regularities in the process of [historical] development. Lamprecht did so, although in other respects he still studied laws, not regularities. To my mind, the identification of similarities and typical events is also a systematic task. In contrast to the view that considers the study of *historical* connections the primary or entire task of the history of religions, I must emphatically assert and establish that, quite apart from the fact that such exclusivity is hardly possible, limiting oneself to purely historical questions will always remain unsatisfactory.[1]

As I have said, earlier scholars, too, found it necessary to supplement historical study with some other approach that aimed at systematic questions. Almost nowhere, however, were the tasks of that other approach specified very precisely[2] and, for reasons given above, it could not be distinguished from the historical study of religions.

At this point, a methodological clarification is required. In the year 1889, Edmund Hardy published a significant essay, "Was ist Religionswissenschaft?" [What is the history of religions?]. Hardy is of the opinion that terms such as *Religionswissenschaft* and *Religionsgeschichte* are in themselves as conventional as terms such as "linguistics" *(Sprachwissenschaft)* and "historical philology" *(Sprachgeschichte)*. He thinks that there are reasons that recommend one term or the other, but that which reasons receive greater weight must be determined by an individual's own preference. Indeed, for Hardy "the history of religions" is a rather vague concept. He adopts this "designation that does not carry any special colorations" only for the totality of studies that deal with "religion and religions," since he feels that there exists a kind of comparison that lies beyond historical treatment.[3] He mentions correctly that while history is a scholarly discipline *(Wissenschaft)*, not everything in a scholarly discipline need be historical, but he does not, as I see it, draw any wider consequences from this. His elaborations offer almost nothing to help establish a systematic study of religions. He limits his consideration almost exclusively to methodological problems pertaining to the historical study of religions.

Tiele, by contrast, at least hints at a systematic study of religions. He states more clearly that the history of religions can never be an exclusively historical undertaking. "But still, I am of the opinion," he writes in his chapter on the concept, aim, and method of the science of religion, "that the history of religions requires a broader basis than mere history, at least than history in the customary sense. Historical studies must take precedence. . . . But even when I have given an exact description of all religious forms that come into view—of dogmas, myths, customs . . .—and when I have given an account of the temporal sequence of the different religious forms, . . . I have still done no more than gather materials with which the science of religion may work."[4] A little later he states, "Just as the precise method of the natural sciences is not suited to the history of religions, the historical method is likewise insufficient."[5]

Of course, the distinction that I have advanced should not *sever* work in the history of religions from the historical study of religions. Their intertwining is not merely the result of historical development nor must one lament it as a practical necessity. There are in theory very close connections between the historical and systematic branches of this as of every other discipline. That is self-evident. Systematization (in my sense of systematization) that exists in isolation is completely unthinkable. Systematization is possible only if it has been prepared for by historical studies. By the same token, the historical study of religions is in the end possible only after systematics has isolated and identified useful categories. Not only should this relationship of mutual acknowledgment and interdependence be recognized; it should be further illuminated by the strict methodological distinction that I require. Of course, in practice this distinction will benefit above all the systematic side of our discipline. Indeed, it may be detrimental to historical work to some extent. But it was and still is necessary to struggle against the hypertrophy of the historical, and not just in the history of religions. The battle against "historicism" is being fought on all fronts. From the very beginning, the goal of Ernst Troeltsch's life-work has been to make the history of religions safe from the relativizing and destructive domination of a one-sidedly historical approach. I have shown above why Troeltsch himself fell short of his goal. But we can and must, nevertheless, refer to him repeatedly.

Hardy recognized one thing correctly, at any rate: "The choice of one term or the other only assumes real significance when one uses the one to deny the findings of the other. At that point, *Religionswissenschaft* and *Religionsgeschichte* are no longer merely conventional labels of equal importance but rallying cries of hostile parties that have no place in scholarly disciplines."[6] Of course, as I have already emphasized, a work in the systematic study of religions that is conscious of its own aims and tasks will never claim that it alone has a right to exist. Here my primary concern is to examine the relationship in which these two subdisciplines stand and ought to stand to one another, and at most to consider their claims for primacy and the problem of nomenclature.

A theory of the systematic treatment of religion has, as I have said, already been anticipated, but even Heiler, for example, who speaks about methodological questions in his *Das Gebet* (prayer), has not defined clearly enough the scope of its tasks. First of all, he equates the history of religions with the philosophy of religion, because "in contrast to both a specialized and a general historical study of religions, *Religionswis-*

senschaft is no longer dealing with individual religions and religious personalities but with religion as such." He continues: "It seeks to understand what religion is, how it arises in the inner life of man, how it develops in communal life, and what it means to our spiritual and cultural life."[7] Such phrases define the task of the history of religions very imprecisely and ambiguously. "What religion is" is at the very least also a concern of the philosophy of religion. At the same time, this definition entirely excludes many themes that are important to the history of religions. Heiler continues: "The modern-day history of religions tries to penetrate the secrets of religion in two entirely different ways: by way of *Völkerpsychologie* (folk psychology) and comparative religion, and by way of a psychological analysis of the individual."[8] Here, however, Heiler takes into account only one method; psychological investigations can never grasp the realm of objective religious forms sufficiently. Furthermore, comparative religion is a subject matter in itself that has nothing to do with questions of psychology. The beginnings and development of religions are, as I have said already, first of all a subject for the historical study of religions, and only secondarily a subject for the systematic study of religions. The reason why Heiler propounds such an excessively narrow definition may be found in his psychological orientation, which narrowly limits his horizons, as it limits Troeltsch's. As a result, in *Das Gebet*, the largest part of the chapter on the subject matter of the history of religions is taken up with enumerating and discussing tasks that belong to the psychology of religion. In the second section of the Introduction, "Die Gliederung der religionswissenschaftlichen Untersuchung" (The branches of the history of religions), Heiler—relying heavily upon Troeltsch—attempts to differentiate the individual subdisciplines within the history of religions. He writes there: "The fundamental component of the history of religions is the purely empirical, historical, and psychological study of religion as one of the great creations of human culture."[9] This definition obviously gives systematic study short shrift. Completely false, too—and I will only mention this in passing—is his assertion that "typology, that is, the classification, description, and analysis of the various forms of religion" is identical with the comparative historical study of religions (vergleichende Religionsgeschichte).[10] That is not at all the case. But Heiler's great accomplishment is to have recognized clearly the importance of studying religious types, to have demanded their liberation from the domination of normative and other heterogeneous points of view, and as a result to have struggled toward the systematic. I can also agree fully with what Heiler has said about the relationship between historical and psychological studies. However, his understanding and classification of the "phenomenology of religion" is less than clear.[11]

Scholz, too, gives attention to a number of tasks that could be tackled within the framework of a systematic study of religions when he describes what he calls the cultural-historical philosophy of religion. Unfortunately, he excludes these tasks from his own philosophy of religion. In Scholz's view, the cultural-historical philosophy of religion studies the "major intellectual problems in the history of religions."[12] Under certain conditions, I could, perhaps, agree with this as a definition of systematic study, as I conceive it. But what problems does Scholz have in mind? He identifies three kinds.[13] First, there is the question of the essential nature and conjectured beginnings of historically significant religion. As we have seen, the question of the essence of religion is really a philosophical problem. The study of beginnings, by contrast, belongs not so much to the philosophy of religion or even to the systematic study of religions as to the *historical* study of religions. Had philosophers heeded this obvious fundamental principle of the history of religions, they could have saved themselves many an erroneous theory. Today, we ought no longer doubt that the beginnings of religion, and consequently of religions, cannot be discovered by speculation but by historical research, if at all.

The second major problem that Scholz assigns to the cultural-historical philosophy of religion is the "classification of religions." I have explained earlier why I would like to see the various modes of evaluative classification excluded from the history of religions. The extent to which these modes are possible and justified in a philosophy of religion need not be decided here. At any rate, such classifications are far removed from anything that the history of religions is able to ascertain. Consequently, there can be no justification for advancing a designation that qualifies a philosophy of religion as "religio-historical" *(religionswissenschaftlich)*. In Scholz's view, "characterization" also belongs to this sort of philosophy of religion, but as we have seen, it is something different. It is a very important task of the historical study of religions and the history of religions.

The third major problem, Scholz declares, is the "logical and psychological clarification of the basic concepts of the history of religions." But his enumeration and closer examination of these basic concepts is most astounding. They fall into three groups, the "cultic," the "dogmatic," and the "psychological." These points of view operate on very different planes. Concepts such as sacrifice, asceticism, revelation, and the mediator belong first of all to the history of religions. Naturally their place in that discipline does not make it impossible to philosophize about them, but one must philosophize in a manner quite different from what Scholz intends. To clarify "what a god, a hero, or a demon is" is first of all the task of the systematic study of religions, to which also belong the works of Österreich and Beck that Scholz cites. The "problem of the savior" *(das "Heilandsproblem")* can be studied by both the historical and the systematic study of religions, but only with regard to much later implications can it become a topic in the philosophy of religion. These three disciplines must also be distinguished with regard to the "discussion of the central religious forces." According to Scholz, these forces constitute a fourth theme for the cultural-historical philosophy of religion. In any case, the concept of a "central force" requires more clarification.

I have already mentioned Max Scheler's ideas about a concrete phenomenology of religious objects and acts. They form a valuable prolegomenon to the systematization of religions. In the end, however, all these proposals leave me dissatisfied. They do not portray clearly enough the nature of and connections among the tasks that are to be assigned to the systematic study of religions.

Let me attempt, first of all, to present what would be the tasks of a systematic study of religions. Once again, it is important to keep in mind that the systematic study of religions is a branch of the broader, general history of religions and as such, an empirical discipline, not a philosophical discipline in either a material or a formal sense. That is, its task is neither to identify "pure" religion nor to work out specific categories for "comprehension" ("*Auffassung*").[14]

As an empirical discipline, the systematic study of religions has no normative character. All attempts to isolate a "natural" religion or something similar are excluded from it from the start. That is true regardless of the particular paths that these attempts might take. Excluded are, for example, all systems of a philosophy of religion, such as the deistic speculations of the seventeenth and eighteenth centuries and the a priori methods of the contemporary phenomenological philosophy of religion (Scheler).

The systematic study of religions, therefore, is not a *pure* theory of religion *(Religionslehre)* in the sense of the attempts that have repeatedly been made to establish a pure theory of jurisprudence *(Rechtslehre)*.

Stammler undertakes to formulate such a theory of jurisprudence.[15] He distinguishes two types of legal theory, a pure theory and a general theory. The latter corresponds to what I have in mind with my systematic study of religions. He defines the former as the "system of the forms of thought that one must observe to determine the legality of a particular desire and to evaluate it according to the fundamental ideas of law." Of this system Stammler writes, "It wishes to be free from all the conditioned matter of the particular experience." The general theory of law, however, offers "a more or less comprehensive presentation of definite legal matters." It identifies "common traits among particular, historical legal materials, for example, the various kinds of constitution and their corresponding fates in situations that are otherwise completely different." What decisively characterizes the general theory of law is thus the "conditioned nature of its object of study." That conditioned character is stripped away by the pure theory of law, which Stammler wishes to conceive, from a clearly Kantian, subjectivistic point of view, as "the investigation of the pure forms of legal thought." These pure forms "never change, but always maintain their identity"; by them, all "legal particulars are determined." Their formal character—and this is naturally important—ensures that the pure theory of law may claim primacy over the general theory of the conditioned. These pure forms make up the "inescapable that rules over every particular legal consideration." In the following statement, this relationship emerges clearly:

> In the analysis of empirical legal matters, the pure theory of law must ascertain those formal modes of thought that are necessary for a unified, legal understanding of a limited situation. The conditioned, general theory of law, however, must deal with the constituents of such legal matters and must seek to identify peculiarities that such constituents have in common. It must deal with thoughts that are contained, to some degree, in every legal concept, but that constitute only a portion of such concepts, namely, the conditioned forms of juridical thought. The other approach takes up the historic, legal creations in their totality, presupposes the formal nature of their unified comprehension, and focuses on legally shaped material as such in the interests of seeing that which is common within the material's particulars.

Accordingly, the two disciplines coexist in a strictly differentiated manner. It is "totally impossible to perform the tasks of the pure theory of law by merely collecting materially conditioned similarities." These necessary forms of thought must be "identified and presented by personal reflection quite apart from the material restrictions of particular legal content; they must not be approached from general similarities within the material."

Stammler's pure theory of law is thus a systematization of the categories of legal thought that belongs, in my view, to the philosophy of law. Likewise, Simmel's categories of religious thought, which were also introduced from the point of view of transcendental philosophy, do not belong to the history of religions but to the philosophy of religion. It is of great significance that the content of a "pure" discipline—pure forms—cannot be attained empirically and inductively. Concerning the comparative study of law, Stammler mentions only very cautiously that it is "not impossible" for it to stimulate the legal scholar to discover and examine critically the pure forms of legal thought. This negative observation is more important to us than his positive answer to the question of how knowledge of these pure forms can be attained. The subjectivistic twist in Stammler's thought, explained by his Kantian philosophical outlook, no longer interests us. I have only tried to illustrate how the concept of a general study of what is conditioned and the concept of a "pure" discipline stand more or less opposed to each other. It would be just as possible to illustrate this point by referring to the theory of a thinker whose approach is phenomenological ("objective" ["gegenständlich"]), such as, to select an example with an eye to the history of religions, Max Scheler's religio-philosophical scheme. It is sufficient here to have shown that a "pure" discipline, a discipline devoted to the a priori, cannot stand as a systematic discipline in my sense. As I have conceived it, a systematic discipline must begin with empirical data.

Hardy, too, is convinced that the history of religions is empirical in the sense of beginning from historical occurrences, as we find in his study of fundamentals that I mentioned earlier. Perhaps he vaguely senses that a purely constructive theory of religion would be an enemy.

It is now necessary to disassociate the tasks of the systematic study of religions from a possible misunderstanding that also results from uncertainty about its strictly empirical character. One often reads and hears that the primary task of the history of religions is to work out the basic, religio-historical concepts. I can agree with this statement only after the nature of these "basic concepts" has been unambiguously clarified. If we are to understand here categories of understanding in the sense of critical philosophy, the statement is, to my mind, false. As shown above, the task of identifying and examining epistemological concepts belongs to philosophy (the philosophy of religion), which will also have to decide how far an epistemology of religion, or an epistemology of particular religions, exists in distinction from general epistemology. Recently, however, scholars within the humanistic studies, such as Wölfflin and Strich, have spoken again about basic concepts in an objective sense. For example, in an appendix to his fine and sensitive work, *Deutsche Klassik und Romantik* (German Classicism and Romanticism, 1922), Strich explicitly demands that thought focused on basic concepts be extended to the remaining "cultural systems," "religion and music." The task of identifying these concepts would belong to the systematic disciplines. In these disciplines one would find the study of certain recurring basic tendencies of human thought and perception—in our case, religious thought and perception—as well as the analysis of certain typical forms of (religious) expression. Such tasks do, in fact, belong in the realm of the systematic disciplines. They do not exhaust their topics and they are not primary; but they are meaningful and important.

Positively speaking, then, what are the tasks of the systematic study of religions? My aim here is to obtain both a material and a formal systematization of religions *(Religionssystematik)*, an approach that first raises the history of religions above the purely historical and then prescribes for it the great systematic task that every humanistic study must perform. To differentiate between a formal and a material systematization of religions, one must first distinguish the essential nature of systematization from that of historical observation. What is it that interests a historian? Development; "Becoming." His work is characterized by a genetic point of view.[16] The systematician, by contrast, turns his attention to cross-sections; he is interested not in Becoming but in what has become *(das Gewordene)*. The historian studies the origin of Islam, its history in time. The systematician hopes to present Islam as a religious system independent of temporal differences. But that is already an advanced goal. He will be satisfied first with studying a portion of the total subject systematically: the theological system of the Qur'ān, or Islamic ethics systematically portrayed. He will subdivide his task according to chronological, geographical, temporal, and factual-systematic points of view. He will study the practice of a religion of a certain time and in a certain realm, land, province, or place. He will seek to describe systematically a specific doctrine and cultic usage: the message of a prophet or the practice of a community in a given period. From all these endeavors the genetic point of view has been excluded.

The preceding would be tasks for a material systematization of religions.[17] This systematization is not, however, the only kind conceivable. It must also be possible to abstract from the particular and the concrete, in short, to pursue a formal systematization of religions. In this kind of systematization we are no longer interested in Islamic theology or in the concept of *bid'a* but in the structure of theologies and in the concept of heresy. The reader should note that this pursuit has nothing to do with a priori or deductive philosophical definitions of essences (which would be the task of the philosophy of religion) but with a kind of abstraction familiar to all systematic humanistic studies. I look for what is similar among theologies known to me; I seek out the principle around which they are all structured and formed. I look for what is identical in the forms and characters of empirical phenomena; I identify the "skeleton" or framework. I compare, and in this way I seek to obtain higher, more abstract religio-historical concepts. It may well be that, as many will object, these concepts have relatively little content and "say nothing," but they are quite important for historical studies. If the historian works continuously with such concepts, his task becomes much easier.

There has been much argument about the nature of these concepts in other scientific disciplines. Most often the reason for misunderstanding has been that the empirical and the philosophical were not distinguished sufficiently. The efforts of the phenomenological school have at least clarified the problems involved.

The difficulty is that categories obtained by a priori means (deductively, whether by an intuition of essences or some other means), never extend down to the individual, concrete object. For example, the concept of mysticism can be deduced, perhaps, from that of religion, but Persian mysticism and its characteristic moments cannot be deduced from these concepts. For this reason, categories supplied by philosophers of religion can never satisfy the scholar who works empirically. He will repeatedly be disturbed at the hiatus, the impassable gap that separates "necessary" concepts from historical reality. This gap cannot be bridged from the top down.

What is the status of the reverse, the attempt to develop these concepts out of the empirical? As we have seen, the material, systematic approach attempts to do just that. But how far can it go? Concepts such as dogma, mysticism, heresy, asceticism, sacrifice, salvation, and reincarnation can be obtained by this empirical and inductive manner, but will such a procedure ever end in a coherent system? Will the concepts thus identified and the relationships perceived ever be necessary as such? No, never. Until now, historians have hesitated to admit this inability, just as philosophers have hesitated to admit the other. But if these difficulties cannot be solved, they ought at least to be recognized and admitted.

From what has been said, it follows that formal systematization must be completed by categories from the philosophy of religion. At the same time, this dependence helps determine the boundary between the history of religions and the philosophy of religion. The means by which historians of religions acquire philosophical categories will always be extremely controversial. There are many methods, and the results are quite varied, despite the apodictic pronouncements of some. Nevertheless, in its formal as well as its material tasks, the systematic branch of the history of religions will, so far as any empirical science can, attain results that will certainly receive widespread support and recognition. Historical and psychological studies will constantly have to modify and improve these results, but from the beginning, practical research will be able to use them with good result.

What methods must the systematic study of religions employ? One method above all: comparison. The importance of comparison is not unique to the history of religions. It is known in all the humanistic studies. But in hardly any other discipline has comparison been put so much in the foreground. Recall, for example, the days of Friedrich Max Müller and H. Usener. The *religionsgeschichtliche Schule* uses comparison as its most important principle of research; the comparative study of myths—Müller, Kuhn, Mannhardt, Schwartz—preceded it. Rarely has this school reflected theoretically on the comparative method in preparation for its practical work. The most important remark may be Rudolf Otto's law of parallels in the "history" of religions *(Religionsgeschichte)*.[18] In the English-speaking world, the history of religions is still [in 1924] called "comparative religion," and among German speakers one also hears *"vergleichende Religionsgeschichte"* (comparative historical study of religions) and *"vergleichende Religionswissenschaft"* (comparative history of religions). These designations are not fortunate. They unjustifiably emphasize a single method, a method that the history of religions shares with other disciplines, as if the very aim of this discipline were to compare.[19] That is certainly an error, for methods can only be means, never ends in themselves.

We shall now examine more closely the function of comparison for the material and formal systematizations of religion, and in doing so we shall learn both the significance and the limits of these two approaches. The material discipline uses comparison to understand the individual phenomenon better by contrasting similarities and differences.[20] The formal approach is interested especially in what two or more phenomena have in common, and thus it uses comparison differently and, if you will, more intensively. To the formal approach, what comparison stresses is quite important. Thus, the comparative method is only accidental to the material systematization of religions, but for formal systematization it is essential. In either case, great dangers constantly threaten any comparison. One need not even look at the histories of the history of religions and other disciplines that have used this method to recall in detail the errors, premature conclusions, and mistaken theories that must be credited to its account.

It is readily apparent that the very idea of comparison conceals several dangers. By its very nature, comparison tends to exaggerate; its results have constantly demonstrated as much. In order not to expose the systematic study of religions to such suspicions and premature skepticism, I must discuss these difficulties here. It would seem obvious that when a scholar becomes interested in studying a particular historical phenomenon systematically, he will want to isolate it from its historical context and understand and describe it first of all on its own terms. That is, he will interrogate the phenomenon about its own unique meaning. At this point it does not matter whether the phenomenon shares this meaning with other phenomena. The immediate concern is to understand the composition and nature of this particular phenomenon. The "here and now" is decisive.

It would seem obvious, I said, that a scholar would approach the systematic study of phenomena with this attitude. But in reality, scholars approach such studies with quite different attitudes today.[21] The immensely fruitful and tempting method that the *religionsgeschichtliche Schule* has introduced into the history of religions has emphasized once again that the particular cannot be understood apart from its context, that it cannot be understood apart from the history of the form (the conception, the custom) and comparison with parallels (a study of types and motifs). When scholars prefer the evolutionary, historical point of view to an excessive degree, little room remains for systematic considerations (cf. Chapter 3). When they emphasize that parallels must be drawn to further understanding and interpretation, the danger is unavoidable that the uniqueness of the phenomenon will not receive the attention it deserves. The results of scholarship during the past several decades have demonstrated that inattention to uniqueness is a real and present danger. So, too, does the recent reaction to the principles of scholarship that were advanced during those decades. We must acknowledge that philology and purely historical studies have obtained impressive results by following the paths that they outlined, but systematic progress properly speaking has been scant. Now there is a dangerous and growing trend of analyzing the multiplicity of phenomena into a mass of elements and atoms, without substituting anything for the particular phenomenon that has been demolished and without contributing to the search for basic principles.

Only rarely have scholars asked the important question of the nature and meaning of parallels, a question of fundamental significance to all comparison. And yet, this question must be answered if the limits of comparison are to be recognized. Scholars have often compared identities, similarities, relationships, and analogies without taking note of the necessary restrictions.[22] As a result, material as well as formal systematization has been neglected. To be useful, a comparison must work within its own limits. One must remember that for a comparison to be successful, certain points must be established as the "bearers" of the comparison. The value of the comparison for understanding will be judged by the weight that these traits carry within the total phenomenon.[23] What is peripheral in one instance may be of decisive significance in another. The integrity (Bündigkeitscharakter) of an individual phenomenon unique in itself, whose elements cannot be eliminated or regrouped arbitrarily, is of the utmost importance. Certainly, it will always be meaningful to reconstruct the background of a particular phenomenon and to identify the strands by which it is anchored historically (in terms of what preceded and what followed it) and systematically. But these investigations are not the major issue.[24] Is it really necessary to point out that identical names alone do not warrant the assumption that the actual objects are identical? But the philological study of myths has frequently violated this basic principle. The difficulty begins with how to *interpret* agreement. The domination of historical interests over systematic interests simply exacerbates the difficulty, for in practice comparison has served almost exclusively to prepare for the construction of historical connections. In such cases the genetic question dominates all.

These, then, are the dangers of comparison that must be avoided. Formal systematization can only begin once the particular phenomena have been comprehended fully, once we have attempted to grasp their unique nature by every means at our disposal, historical and psychological. Only then is abstraction justified. The particular may be left behind only after it has received the attention that it deserves.

The formal systematization of religions has two primary tasks. First, it must formulate abstract, ideal-typical concepts, and second, it must identify the regularities and principles that appear in historical development.

Let me make clear once more the logical nature of these "systematic" concepts. They are derived from experience. In studying Western monasticism, we seek to grasp its fundamental traits from certain essential points (moments) and from these points to understand and portray in turn the individual phenomena and their modifications. We develop the concept of "Western monasticism" that we will employ from various historical expressions of the monastic ideal.[25] Then we compare Western monasticism with Near Eastern monasticism. We drop whatever characteristics are not common to all; and from the total picture that the common characteristics provide we obtain our concept of "monasticism." Philosophers will tell us that our procedure is insufficient for grasping the "essence" of monasticism, but their "essence" is of no concern to scholars of religions. We are interested first in the historical phenomenon and then in what is common to these phenomena. If the philosophers object: "You really would not have recognized that first phenomenon as monasticism had you not presupposed its philosophical 'essence,'" I would reply: Certainly we approach things with a certain mysterious foreknowledge *(Vorwissen)*. But that belongs to the "prelude"; it precedes the historical knowledge upon which systematic understanding rests. It will always be up to the philosophers to clarify the nature of this foreknowledge. I concede further that, as we have seen repeatedly, the study of religions must be supplemented by the philosophy of religion. To continue the same example, it is up to the philosopher of religion to tell us what, for better or worse, "monasticism" is, whether from deduction, eidetic abstraction, or some other means.

But it is material systematization that is the central task of the history of religions. It is more important than formal systematization, for it operates more deeply in the empirical and concrete, which is the root of the entire discipline. Formal systematization is important and necessary for overcoming the historical; material systematization cannot accomplish this task, even though it overcomes the "absolute" relativism of the historical study of religions. Only both approaches together will do justice to the demands of life and of historical reality: to understand the particular for what it is, and to order the manifold, to see it together as a whole. The foundation for both is the historical study of religions. Just as formal systematization cannot be conceived apart from material systematization, so both systematic disciplines are inconceivable apart from the historical approach. We have seen how in history itself something drives us beyond a purely historical treatment, how the historian is confronted by similarities and common principles. Research in the historical study of religions repeatedly demands a holistic or systematic vision (Zusammenschau) and holistic or systematic ordering (Zusammenordnung). It has not always been recognized clearly enough that the unavoidable prerequisite for such a synthesis is a thorough understanding of the particular, but scholars have sought to overcome the merely historical in the most different ways. Among them are the study of types and the search for rules or principles of religious development. The realm of material systematization includes the identification of historical types (of individual personalities or of objective phenomena); formal systematization includes the psychological study of the modalities of a life "in tune" (Lebensgestimmtheit) (Siebeck), of religiosity (Höffding, James, Scholz), and the identification of typical forms within objective religion. Scholars began to study regularities in the development or evolution of religions (stages, epochs, and processes) long ago. Hegel and Herder were the forerunners in this endeavor, but their interest in speculation and construction was still too strong, and the materials had not yet been sufficiently studied either historically or systematically for them to proceed with the needed care and precision.

Then came the mythological school (Max Müller), which depended too heavily on other disciplines, above all, on the study of language, to be able to work unhindered. We have seen how the humanistic studies, including the study of religions, were empiricized in the course of the nineteenth century. Positivism, too, produced an interest in identifying developmental principles, stages, and schemas. But then came a period of calm. Tiele's *Einleitung in die Religionswissenschaft* was one of the few comprehensive attempts to find regularity in the evolution of religions.[26] Otto's "law of parallels" also belongs in this camp. Today, Spengler's idea of a morphology of the "history" of religions *(Religionsgeschichte)* has made such thoughts once again of more concern to the scholar. But surprisingly, the works of historians (Lamprecht, Breysig, Eduard Meyer), psychologists (Wundt, Krueger), and ethnologists have influenced the history of religions very little. Weber's interest in the theory of science led him to tackle this entire set of problems, and his works combine typology with a theoretical concern for evolution. The time is coming when historians of religions will continue the discussion, outside the realm of philosophy, of what sort of regularity governs the Becoming of religions. Positivism sought to delight us with "laws" of the sort found in the natural sciences. The time for such laws may not be past, but loud voices have been raised in favor of replacing them with discussions of morphology. It is with morphology that the debate will have to begin today.

Monographs about prayer, ecstasy, cult, salvation, and other moments of religion manifest a systematic interest. An immense amount of historical and psychological material still awaits treatment.

One of the most noble and important—and last—tasks of systematization will be to teach us about the formation of religions. We shall discover what factors work together to form a religion; we shall learn about the relationship of the forces in which these factors are active; we shall perceive which "moments" constitute religions structurally; and we shall investigate the relationship and modifications of religious forms. Every attempt made so far to describe the structure of the various religions could not help but be fragmentary, for the principles underlying the internal formation of religions have not yet been discovered. The most monumental attempt, Wundt's *Mythus und Religion,* has performed the service of once more emphasizing and working out the manner in which the various forms of religious expression or the various religious moments relate to one another. That had not been done since the collapse of the various speculative systems. Historical research had concentrated on the study of particular problems or areas rather than on larger structural connections. Psychologism, too, was an obstruction to such an undertaking (see the Appendix to Part One). As we have seen, structure in the sense of a framework *(Gefüge)* is not at all psychological. Wundt, however, still took a psychologistic stance toward the phenomena of religion. As a result, he too has been unable to help us understand the nature and structure of the moments that form and constitute religions. Moreover, Wundt's constructionism also stood in the way (see Chapter 3). What is important is the context; in Dilthey's words, "structure is everything." Edward Lehmann's comprehensive outline, "Erscheinungswelt der Religion," attempts to present a vision that is comprehensive in scope, but on reading his overview, who could not wish that Lehmann had described the internal connections between particular religious instances and manifestations?

The systematization of religions must proceed systematically. For a long time now, scholars have worked systematically at various points, from various directions, and with varying success. Now it is time to integrate these isolated instances of systematic work in accord with a systematic point of view. Everything must be subordinated to the study of the formation *(Bildung)* of religions. Recently, a scholar of religions spoke from a high vantage point of the tasks and goals of the history of religions, criticizing the procedure of the historical study of religions. He mentioned a number of important issues relating to the study of primitive religions: "The question of the religious object, the differences among various forms of this object; what is psychologically significant in the formation of such objects; the other factors—climatic, social—that influence their arising; the instincts that underlie cultic institutions and the varied cultural structures that result from these instincts; the nature of myth, its significance for cult and its significance as the predecessor of religious thought; the beginnings of notions of an afterlife and belief in gods"; and so on—all important problems. But this student, too, has overlooked the manner in which all these moments are interrelated. Let us reminisce once again. Hegel, with a deep personal vision and feeling for the "objective," sought to connect internally the forces, powers, and principles of religious formation—speculatively, of course, and, despite all his sense for historical reality, in a forced and one-sided manner. Prior to Hegel, Herder had anticipated and suggested many things. In the Appendix I shall show the extent to which emphasis then shifted to the study of the subjective life in history and the humanistic studies, and how psychological concerns have dominated. I shall also mention there that a reaction has set in recently, a turn to the objective. As a result, the entire "world of religions" has once again become visible. This turn to the objective yields a group of questions that no longer concentrate in a one-sided fashion either on understanding religiosity—pious feelings (Schleiermacher), their development, their principles and modalities—or on objective forms—cults, rites, and myths. Attention has turned to a midpoint between these two: the question of the formation of religions, which can be answered in full only through the cooperation of the historical and systematic studies of religions. To the results of these studies we must also add considerations from the point of view of the philosophy of religion.

Thus, at the end, we raise once more the question of how the historical and the systematic branches of the history of religions relate to one another. Now, after the scope, tasks, and peculiar nature of each has been clarified, we can answer this question more thoroughly than in the beginning. Then, for the sake of clarity, we had to isolate; now we may see the parts together.

The history of religions seeks to study, understand, and interpret religions. Thus, it will first seek to clear up their becoming, their arising, their waning—in a word, their history. But the history of religions cannot be satisfied with purely historical sequences and with tracing developments. Cross-cuts must be made. Systematic study, interpretation, and presentation must proceed from decisive, central points. Such a study transcends the historical to supplement or complete it; but in fundamentals it points back to the historical as its source, its home. As a result, systematization is not the ultimate; in some sense, it is circumscribed by history. The old tension between knowledge and life that keeps philosophers so busy emerges here, too. In order for understanding to plumb the depths of the stream of Becoming, we must choose and mark anchor points. But life flows onward, and we must follow. We seek to grasp its movement as well as we can, but still we will never see more than a dim reflection.

The history of religions, however, is prepared to cooperate in the task of human knowing, in its own place and with its own means.

Appendix

PSYCHOLOGISM AND THE HISTORY OF RELIGIONS

MAX SCHELER HAS perceptively criticized the psychologism of which philosophers of religion have been guilty in recent years.[1] He has especially pointed out that these philosophers have ignored the intentional nature of religious acts and the relation of these acts to the objective world (cf. psychologism proper). Here I wish to point specifically to another, closely related phenomenon that Scheler, too, has occasionally noted: the study of religions has generally overemphasized the psychological dimension. This is not a matter of distributing emphases for practical or other opportunistic reasons; it is a question of fundamentals. The overvaluation of the psychological and the concomitant undervaluation or rejection of the significance of objectifications—of objective manifestations of the spirit *(des objektiv Geistigen)*—are associated most closely with the contemporary worldview. When such a (psychologistic) tendency flourishes, it is always grounded in a larger constellation, a constellation in the history of ideas.

It is important for the history of religions to eliminate the dangers of psychologism, for the sake of both historical and systematic studies. The subjectivism that psychologism implies threatens to limit our vision drastically. If the scholar wishes to do justice

143

to the whole phenomenon of religion, the entire expanse of the objective religious world must be open to him.

My specific attempt to point out the significance of objective religion is in harmony with a more general tendency in related humanistic disciplines. Philosophy seems to have taken the lead here. Its interests were for a long time dominated by purely epistemological and logical problems, but now once again it is energetically pursuing problems of culture; it is becoming, once again, a philosophy of the historical world.[2] In the process, a concept has come to the fore that it is of the utmost importance for all the humanistic studies to study and clarify: the concept of the objective spirit.[3]

Following Herder's lead, Hegel was the first to formulate the concept of the objective spirit, which he placed within the immense system of his philosophy of spirit. When his mighty structure collapsed, Dilthey took up this most important concept and sought to reestablish it apart from metaphysics. One of the most important themes of Dilthey's work was the connection between the psychological world and objective reality. He treated this theme repeatedly from the points of view of psychology, logic, and epistemology, whether he was drawn to it by a concern for connections between the collective soul and the objective spirit, or whether the biographical and psychological study of individuals led him to explore such questions historically and psychologically. But, in spite of his thorough understanding of the history of religions, and in spite of his remarkable training in theological matters, Dilthey has thus far exerted only a slight influence on the history of religions. In recent times, his thoughts have come to us via the philosophy of religion.

Before Dilthey's followers renewed our interest in Dilthey's problems—consider Spranger, for example—it was primarily Siebeck who thought about the relationships with which we are concerned here. To a great extent his clear approach prepared the way for more thorough studies. The fourth chapter of the third section of his *Religionsphilosophie* is devoted to presenting the relationship between the subjective and the objective sides of religion. He develops and establishes there—profoundly and brilliantly but unfortunately only in summary fashion—the relationship betweeen the subjective and the objective from the point of view of a philosophy of life that seems very modern. He writes:

> Knowledge of this state of affairs contains the further insight that neither the subjective nor the objective is prior factually or temporally.

Inner subjectivity has never been found apart from a corresponding objective manifestation, and vice versa. The corporeal and the spiritual coexist in a living organism from beginning to end . . ., and the concrete formations of cultural life must be understood in the same way. Subjective and objective, ideal and real, are inseparable manifestations of a unified life expressing itself. The best term to designate conceptually the basic force underlying both aspects is the term "Idea," already introduced by Plato in a related sense. It signifies the substantial and essential content of a certain realm of reality—in nature as well as in mental and cultural life—that expresses its essential nature both in subjective units of consciousness (concepts) and in the objective portions of external reality that are conceived and influenced by concepts. This happens in such a way that the life of subjective consciousness develops in a manner that corresponds, step by step, to the way in which the Idea realizes and presents itself in objective reality. The Idea of each object must, therefore, be recognized not only by considering its particular aspects in their given uniqueness but also by understanding the universal unity of both. Only in this unity does that which is unique to a given Idea gain sufficient expression.[4]

Siebeck designates these two sides with the fortunate terms "religiosity" and "objective religious matters" *(objektives Religionswesen)*.

Religion as a whole finds its life and historical activity in the religious inwardness of individuals and in the realm of doctrines, symbols, cults, and ceremonies that are all essentially related to inwardness, and in which religious inwardness is outwardly recognized as being at work. The first is essentially a disposition, a mood *(Stimmung)*, and thus always more or less fluid, indefinite, and, although it carries a set fundamental emphasis, always changing in height and depth, in degree of certainty and satisfaction. The second, however, represents object *(Sache)*, work, accomplishment, in which the content of the disposition has attained visible and tangible shape and has crystallized itself into clearly discernible objects.[5]

The subjective, as distinguished from the objective, side of religion may be defined as the realm of religious thoughts, feelings, moods, and inclinations. They appear as the content of both individual and communal consciousness and as such distinguish themselves from other contents of consciousness. The objective side appears as the region of orally or scripturally transmitted doctrines, dogmas, commandments, and promises, and also a number of acts, in part symbolic and in part substantial, that identify a community as of the same religious spirit, strengthen it, and maintain it.

The various modalities of the objective side can only maintain their
character and value in permanent relation to the spirit or the subjective
side. Similarly, the subjective can maintain and preserve its uniqueness
and distinctiveness as religious consciousness in the full sense only
through its inherent tendency to manifest itself through objective forms
and activities, through which it becomes the vehicle of the religious
community.[6]

An approach that focuses on the study of these data will bring the
philosophy of religion and the history of religions together. Not
only will the scholar and the philosopher trace changes in objective
religion out of a concern for "the" genesis of "religion," as a
preparatory study for the psychology of mysticism, as now happens
occasionally; they will also work with a quite definite presupposition:
in these objective religious forms a unique and irreducible value
is given; in the anchoring of cultic practices, in the persistence of
concepts found in archaic legends, in the stringency of dogmatic
commitment—among others—must be seen not only a necessary
moment of inertia *(Trägheit)* but also positive factors that prevent
a religion from fragmenting into a thousand particular configurations and falling into an ultimately hopeless subjectivity. These
factors make possible the inner coherence upon which the religious
life of a community rests.

Of course, the history of religions does not evaluate. But when
it observes the history and destiny, the structure and formation of
religions, the history of religions cannot avoid learning what has
been for good or for ill in a religion's development. At this point,
experiences will supplement and confirm one another. The *philosophy* of religion will draw its conclusions, and in this manner the
results of the history of religions will be of "political" and "pedagogical" significance, if only indirectly.

Psychologism has probably dominated no other philosophical
discipline so powerfully as the philosophy of religion. At most, only
its role in aesthetics may be comparable. In the philosophy of
religion, psychologism has not only determined the approach to
research and thought, forcing the entire enterprise into the path
of psychological observation; it has also influenced the scholar's
evaluations.

A glance at intellectual history explains this development. It is
not by accident that it was the Protestant philosophy of religion
that entered upon this path. From the beginning, it has greatly
esteemed the psychological dimension. As often noticed, the uniquely

Protestant approach to the internal and subjective that reached its peak in Pietism was powerfully supplemented by the development of spiritual introspection, self-analysis, biography, and similar activities. The first significant philosophical formulation of this attitude came with Descartes, and the psychological philosophy of religion found its first great systematician in Kant, who was followed by Fichte. Schleiermacher stands at the apex of this movement. Schelling and Hegel were unable to put a stop to it, and this development continued in Feuerbach, Pfleiderer, von Hartmann, Höffding, and in Americans influenced by Schleiermacher, such as William James. To the explicitly subjective doctrines of systematic theology during the second half of the nineteenth century corresponded a one-sided psychological, or even psychologistic, philosophy of religion. A typical development was the creation and formation of a "psychology of religion" that, as conceived and developed, seems possible only on a Protestant foundation. Interests centered almost exclusively on the study of psychological relationships, even in the nascent history of religions. Symbolics (in the sense in which the Romantic philosophy of religion used this term) and the interpretation of objective forms were pushed aside and entirely neglected. These objective forms continued to receive consideration longer in all the other humanistic studies than in the philosophy of religion and the history of religions. Indeed, disciplines such as the history of art, Germanic studies, and ethnology (in the study of myths) never lost sight of the objective, and from them the history of religions has repeatedly derived inspiration in this regard. It might be said that what the history of religions has accomplished with regard to the objective has resulted from the inspiration of these other disciplines.

The issue of individualism is closely associated with subjectivism.[7] The extent to which individualism has dominated recent Protestant thought in the philosophy of religion (liberalism) is plain to see. The result is that only the individual is thought to be important for the study of religions.[8] Given such an extreme concern for the individual, concern for the community—the people, the masses, in short, every collective bearer of religious movement—vanishes. Here I am only interested in the way this attitude has affected work in the history of religions. It is clear that individualism is closely connected with the basic position of Protestantism: what is decisive is the individual who struggles by himself for his faith, who knows his calling, and who stands before God alone. Kierkegaard has expressed this solitude before God most beautifully and powerfully. Today even foreign religiosity is measured and evaluated by the degree to which it approximates this idea. Individualism has thus dominated the choices, interests, and procedures of thought in the philosophy of religion (and the history of religions). It now seems so obvious that "inwardness" is of the highest value that hardly anyone thinks of measuring a religion by any other scale. As a result, whenever objective religious forms stand out, they are immediately identified as the products of alienation or "petrification." It is assumed that the objective is of secondary importance, that it not only arises later than the subjective but is also less important and less valuable subjectively and objectively.

The approach of the *religionsgeschichtliche Schule* has always been a little less rigid. This school has altogether abandoned an individualistic subjectivism, but it has at least broadened its attitude in practice, if not in theory. Through studying the multiplicity of the empirical religions, its members have learned to recognize and value the objective (myth, cult, ritual) as a significant aspect in the life of religions. Nevertheless, the philosophy of religion of this school's theoretician, Ernst Troeltsch, expresses most strongly the psychologistic, subjectivistic, and individualistic attitude, whose proper significance for the history of religions I have tried to indicate here. Significantly, Troeltsch himself did little actual work in the history of religious or the historical study of religions proper.

The situation will improve only if the history of religions studies the process of religious objectification more than it has in the past and turns its attention to the laws that govern the development and structure of religion as a manifestation of the objective spirit. Many good beginnings have been made in both theology and the history of religions. Several examples come to mind: Harnack's *Einleitung der Dogmengeschichte* (Introduction to the history of dogma), which outlines the factors that lead to the formation of dogmas; Heiler's study of prayer; and especially Wundt's studies in *Völkerpsychologie*. Wundt makes a grand attempt to depict the process of objectification by approaching it as if it were only an ethno-psychological phenomenon. Wundt's great error, as his critics have shown, lies in conceptualizing the problem in one-sidedly psychological terms. Otto in particular has demonstrated this.

Much richer material is now available for studying the laws that govern the development of objective religion than for studying the process of objectification. To the former both the historian of religions and the philosopher of religion have contributed their shares. Usener's *Götternamen* has been of great significance, for despite several errors in detail, it broke new ground in the matter of studying objective changes in the names of deities.[9] As a result, Usener revealed how important changes in language could be to the development of religion. The significance of the principles Usener discovered may be less far-reaching than he himself assumed, but the innovativeness and the breadth with which he posed the question were decisive. Usener's investigation centered on names and the changes they underwent, while Wundt's primary concern was the evolution of (religious) conceptions, to which he devoted the major portion of his ethno-psychological description of myth and religion.

The study of cultus has also not stood still. To date, however, it has yielded more content-laden monographs than contributions to the theory of the development of cult in general. The study of classical religions has taken the lead in this area; but one should also note the works of Wellhausen and Smith and, to do justice to a more specialized field of study, research on the Catholic liturgy.[10] Consider, too, von Hartmann's, Pfleiderer's, and Siebeck's philosophies of religion, Wundt's and Krueger's psychologies, Tiele's and Söderblom's histories of religion, Vierkandt's works in sociology, and studies by ethnologists such as Frazer, Preuss, Ehrenreich, and Frobenius. Once we pose in principle the weighty question, long recognized as significant by philosophy, of what factors ᵢinfluence the development of cult—to answer this question the history of religions has not progressed far beyond the alternative between the great man and the community—our chief question becomes: How does the development of religion proceed as a manifestation of the objective spirit? Through an internal logic (dialectic), through human interference, or both? Hegel did justice to both psychological and philosophical explanations by invoking a necessary progress of the Idea. The development after Hegel that I have alluded to several times above has increasingly excluded philosophical explanations. The *Völkerpsychologen* represent a specific stage in this movement, too. They underscored the significance of psychological explanation, and they directed all their efforts and attention toward elucidating it. This tendency toward the psychological characterized both those who placed more weight on the individual and those who emphasized the community, those who attributed the primary scholarly task to the psychology of the individual and those who assigned it to ethno- (social) psychology. If we are to reflect on the approaches and tasks of the various humanistic disciplines, we must be clear about this development and its causes. There is no question that, in contrast to the study of psychological facts, objective factors have been neglected by the philosophy of religion in its theory and by the history of religions in practice.

I would certainly not wish to fall into the opposite error and underestimate the importance of the internal or the subjective in the development of religions, nor would I wish to endorse a dialectic at any cost. That error brought about the demise of Hegelian philosophy and its disappearance from research in the various disciplines. Hegelianism did not derive its categories and laws from the course of history but imposed them on it from above. It is nevertheless possible to inquire, quite apart from metaphysical speculation and construction, into the principles according to which religion as a manifestation of the objective spirit evolves historically. Certainly, the study of religion will never be able to undertake this inquiry alone. In the other humanistic studies, too, these tasks were recognized long ago, and sooner or later, more or less consciously and more or less directly, scholars will enter upon these paths that, while new, are yet so old.

PART TWO

Essays from *Die Religion in Geschichte und Gegenwart* 1928–1931

UNDERSTANDING *(VERSTEHEN)*

THE THEORY OF understanding arose from the associations and needs of daily life. Methodically ordered and pursued as an art or technique, understanding has assumed special significance in those disciplines that are concerned primarily with interpreting the expressions of the mind or spirit: theology (doctrine based upon an understanding of sacred scriptures), jurisprudence (the interpretation of laws), and philology (the understanding of texts). To these must be added the contributions of philosophy, which is interested in the process of understanding as such (epistemology), and of psychology or anthropology, which analyzes the life of the psyche and the forms of its manifestation. In these intellectual disciplines, a "hermeneutics" has developed.

The history of hermeneutics begins in antiquity. The field achieved considerable depth in the Middle Ages. Then the modern world created new foundations for it. Dilthey has shown the extent to which Protestantism led to a revival of hermeneutics. The universalistic scholarship of the seventeenth and eighteenth centuries sought a universal theory of human

153

expression, and even the Enlightenment held to the ideal of a unified theory of understanding. But in the subsequent period these efforts fell apart. The reestablishment of the humanistic studies in the German Classic-Romantic movement at the beginning of the nineteenth century has revived the theory of understanding, drawing its primary stimulus from Herder. The historical school has been more important in this development than transcendental philosophy. Borrowing from F. Schlegel and F. A. Wolf, Schleiermacher sketched out his own comprehensive hermeneutics, a hermeneutics that A. Boeckh fashioned into a system. These ingenious attempts still preserved the idea of unity, but nineteenth-century theology distinguished between a general and a special hermeneutics, in accordance with the attitudes that were held at that time toward the object of theological interpretation, the Bible. I need not discuss the further development of philological hermeneutics, or even of legal hermeneutics, here. The various studies of art *(Kunstwissenschaften)* that are now independent were concerned with a theory of the interpretation of art. In the field of history it was Ranke and above all Droysen who in the nineteenth-century thought about the understanding of historical processes, persons, and manifestations. Studies of the contribution of "positivism" to the theory of understanding have not yet been completed. Today, however, interest in hermeneutical problems has been revived by the historical and systematic works of Dilthey, his pupils, and his successors.

"Understanding" pursued as an art or technique rests upon the kind of understanding that we practice in daily life. Even in daily life subjective *(Seel-)* and objective *(Sach-)* understanding occur side by side. Because there is always the possibility of misunderstanding, there has arisen a concern to guarantee that understanding is adequate ("objective," binding). Scholarship *(Wissenschaft)* relies upon such understanding and at the same time proves that it is possible. A special discipline— hermeneutics—has the task of formulating a theory of adequate understanding.

Every hermeneutics that goes beyond a theory of techniques and methods is grounded in certain metaphysical convictions, for example, the convictions of a philosophy of life or of spirit, according to which the idea of participation, based on an essential commonality *(Wesensgemeinsamkeit)* is the presupposition of all understanding. In this connection, the nature and meaning of an objectification of life or spirit (the "expression") may be determined. Since we can participate in the life of another, we are able to understand its manifestations through a psychological understanding that is directed toward internal motivations. (I will discuss the extent of this understanding later.) Important in this regard are the bounds that distinguish the meaningful from the meaningless expression and expressions that are more objectivized from those that are less so. Given the current debate over the "broad" and the "narrow" sense of "understanding," it seems best to reserve the term understanding *(Verstehen)* for subjective and objective understanding *(Seel- und Sachverstehen)* and not to speak of the comprehension *(Verständnis)* or even the exposition *(Auslegung)* of life, life contexts, and so on. Complexes of meaning of this sort are no longer to be "understood" but "interpreted."

It is the task of the theory of cognition (epistemology, *Erkenntnistheorie)* to illuminate understanding as a human activity: the actual moment of intuition in which understanding occurs, the connection between the various psychological powers (the relations of emotional, affective moments to intellectual ones), and the methods that lead to it. Modern epistemology, phenomenology, and psychology have analyzed both the prerequisites and the nature of the way we understand a foreign *"Thou,"* its nature, experience, and activity. The methodologies and hermeneutics of the various human studies—theology, law, philology and linguistics, the historical sciences—study and describe the understanding of objectifications as a methodical procedure, an understanding which ranges, as Dilthey said, "from comprehending children's cooings to understanding Hamlet or the Critique of Reason." In regard to the possibility and extent of understanding, the theoretician must strike a balance between overenthusiastic optimism and unlimited skepticism. "Precisely where are the qualitative and quantitative limits of human understanding?"—this is a central question for all hermeneutics.

But to what extent can we understand another individual at all? How can we overcome the difficulties that derive from belonging to a particular time and space, to a specific culture? In brief, how can we overcome the limits of the "relative a prioris" that condition not only our own understanding but also the life and expressions of others? An understanding completely free from presuppositions is out of the question. But similarly, the radical subjectivization that characterizes some modern trends has no place in a sensible hermeneutics. The aim of hermeneutics will always be to develop tools that, in full awareness of the limitations under which understanding proceeds, help us overcome these limitations in both theory and practice. The final product will thus be a "result." Understanding does not "mirror" reality. It refers to a never-ending process that must be carried out anew in every age, by every group, and by every individual.

The great task of understanding others (fremde Individualität) is entrusted to all the humanistic studies, especially the historical disciplines ("psychological interpretation"). Hermeneutical questions are especially important in writing various kinds of biographies. Every discipline that deals with human expressions must contribute to this task. Hermeneuticists have always known, however, that to understand the individual, we must also be able to think typologically, to relate the specific to the typical. To understand the psychological states and developments not only of individuals but also of groups, communities, and peoples, we must be aware of our presuppositions, possibilities, and limitations.

In addition to understanding the subjective, the humanistic studies also attempt to understand the objective. The history of religions, for example, seeks to understand foreign religions: on the subjective side, their piety; on the objective side, their expressions. Its ultimate goal is to comprehend the spirit that is active in the totality of a religion's manifestations. Consequently, it seeks to understand the whole from the parts, and then again to understand the parts from the whole. This basic procedure entails a great deal of philological and historical work. A primary task, naturally, is the attempt to understand sacred scriptures; but in seeking to understand a foreign religiosity, the historian of religions must not overvalue theoretical expressions to the detriment of the practical (cult, ritual). The hermeneutics of religious documents, which is still in its infancy, should make such understanding possible.

The Christian theologian desires to understand the Bible. How he views the essential nature of this book will help determine the kind of hermeneutics that guarantees understanding. Even in this case, however, where practical, normative interests complement theoretical interests, the goal of understanding is to comprehend the word of God as completely and adequately as possible. The methods developed by the science of interpretation seek to lead from linguistic proficiency to a factual, a generic, a historical, a psychological, and finally to an integral understanding. This goal provides hints of what is necessary if we are to understand someone or something. Beyond the factual prerequisites, we must have an affinity with the subject matter, an affinity that in general hermeneutics is expressed in terms of kinship of spirit *(Geistesverwandtschaft)* or congeniality, and that in theology is conceived of as an "attunement" of spirit *(Geistesbestimmtheit)*. Each scholarly discipline adjusts the specific demands of its hermeneutics to correspond with what it perceives to be the structure of its subject matter.

THE HISTORY OF RELIGIONS
(RELIGIONSWISSENSCHAFT)

Concept and Nature

The designation *"Religionswissenschaft"* is of recent date, and its usage is not uniform. Not long ago, it seemed that a history or science of religions might displace theology. Now theology occasionally denies that the history of religions has a right to exist. Thus, we must first clarify what we mean by "the history of religions."

"The general history of religions" *(allgemeine Religionswissenschaft)* is the inclusive designation *(Inbegriff)* for the scholarly study of religion. It includes, to begin with what is not disputed, the study of the nature and form of historical religions. Whether Christianity should be among these religions is a matter of debate. Many incline toward including it, but in practice a specific, independent, scholarly discipline devoted to Christianity has been developed: theology. Theology's central task— the normative treatment of the Christian religion—gives it an exceptional position with respect to religio-historical work. The history of religions is not a normative discipline. It is, therefore, just as impossible for the history of religions to undertake and accomplish theological goals as it is for theology to replace the history of religions. If nothing else, the immensity of the material prevents the latter from happening.

The next question that we must consider concerns the extent to which the history of religions should undertake tasks that lie beyond historical investigation proper. Should historians of religions explore the essential nature *(Wesen)* of religion? Should they identify typical regularities and evaluate various religious forms? Clearly, such questions lead more or less directly into philosophy, so that here the history of religions shades off into the philosophy of religion. It is possible to argue about whether all philosophy of religion should not be included within the history of religions, but despite their interconnections, scholarly study *(Wissenschaft)* and philosophy are distinct. Therefore, we must clearly recognize that the tasks of the history of religions and those of the philosophy of religion are fundamentally different. If historians of religions are allowed to proceed unhindered, it is not so important whether issues in the philosophy of religion are included within the history of religions or whether they stand beside it and constitute an independent discipline. In the final analysis, it is up to the discretion of the individual scholar to determine to what extent a particular problem or task becomes philosophical. These scholars, however, will have to modify the criteria for the history of religions accordingly.

In any case, there can be no doubt that in studying foreign religions the history of religions must proceed in a manner that is analogous to the other humanistic studies. The history of religions cannot simply be equated with these studies. In every realm of the spirit—law, art, morals—the process of objectification is unique; so, too, religious expression follows its own laws. It is extremely difficult to reason back from religious forms to what is internal—and a great deal of religio-historical work consists of just such reasoning. Ultimately, religious experience is beyond description, and the expressions that proceed from it are inadequate. When dealing with nonreligious cultural experiences, one is dealing with the relative; religious experience, however, relates to the absolute, however that absolute may be constituted or defined. As a result, the categories with which scholarly disciplines generally attempt to characterize expressions of the human spirit cannot be applied directly to the history of religions. One of this discipline's most important tasks is to develop categories specifically suited to the subject that it studies.

Recently theology has become aware that its task is unique; now theologians often deny that scholars have the right to create general categories that apply to religious phenomena. General categories such as religion, cult, and prayer are unwarranted, they say; at least these categories do not apply to Christian phenomena. We do not need to bother with the specific assertion here, but we must insist strongly that the history of religions has a right to develop general concepts, whether through generalization, phenomenological analysis, or some other method. What Schleiermacher recognized in his *Speeches* must never be forgotten. Historical work, which is naturally basic to the history of religions, absolutely requires us to formulate general concepts if we are to structure and examine historical phenomena.

Today, those who are familiar with the history of religions can no longer dispute that it is necessary to formulate this discipline as an independent, well-structured context for research and understanding. One must grant to theology the right to treat the results of religio-historical work in a "theology of religious history" and grant to philosophy the right to interpret such results in the light of certain philosophical convictions. Obviously, however, such "applications" will never replace research in the history of religions itself, which is indispensable. The development of this discipline has been slow but steady. The nineteenth century saw the emancipation of the history of religions from its various "parental" disciplines. The twentieth century is witnessing its constitution as a scholarly discipline.

Subject and Method

The history of religions studies the multiplicity of empirical religions. It aims are to *explore, understand,* and *portray* the empirical religions, both with regard to their development—

"lengthwise in time" or diachronically—and with regard to their being—"in cross-sections" or synchronically.

First, the history of religions must *explore* the empirical religions. It does so first of all with the historical-critical method developed in the humanistic studies. If a living faith—which is always the most fruitful source of knowledge—no longer survives, scholars must take recourse to the artifacts and accounts that have been left behind. Archeological, philological, and historical interpretation of the evidence is, therefore, indispensable.

After exploration, historians of religions must try to *understand* foreign religiosity and foreign religious forms. In understanding, the interpretive effort is intensified: the exegesis of sources is carried out from every angle; particular moments and views are related to others. Above all, the specific character of the object of religio-historical consideration is taken into account. A religious manifestation must be understood as a religious manifestation. Thus, whoever wishes to deal with such data must possess a certain sensitivity for religious feelings and thought. Moreover, a hermeneutics of religious documents will have to reflect on the prerequisites, conditions, goals, and limits that govern the scholar's understanding of such documents. There is also a constant interchange: from particular phenomena the student seeks to penetrate more central concerns and so to grasp something of their spirit; at the same time, he seeks to understand each individual manifestation, whether central or peripheral, on the basis of the spirit.

Finally, after exploration and interpretation comes *presentation*. The scholar must communicate his results in a manner that is suited to the subject and at the same time informative to the reader.

After studying the multiplicity of religious forms, it is only natural to contemplate evaluating and comparing them. In the past, comparison has perhaps been overvalued, but it will always be an important and instructive research tool. Our use of comparison must always be guided by an important principle of careful criticism: similarity of form does not always imply similarity of meaning. Comparison should help us see not only what is common, but also what is distinct and different. We must always note carefully the weight and significance of the individual features that we are comparing in the entire phenomenon in which they occur. But if we try to evaluate on the basis of our comparisons, the question arises what "yardstick" or norm we shall use. It is possible to evaluate directly from one's own point of view; to do so leads straight to apologetics. Under the banner of (methodologically) "bracketing" one's own point of view, one can try to apply an immanent scale (for example, the degree of ethical perfection or aesthetic form) or a transcendental principle of a metaphysical sort (say, the idealism of the philosophy of mind or spirit *[Geistesphilosophie]*). Within the bounds of the history of religions itself, it does not seem possible to decide on or justify such a principle. The history of religions can neither ask nor answer the question of truth. The field of scholarship does not deal in personal decisions but in generally valid research.

The principle of "relative" objectivity (the greatest possible objectivity) must be as decisive for the history of religions as it is for all the humanistic studies. The methodological criteria that apply to these other disciplines apply to the history of religions as well. In following this principle, it is necessary to neutralize subjective factors as much as possible. Only if we abstain from personal opinions and convictions can we ever fully understand the intentionality of the phenomenon at hand. We may never actually realize this ideal, but it must still guide scholarly work. There is no need for us to renounce personal convictions altogether; it is only necessary to be methodologically clean. We can and must remain aware of the "perspectivism" in our own knowledge, but our awareness does not excuse us from the obligation to prepare as pure a field of research as possible. Still, there is little hope that we will ever free ourselves completely from the conditions under which we work.

Task

The task of the history of religions is historical understanding in the broad sense of the term. Historians of religions study the development—the Becoming—of religions, their forms and their destinies in the world. The philosophical and psychological problem of the origin of religion lies outside this discipline's competence. The history of religions tries first of all to understand a religion by itself, to study the unfolding of religious ideas in the multiplicity of their empirical forms and the interconnections and interactions of these forms with the other manifestations of the socio-historical world. Beyond this, the development of a particular form must be placed in a higher order, until the question of the development of religion itself transforms the history of religions into the philosophy of religion and the philosophy of history.

But the history of religions does not limit itself to historical investigation, to studying how this or that religious phenomenon was constituted at one time or another, how it manifested itself and how it wielded its effects. The history of religions also formulates comprehensive, comparative, systematic insights. It attempts to use research into particular concepts of the divine, particular rituals, and particular forms of religious association to clarify our thought about the divine, prayer, and the religious community. To be sure, pure abstraction or generalization—simply excluding historical particulars—would not produce satisfactory results. It must be supplemented by a phenomenological treatment that transcends the descriptive and leads to the "idea." In this endeavor, the history of religions still has very much to do. Although some have expressed doubts about and even rejected the possibility of speaking about what is beyond the individual, the history of religions will continue to follow the successful path it has already begun. Here, too, the history of religions merges with the philosophy of religion.

The religious event (*Vorgang*) is an internal matter, all objectification notwithstanding. Consequently, historians of religions must penetrate the inner religious state (*Verfassung*) that lies behind objectifications. They must pursue regularities or types of religious experience—a task apart from which historical and systematic work is unthinkable. Penetrating the inner religious state is the concern of the psychology of religion. For some time, scholars thought of psychology as a key that could open every door. Today, we have come to recognize its uses and its limits.

Religion is not only and, from a genetic point of view, not originally a matter of the individual. At the very least, it is also a matter of the community, it is also social. Just as religion can unite a group of prople, it can itself also be conditioned by the character of the community. A special branch of study is devoted to these reciprocal relations: the sociology of religion.

In sum, we may say that the history of religions studies religion as an internal and external phenomenon, and it studies the latter in terms of theoretical (myth, doctrine, dogma), practical (cult, rite), and sociological forms (religious community, congregation).

History

Already in antiquity people were interested in foreign religions. Travelers, philosophers, and historians fostered and contributed to knowledge of such religions. Here the intellectual flexibility of the Greeks and their openness to the world had beneficial results. Scientific sensitivity first began to stir in the Greek world. In some areas of study, the value of information provided by ancient authors is still inestimable. In contrast to the Greek pursuit of knowledge for its own sake, the concern for foreign religions among early Christian writers was purposeful and oriented toward their own interests. It is true that we owe a considerable amount of important information to apologetic zeal. During the Middle Ages, three major movements of expansion added to knowledge of non-Christian religions: the crusades, missionary enterprises conducted by religious orders, and travels such as those of Marco Polo.

More recently, our knowledge of these religions has grown immensely. Discoveries, a new interest in antiquity (the Renaissance, humanism), and a new interest in matters of faith as a result of schisms within Christendom, have intensified both practical and scholarly interest in religion and religions.

The age of the "system of nature" (the Enlightenment) marked the dawn of a new day in the history of European concern with foreign religions. The Enlightenment distinguished between natural religion and positive religions, and it sought to probe natural religion philosophically. In addition, the amount of information about positive religions was growing steadily. But still, there was no single point of view that could unify studies motivated by philosophical, theological, philological, antiquarian, and exotic interests. Herder, a German driven not by clear systematic interests but by an anticipation of what was needed, full of enthusiasm and full of ideas, became the actual father of the modern history of religions. His extremely fascinating personality combined tendencies that would soon cause scholarship to fragment in many different directions: religious and aesthetic, philosophical and psychological, philological and archeological, historical and ethnological. After Herder, only Hegel and Schleiermacher displayed a similar universality. But these two men were, and wanted to be, primarily philosophers or theologians. They provided much stimulus for the history of religions, but they could not develop it into an independent discipline.

Schleiermacher's *Speeches* stand at the beginning of the nineteenth century. This century presents us with an immense amount of research, but research that is still quite diverse. The powerful development of philology, above all the study of Oriental languages and cultures, was of great significance for the study of religions, even though this study was not immune from the excesses of philologism. Ethnology has continually broadened our knowledge of primitive peoples; it has made an immense amount of material available for the study of religions. Archeology has unearthed monuments, and the study of prehistory has revealed previously unknown epochs. To all this, the nineteenth century added the work of the two great parental disciplines of the history of religions, theology and philosophy. Theologians have taken part in defining and studying many important religio-historical problems. They have also frequently attempted to penetrate from particular points of view the massive amount of material that is available. In recent philosophy, interest in the problem of religion has moved along traditional lines. Ever since Hegel's philosophy of religion there has been a lively interchange between the history of religions and the philosophy of religion.

In the nineteenth century, a number of individual scholars and thinkers played decisive roles in constituting the history of religions, even though some of their work now seems out of date. After Schleiermacher, I must mention Max Müller, Lagarde, and Usener. Throughout their lives, these men subscribed to very specific models of the history of religions. Today a number of great scholars have dedicated themselves primarily, or exclusively, to the study of religion—scholars such as Nathan Söderblom, Ed. Lehmann, Rudolf Otto, F. Cumont, R. Reitzenstein, K. Beth, A. Bertholet, H. Haas, F. Heiler, H. Frick, J. W. Hauser, C. Clemen, Wilhelm Schmidt, Gerardus van der Leeuw, and Raffaele Pettazzoni.

THE PHILOSOPHY OF RELIGION

Philosophical Consideration of Ultimate Questions from the Point of View of a Historical Religion

Practically every positive religion, including every primitive religion, contains the beginnings of a philosophy of religion. Myths frequently hint at such beginnings. Wherever theoretical convictions are consolidated into a developed, systematized doctrine, a development in the direction of the philosophy of religion has already begun. Where there exists an explicitly formulated dogmatics—the most intense refinement of doctrine—as in Christianity, Judaism, Islam, and Buddhism, the philosophic tendency serves first of all to develop and support statements of faith, but it also critiques, opposes, and dissolves dogmas from within and without. Frequently, it is difficult to decide whether to call a certain religious phenomenon a theology or a philosophy of religion. Such ambiguous phenomena are found in the Vedic and Brahmanic religions, Jewish philosophy, Muslim philosophy, and Christian Scholasticism. Even among the religions of higher cultures where for some reason or another a full-fledged philosophy of religion has never developed, sporadic reflections of a philosophic sort may nevertheless be observed, as in the religions of Egypt, Babylon, Iran, Japan, and Mexico.

169

"Philosophic" denotes, then, both the systematic inclination, which may, of course, manifest itself in a "systematic"
(dogmatic) theology but which may also go beyond it at some
points, and the use of rational arguments and methods. From
these two endeavors arise a number of characteristic difficulties.
Human reasoning tends to autonomy and exclusivity, and this
tendency repeatedly conflicts with the source and norm of a
believer's knowledge, revelation. Thus, we see in the Christian,
Jewish, Islamic, and Indian philosophies of religion a struggle
between reason (philosophy) and faith (revelation). Only in
the first of these philosophies has this struggle led to an
emancipation of philosophy, but in that case emancipation has
surpassed even the freedom achieved in Greek thought. In a
religious community in which revealed doctrine is developed
and defended dogmatically, a rational critique advanced by
the philosophy of religion easily becomes heterodox and he-
retical. The amount of tolerance that orthodoxy is willing to
grant to philosophy varies from case to case and from one
set of principles to another. It is often sufficient simply to
have a point of contact with the religious norm, as, for instance,
in the Eastern philosophy of religion, which poses as the
interpretation of sacred scriptures (compare, for example, the
orthodox and heterodox systems of India).

What I have said so far applies not only to the rationalistic
philosophy of religion but also to a second type of philosophy
of religion, which derives from positive religions (theology),
the mystical type. A rationalistic philosophy of religion has
developed in every cultural context in which thought has
achieved the emancipation that I mentioned above—beginning
with the Mutazilitism of Judaism and Islam, the Ionic philosophy of nature in the Greek tradition, and already during the
so-called Brahmanic period in India. Mysticism has developed
in many areas—in China, India, and Greece, in Christianity,
Judaism, and Islam—and out of mystical piety there has arisen
a mystically oriented philosophy of religion. Where mysticism
is not simply identical with the root or core of the religion
concerned, it grows directly out of that religion. As a result,
a distinction between orthodox piety and mystical piety often

arises very late, if at all. More clearly than in a rationalistic philosophy of religion, a mystical philosophy of religion displays a distinctive attitude toward life *(Lebensgefühl)*, an attitude that is bound up with certain conceptions of God, the world, nature, and humanity. As long as mysticism remains within certain qualitative and quantitative bounds, it may be satisfied with the positive religion with which it is associated; but frequently mystical piety transcends these bounds, and then there are great conflicts between mystics and the religious community. Such conflicts are familiar from the histories of Christianity, Judaism, and Islam. The consequences of these conflicts can be devastating, because in contrast to the rationalistic philosophy of religion, a mystical philosophy of religion exercises a direct effect on practical life. In spite of the mystic's basic mistrust of reason, philosophically inclined mystics work by rational means. Paradoxically, mystical doctrine becomes developed into a full-fledged philosophy of religion. Mystics such as Eckhart, ibn Arabi, Shankara, and Ramanuja rank with the most outstanding thinkers in the history of human thought.

Of course, these two types of philosophy of religion—rationalistic and mystical—are not absolutely distinct from one another. Just as a mystical philosophy of religion often displays the influence of the rational, so the rationalistic approach is affected by mysticism. Consider Thomas Aquinas, al Ghazali, and Nagarjuna. But every philosophy of religion, whatever its stance toward the positive religion—interpretive, critical, or opposed—has an affect upon the positive religion from which it derives.

As I have discussed it so far, the philosophy of religion works on the whole to support and develop the truth contained in revelation. In no way does this activity exclude criticism of or opposition to dogma. This sort of philosophy of religion must elaborate and analyze religious knowledge (epistemology); it must formulate the view of nature and destiny contained in positive revelation (cosmology; philosophy of nature; philosophy of history); and it must formulate the implicit view of humanity, its nature and disposition (anthropology and ethics). As long as the philosophy of religion is concerned with elaborating dogma in the narrower sense, it simply continues the dogmatic task with other tools (philosophical tools). Where, however, the "expansion" of dogma leads to a systematically developed worldview, albeit a worldview derived from a particular revelation, criticism, discussion, and opposition will arise. This stage has been reached by Christianity, Judaism, Islam, Zoroastrianism, Buddhism, and Hinduism, and also in China. From this situation of conflict arises the need for polemics and apologetics; where a philosophy of religion rooted in revelation is put on the defensive, apologetics and polemics become decisively important religio-philosophical tasks.

Philosophical Consideration of Ultimate Questions Independently of a Positive Religion

The emancipation of philosophical reflection from concrete religions and from worldviews based on them has taken place, strictly speaking, only in the Western world. Of course, in East Asia, thought is in general less constrained than anywhere else in the Orient, and there we do encounter "autonomous" thought. In India, too, individual movements and persons have freed themselves from traditional speculations. But except for sporadic occurrences, such as mysticism, Greek influence on Judaism and Islam has led to no fundamental separation of philosophy from religion. In the West, by contrast, a unique "theoretical" and then a "scientific" attitude flourished first in Greece, and a radical separation of thought from the inherited faith was the result. Critique and opposition appeared alongside the defense, elaboration, and transformation of the religious view—that is, alongside interpretation. In addition to a philosophy of religion profoundly oriented toward revealed faith (both Greek and Near Eastern), then, late antiquity also knew autonomous speculation. In the East such independence has scarcely ever been achieved, even if we keep in mind that often in the East, especially in Islamic countries, the political situation has necessitated dissimulation, so that thinkers have worked with veiled terminology and concepts. In contrast to ancient Greece, the Christian Middle Ages possessed a specifically Christian philosophy in its grand unity. Only toward the end of this period do we encounter thinkers who began to leave the ground of religion. Finally, Dilthey has demonstrated how, in the recent history of European thought, the specifically Christian understanding of the world was pushed aside by the development of principles of reasoning for use in the natural sciences, especially mechanistic principles, and by the exclusion of teleological points of view. The attitude toward life *(Lebensgefühl)* that supported the Renaissance and humanism pressed forward to philosophical positions that often could be harmonized with fundamental Christian views only with great difficulty. Still, Christian impulses and motives had a strong influence on the religio-philosophical ferment of the Renaissance. The Reformation was the grandest among many attempts to renew the teaching of the Gospel. It opened up the possibility of a new beginning for the philosophy of religion, the Protestant philosophy of religion.

At first, philosophical discussions were governed by the specifically humanistic impulses of the Renaissance. The new conception—alongside (and in) which philosophy still proceeded on a thoroughly Christian basis—was given a sort of foundation in the "system of nature," which was introduced 'into the humanistic studies. Thus, efforts to understand natural religion, efforts often linked with tendencies from late antiquity such as Stoicism, formed a new beginning in the history of the philosophy of religion. The climax of these efforts came with Herbert of Cherbury, Spinoza, and, above all, Hume. In the major European countries, the Enlightenment continued this movement on a massive scale. From the first there were two possible courses: either reveal the contrast and even the contradiction between positive and natural religion by pitting the latter against the former, or overcome and hide the contrast by means of a harmonization that frequently slights the historical religion. By and large, French philosophy chose the first path, but during the Enlightenment German philosophy of religion sought to reconcile the religion of reason and the religion of revelation, and in this course it was followed by the idealism of German transcendental philosophy. Herder's, Lessing's, Kant's, Fichte's, Schleiermacher's, Schelling's, and Hegel's philosophies of religion mark the climax of this effort. Obviously, different thinkers conceived of "rational" religion differently and accordingly stood at varying distances from Christianity. Consequently, their harmonizations differed in detail. But in the thought of German idealism, the motives of the Enlightenment merged with Christian philosophy of a Protestant bent. More radically than the thinkers just mentioned, people like Hamann and Fr. H. Jacobi voiced the concerns of Protestant philosophy. As the classical philosophy of religion dissolved, however, the critique and abandonment of Christianity gained momentum (for example, D. Fr. Strauss). It was not simply that materialism became fashionable (as in the French Enlightenment), for in any case materialism is by nature fruitless for a philosophy of religion. The movement was led by thinkers like Feuerbach and Nietzsche who were searching for a non-Christian, that is, an a-Christian or anti-Christian, world-immanent, "humanistic" philosophy. As a result of this development, the emancipation of philosophic thought from religious tradition has attained a level never before reached. School-philosophy in the second half of the nineteenth century kept to the traditional paths, and a less original philosophy of religion prolonged its existence on the sidelines, but the late idealistic tradition of the philosophy of religion—Krause, Weisse, Lotze, Feichner—continued the earlier movement. Kant and Hegel exerted their influence more broadly, or rather, anew (as in neo-Kantianism), and popular thought was influenced increasingly by the primitive "philosophy" of naturalism in various forms, such as Darwinism, monism, evolutionism, and the economic theory of history. By the turn of the century it had become evident that positivism, which had dominated the preceding decades, and the naturalism that, with its evolutionism and its theory of illusions, had opposed religion in general could achieve no final victory. Under the impact of a flourishing history of religions, various thinkers—Vatke, Pfleiderer, Wundt—sought to broaden the base of religio-philosophical reflection. Neo-Kantians developed a philosophy of value (Windelband, Rickert). Epistemology and the psychology of religion came to occupy an increasingly large place in the study of religion (Simmel, Troeltsch, James). However, there was no original achievement on a grand scale in the philosophy of religion. Recently, phenomenology and dialectics have also influenced the philosophy of religion (for example, Heidegger). The more the anarchy of worldviews and interpretations of life increases, the less will contemporary philosophy—itself divided among a number of schools, none of which enjoys far-reaching authority—be capable of creating an imposing system of norms. The more philosophy is forced to retreat before the onslaught of the various specialized disciplines, the more the philosophy of religion will become a philosophy *about* religion.

The attempt to establish ultimate truth independently of all revelation is the decisive characteristic of an autonomous philosophy of religion. The foundation of this enterprise is confidence in the human ability to comprehend the truth. Optimism with regard to this ability corresponds to optimism with regard to the human makeup and its evolution, as well as to optimism with regard to the destiny of humanity. Even where a pessimistic philosophy of religion (Schopenhauer, von Hartmann) emphasizes human finitude and incompleteness, human beings cooperate decisively in their salvation through knowledge and action, even though no consistent doctrine of salvation may be present. Within the bounds of an autonomous philosophy of religion, the belief in human dignity and greatness that characterizes "humanistic" and most idealistic philosophy of religion leads to an anthropocentric orientation opposed to the ideal of perfection that in extreme form is magnified into a Promethean stance.

Because it adopts a more or less positive view of human abilities, the autonomous philosophy of religion sees human beings as essentially successful in answering ultimate questions. In the previous section I discussed a kind of metaphysics that supports and elucidates revealed wisdom. In an autonomous philosophy of religion, metaphysics becomes the representative of or substitute for religion. If religion is not rejected completely, it now appears as a low, preliminary stage, as an esoteric form of philosophical knowledge, or as an expression of the truth of philosophy that uses a different language and different means. All in all, the autonomous philosophy of religion strives to grasp a more or less systematic cognitive whole *(ein Erkenntnisganzes)* that provides the normative context from which cosmology, the philosophy of nature, the philosophy of history, anthropology, and ethics are derived. We can also distinguish certain types of basic conceptions within such philosophies on several bases: on the basis of the concept of the absolute and its relationship to the finite; on the basis of the conception of human beings and the value of human activity; and on the basis of the configuration *(Stimmung)* in which development, the world, and life appear. The extent to which a philosophy that addresses ultimate questions in this sense can still be called a "philosophy of religion" is debatable. At any rate, some metaphysical systems can hardly be distinguished from religion, and there are many "philosophies of religion" that are hardly concerned with answering ultimate questions. In general we may say, on both historical and systematic grounds, that so far an autonomous philosophy of religion has appeared only in initial attempts and that it has sought, often quite unexpectedly, to associate itself with religion—and tradition. It is not easy to find a common denominator for the extremely varied movements and teachings that make up this approach to the philosophy of religion. At the present time we can discern that new fundamental deliberations in this area have just begun, influenced by new tendencies in the Protestant philosophy of religion.

Philosophical Consideration of the Nature and Form of Religion as an Objective Phenomenon

It is possible for both types of philosophy of religion discussed so far to study the nature and forms of religion as an objective structure. After the concept of natural religion had been formulated, it became possible to think about religion as such. Before that, thinkers generally absolutized, more or less naively, their own religions, a procedure that made it unnecessary or impossible to look for "religion" anywhere else. To the extent that it was possible at that time to talk about religion in general terms, one's own religion provided the standard against which all others were judged. The basic reorientation that provided the philosophy of (or about) religion with the concept of natural religion also brought with it a deeper awareness of historical forms. Just as it had increased earlier in the wake of crusades and pilgrimages, historical awareness was fostered again at the beginning of the modern period through research, travel, and discoveries, through the rediscovery of antiquity and through ecclesiastical schisms. It came to be expressed in historical, linguistic, and ethnological studies and in the study of religion's psychological nature and laws. In the eighteenth century, thinkers generally assimilated thoughts and paradigms associated with the "system of nature," and the result was the first significant attempts at a philosophy that examined objective religious structures. Hume and Herder prepared the way, but the actual founders of a systematic philosophy of religion were Schleiermacher and Hegel, the one thinking in more psychological, the other in more historical terms. Schleiermacher's *Speeches* and Hegel's *Philosophy of Religion* have exerted a great influence on subsequent developments. Under their influence the embattled philosophy *of* religion of the nineteenth century—scarcely holding its own against its opponents—became a philosophy *about* religion.

The development of a philosophy about religion raised a number of significant problems and tasks. How has religion developed and what laws governed that development? What is the basic structure of religion (the analysis of the religious act)? What types of religion are there and what are their characteristics? How does religion relate to other manifestations of the life of the human spirit, and how has it come to be expressed in history and culture? Finally, how does philosophy evaluate and characterize religious forms? These ques-

tions can be addressed in many different ways. Hegel's philosophy of religion attempts—sometimes in a one-sided manner
but with an amazing speculative power—to construct a unified,
philosophical vision of all of religious history. Vatke and Pfleiderer were guided by a theological point of view but they
were also affected by Hegel. Pfleiderer has sought to embrace
the results of the historical study of religion without surren-
dering an idealistic construction according to which all of
evolution has proceeded along a single path. With Wundt's
mammoth undertaking, *Völkerpsychologie: Mythus und Religion,*
the quantity of empirical data has become immense, but the
work as a whole is structured by only a few psychological
categories. Spengler's philosophy of religious history is developed within the framework of a pluralistic philosopy of culture
and metaphysics.

In the final analysis, the standard to be used for evaluation
will always be a problem. Philosophers can construct series of
values only after they have accepted a set of norms as a basis.
These norms can be derived from either a positive religion
or an autonomous philosophy. Today, for example, attempts
to interpret religious history from the point of view of Christianity stand opposed to attempts that try to adopt the view-
point of some future religion. But the more the philosophy
of religion immerses itself in the multiplicity and uniqueness
of religious forms, the more it will prefer a typological approach rather than hasty absolutizing. A typological approach
leaves the ultimate differences among religious expressions
and their subtle characteristics in place, and these differences
and characteristics reveal to us religion in its essential nature
and manifestation. In so far as it is necessary to do justice to
particular religious phenomena—and only a philosophy of
religion that takes these phenomena into account can be taken
seriously—the desire for a more or less unified, comprehensive
conception *(Gesamtauffassung)* of the world of religion, in terms
of both Being and Becoming, will always assert itself. Attempts
to see the multiplicity of religious phenomena as a whole and
to construct their evolution will always continue.

THE SAVIOR IN THE HISTORY OF RELIGIONS

The Concept of the Savior

The presence of a savior is a mark that distinguishes religious from philosophical doctrines of salvation. Philosophical doctrines teach that human beings are saved by their own efforts; religious doctrines proclaim the principle of salvation by another. The experience of finitude, limitedness, and nothingness that makes itself felt in the "boundary-line situations of humankind" *(Grenzsituationen)* is inseparable from religious experience. It leads directly to the need for salvation that is formulated more or less explicitly in all the higher religions. Similar to this need is the desire for help that is embodied in savior figures, mediators, and divine incarnations. We can already detect the beginnings of such notions in the religious beliefs of primitive peoples, for example, in the various sorts of culture heroes *(Kultur- und Heilbringer)* that we find among American Indians such as the Algonkins. Certainly, the saviors of the higher religions have traits that come from very different origins. It will never be possible to reconstruct an unbroken evolutionary sequence from these primitive *Heilbringer* to Gnostic, Buddhist, or Christian saviors. The ubiquity of the savior may be understood instead in terms of the necessary role that this figure plays in the universal human idea of salvation, a role that derives from the longing that the assistance of grace be incarnate. Such an explanation does not, however, excuse us from the task of studying the particular manifestations and characteristics of the savior figure as an individual phenomenon and in the light of historic and genetic relationships. At the same time, the polymorphous nature of the belief in saviors need not lead to a skeptical relativism: dogmatics identifies the particular significance of a savior for faith; the historical study of religions determines only what has been, is, and can be believed, not what ought to be believed. The historical study of religions discovers the plurality of saviors in the beliefs of different peoples as a historical fact.

Savior Figures

The historical study of religions uncovers varied and yet quite similar concepts of the savior in primitive religions. The savior may appear as a liberator from want and misfortune, as a comforter and giver of aid, or as a bringer of immortality. Often he appears as an animal, as a human being, or as a god: the Yelch of the Tlingit Indians, the Michabozho of the Algonkin, the Yokesha of the Iroquois, the Edshu of the Yoruba, the Maui of the Polynesians, and the Viracocha of the Peruvians. The main emphasis is placed on this figure's armament, his abilities, and his gifts (fire, tools, or culture). He is one of the central figures in mythology.

Purely mythological, too, is, the savior figure that is found in the religions of the Near East: Osiris of the Egyptians, Marduk and Tammuz of the Babylonians, Esmun and Adonis of the Syrians, Attis and Sabazios in Asia Minor, Mithras of the Iranians, Manda d'Hajje and Hibil-Ziwa of the Mandaeans. The same is often true in Indian religions, for example, Vishnu-Krishna-Vasudeva and Shiva. This savior is a divine being, often closely associated with the life of nature as a vegetation deity. He grants and guarantees immortality, and the faithful take part in his suffering and victory. Thus, the Near Eastern savior is often a "saved savior."

A third type of savior has also appeared: historical persons who come with a message of salvation or who are honored as saviors by their followers more or less against their will or after their death. To these saviors belong the many myst-agogues and teachers of salvation in late antiquity—Pythagoras, Apollonius of Tyana, Alexander of Abonoteichos, Simon Magus, and so on—as well as Mani, Zarathustra, and Muhammad, who were transformed from prophets into saviors by their communities. The Buddha and the Jina are saviors in a deeper sense for those who have attained liberation through their assistance. The history of dogma in the different Buddhist groups and schools illustrates well how the belief in a savior is formed and develops. Buddhist beliefs range from thinking of Gautama as simply a teacher to thinking of him as a supernatural and divine savior. Jesus Christ, who counts as a savior to his followers, is a historical personality, too. St. Paul and the evangelists, especially Luke, have described him in historical terms. Christian theology has tried for centuries to understand his person and work ever more profoundly as those of a historical personality.

Myths of the Savior

In connection with these historical personalities myths often grow up, as has happened even in our time, for example, in the mission of the Bab in Persia. Occasionally, the overgrowth of mythology obliterates everything historical, as has happened with the saviors of Mahayana Buddhism: Amida and Amitabha, Avalokitesvara and Manjusri, Maitreya and Vairocana. In these saviors, we can discern very little of the historical Buddha Gautama, from whom, in combination with ancient mythical figures, they first arose. Sufic piety has transformed Muhammad, originally far from a savior, into the central figure of a savior cult, associated primarily with the miracles of his birth, his splitting of the moon, and his heavenly journey. The Shi'a, in turn, has nearly made Ali into a savior. The same appears to be the case with the many colorful saviors of Gnosticism: the Gnostics derived a variety of mythical figures from the historical Jesus, as in the christologies of Valentinus, Basilides, the Pistis Sophia, and Mani.

A distinct type of savior is constituted by those saviors who were never active in the past but who are expected in the future. The transition from the idea of one who rules over a coming era of happiness, often based on a historical person such as Assurbanipal or Augustus, to the divine savior is just as fluid as the transition from the primeval mythical king to the savior who "was from the beginning," such as the Messiah of the Jews and the Imam of the Shi'ites. Several ideas combine when followers expect a savior who has already appeared to return, whether in the same or altered form or in a new incarnation: Saoshyant of the Iranians, the Buddha Maitreya, Viracocha of the Peruvians, the *Heilbringer* of the Algonkin, and the Aztec Quetzalcoatl. It is also possible for the savior to have both predecessors (Elijah, the Messiahs ben Joseph and ben David) and adversaries (Ahriman, the Antichrist, the "false Messiah").

The Nature and Essence of the Savior

As we have already seen, conceptions about the nature of the savior vary greatly. Some saviors have been thought to be human, others divine. Where both views have been combined, difficult problems arise, such as those that vexed the early Christians—questions about hypostatic union and the divine versus the human will. Docetism forms an interesting, intermediate stage: the savior, a divine figure assumes an earthly or human body that is not real but only apparent. Docetic conceptions are often found in Gnosticism, in the teachings of Mani, and in certain branches of Sufic and Shi'ite thought. The theory of avatars, developed in classical form by Vaishnava Hinduism, is rather similar: the savior—or the "saving light" or "saving substance"—has undergone a series of incarnations (compare Gnosticism, the Shi'a, and Tibetan Mahayana). In the doctrines just mentioned, we find, then, a plurality of saviors, a principle that Mahayana Buddhism has developed most clearly and that is also not unknown to the Jains.

Myth modifies these figures continually, working especially on the great moments of a savior's life: conception, birth, childhood, calling, and death. In this way, the natural biography is transformed into a supernatural one, which may be canonized and become the basis for a cult. In general, myths conceive of the nature and work of a savior in terms of specific motifs: a battle, whether against chaos or a monster; descent from and ascent to heaven; participation in creation and the new creation; suffering and distress. The most important event in the life of a historical savior is the call or the beginning of his mission. The idea of sacrifice, too, is often alluded to, but nowhere with such depth and variety as in Christianity.

In the life stories of Christian, Buddhist, and Iranian saviors we find tales of their temptations. The savior is often perceived in terms of such common images as the healer, the teacher, the shepherd, and the king, and the cult of the savior is frequently attached to particular portions of his nature, or rather, his body, such as the feet of Vishnu and the heart of Jesus. There are also female saviors: Kwan-yin, the Chinese form of Avalokitesvara; Sri in Vaishnavism; Ishtar in Asia Minor—all of whom are associated with a male earth deity. Even in Christianity Mary has come to be regarded as a savior, a *corredemptrix*.

Development of the Concept

As a religion centered on a savior develops, myth retreats. The savior is deprived of mythical characteristics, and the faithful find it necessary to guarantee their belief in the savior in the face of learned criticism and rational enlightenment. Christian, Indian, and Islamic theology have tried two different paths in this situation. Some have stylized the savior as an empirical, psychological, and ethical example (the "exemplar" who leads a model life); others try to establish a dualism in which the profane world is subject to the law of causality, but the religious world, in which supernatural and divine power is manifested, is more or less autonomous. In Christianity, it was especially Søren Kierkegaard who traced these two possibilities and described their ultimate consequences. Schleiermacher was the preeminent advocate of the first possibility, which dominated Protestant theology during the nineteenth century. Kierkegaard has become the spokesman for the second approach, which has become prominent in our own time.

SALVATION

Salvation in the History of Religions

TYPICAL AND SPECIFIC FORMS OF THE IDEA OF SALVATION

The idea of salvation stands at the center of religious thought and activity in the so-called religions of salvation or soteriological religions. If one conceives of salvation rather broadly and includes in it all concepts of rebirth and immortality, concepts that are found even in the most primitive religions, then salvation may be regarded as a central concept of religion in general. As a result, there are two distinct tasks for historians of religions: (1) to study the development and nature of the specific forms that ideas of salvation assume in historical religions; and (2) to determine through comparison whether individual forms of salvation can be grouped into structurally and qualitatively similar types—types of soteriological ideas. Of course, historians of religions must also be attentive to the historical migrations of motives, ideas, forms, and practices. They will have to guard against drawing hasty equations and parallels. The apparent identity of individual surface features in the soteriologies of various religions must never be allowed to distort the different values that are found in individual religious systems. In fact, once someone recognizes that all human beings ultimately and profoundly depend upon and require the idea of salvation, that person will naturally strive to do justice to the particular historical forms of that idea. He will attempt to understand these forms within their physical, historical, cultural, and ethno-psychological context, but he will also try to grasp their uniqueness and individual significance.

INDIA AND THE NEAR EAST

The idea of salvation in India assumes quite different forms in particular Indian religions, but it still exhibits certain characteristic traits. Typically, Indians conceive, evaluate, and to a large extent explain worldly suffering—the experience of boundary-line situations—in terms of *karma* and the transmigration of souls. The description of the world and humanity as standing in need of salvation is very similar in Vedanta and Samkhya, Hinayana and Mahayana Buddhism, Vaishnavism and Shaivism. Differences in detail exist primarily with regard to the path that is eventually supposed to overcome suffering. And yet, in the path of action, the path of knowledge, and the path of love [devotion], one finds typical, fundamental possibilities that recur in Brahmanic religion, in Hinduism, and in Buddhism. In their various combinations, the stages leading to salvation in Samkhya and Yoga, Buddhism and Jainism, reveal surprising parallels. And although specific theories of suffering in the world and specific definitions of the ultimate goal of salvation vary on many points, statements about the nature of temporary or final salvation *(moksha, vimukti)* and descriptions of what constitutes salvation are quite similar *(kaivalyam, nirvanam)*.

Another concept of salvation is found in the Near East. Many similar traits in the religions of this region may—or may not—rest on relationships that can be traced historically, but the idea of salvation—as developed in Egypt, Babylon,

Syria, Palestine, Iran, and Asia Minor, and to some extent
also in Greece, and later by the Gnostics and by Mani—reveals
similar basic conceptions about the human need for salvation
and about the world. We also find far-reaching agreement on
the relation of the soul to the body and of spirit to matter,
on the path that leads to salvation, on the kind of assistance
given to those in need of salvation, on the various means
available (magic, sacraments), and on the goal of all salvation
(immortality).

DEVELOPMENT AND SYSTEMATIZATION

From the preceding brief survey one can see that scarcely
any of the higher religions is unfamiliar with the idea of
salvation. This idea is found in the religiosity of the most
diverse peoples and tribes—for, of course, the idea of salvation
has taken root and spread far beyond the areas mentioned
above. Its Christian form has conquered part of the East and
at the same time prevails in the West. The degree to which
the idea of salvation has been cultivated depends upon historical development, physical circumstances, and spiritual ap-
titude. In some higher religions, the idea of salvation has
receded into the background: for example, the religions of
ancient Greece and Rome, Islam and Judaism, and Japanese
Shinto. But still, the Greeks developed the idea of salvation
in Orphism and in the neo-Pythagorean and Neoplatonic sects;
Islam developed it in Sufism, Judaism in apocalyptic writings
and mysticism (Kabbala, Hasidism), and Japan in the Buddhist
schools. Beyond any doubt, certain fundamental religious concepts are also closely related to the idea of salvation. Where
this affinity is not clearly manifest from the beginning, special
efforts, movements, and doctrines place salvation back in the
center and endow it with depth. Mystical movements have
especially preferred to cultivate the idea of salvation; for them,
it is central.

Thus, most soteriological religions have developed a systematic theory of salvation, a soteriology that determines the

way believers understand the cosmos and its origin and dissolution, and the way they understand humanity and its nature
and destiny. Oddly enough, there are even atheistic (philosophical) soteriologies. But in general, soteriological notions
are found in close conjunction with notions about a deity.
Human beings are allotted greater and lesser roles to play in
saving themselves or the world. Even when we encounter a
savior, human cooperation can be granted more or less space
in which to operate. Consider, for example, the debates on
the nature, necessity, and efficacy of divine grace (the syn-
ergistic controversies) in Christianity, Islam, Hinduism, and
Buddhism. Human cooperation is usually linked more or less
to objective requirements, such as participation in certain rites
and practices or membership in certain communities. I have
already referred to the three major paths to salvation, whose
requirements are at times entirely practical (works), at times
entirely theoretical (intellectual knowledge or emotional faith
and devotion), and at times a combination of the two. In some
soteriologies artificial means, such as narcotics, play a part.
They induce a state of ecstasy that appears to guarantee the
desired condition.

In many religions we encounter the idea that human beings
may attain and become conscious of a kind of "preliminary"
salvation in earthly life (in India, the *jivanmukta*; in Christianity,
the state of grace and reconciliation). Even so, final salvation
is achieved only by passing from this life. Various religions
and different branches within the same religion differ on the
conditions from which salvation is sought and found: objective
evil, subjective errings in an external sense (ritual and moral
sin), or a thoroughly sinful disposition *(habitus)*. They also
conceive of the goal of salvation differently. A variety of
statements may be found side by side: positive—being in, with,
or in the presence of God; *unio substantialis*—and negative—
extinction, dissolution. Sensually perceived conceptions are
found next to such abstract ideas as immortality, reincarnation,
and nirvana. The metaphysical, psychological, and ethical over-
tones of the idea of salvation become evident whenever the

goal of salvation is defined. This fact is the mystery of all doctrines of salvation.

Salvation in the Philosophy of Religion

THE IDEA OF SALVATION AND ITS NECESSITY

The idea of salvation, which can be seen as constitutive of all religion, is of great significance to the philosophy of religion, too. It arises from the conviction that human beings fundamentally stand in need of salvation, that is, from the general experience of suffering, which may have many sources and causes, from accident and misfortune to an all-encompassing anxiety *(Weltangst)*. Schelling designated this *Angst* as the *Melancholie* that is spread throughout all creation, and it has been interpreted in a variety of ways, in cosmic terms as fall, alienation, and corruption *(Verführung)*, and in psychological terms as error, ignorance, sin, and guilt. As varied in details as the awareness of the depth and significance of the need for salvation may be, the earliest stirrings of this sentiment among primitive peoples—and these stirrings appear quite often—lead in a straight line to the deeper and universal conceptions found among the most highly developed cultures. The intensification of this awareness and the gradual development of the idea of salvation is one of the most important regions for the development of the spirit *(Geist)*. Naturally, we must conceive of the development of this idea not as an even continuum but as proceeding by pushes and shoves. If the need for salvation were not deeply rooted and, indeed, universally human, we could never account for the massive amount of attention—thoughts and concepts, hopes and wishes, ideas and doctrines—that the human mind has devoted to the idea of salvation. Religious geniuses have devoted themselves to this idea repeatedly. Countless great and lesser preachers and prophets have proclaimed it and modified it. And wherever human beings have abandoned positive, historical religions, philosophers have continued the efforts of the *homines religiosi.* Massive religious systems have arisen whose theoretical bases often include doctrines about the origin and end of the cosmos and about the nature and destiny of humanity. In these systems cosmology, anthropology, and eschatology culminate in soteriology, and practical instruction consists of showing the path that leads to salvation from the evil whose nature and origin the doctrines explain. These religious systems assume concrete shape in cultic and ritual forms and institutions; their sociological power is manifested in large and small groups, in schools, churches, and sects. When that happens, in Asia (India, Islam) as well as in the West, the theoretical problem of salvation is taken over by philosophers, that is, by philosophers of religion. This has happened even when philosophers have left the religious community and have rejected religious solutions to the questions they raise. I explain below that the philosophers who have been especially concerned with the idea of salvation have also been the most sensitive religiously; therefore, they have repeatedly returned the philosophical enterprise to the neighborhood of religion. For a time positivism fostered the misconception that religion and philosophy are temporary phenomena that humanity will eventually outgrow, but the temporal and spatial universality of the need for salvation shows that this contention is false. The idea of salvation has developed by degree at different places, and it has received a unique stamp in each of them. In one place the idea of salvation may stand out quite distinctly; in another it may have reached only the initial stages. But it will never disappear again. Creatures always hope for salvation; that is their nature.

THE PHILOSOPHY OF SALVATION

The need for salvation rests, we have seen, on the experience of suffering and evil in the world. Suffering may take many forms: poverty and toil, disease and misfortune, shortcomings and sin. It may be expressed in the contrasts between body and soul and between reason and passionate drives or in transitoriness and death. Following Jaspers, I designate the crucial events and moments in human existence, when persons experience suffering and become aware of the need for salvation, as "boundary-line situations" *(Grenzsituationen)*. Situations of suffering can motivate human beings to leave behind their natural states of existence, the finite world and its relations, and turn to the eternal. In doing so, they discover a new transcendent relationship among things: world and humanity appear in a new light, and meanings and values are stressed differently than in the configurations of "natural" existence. Consequently, depending upon whether the interpretation of the experience of suffering emphasizes man's relationship to the eternal (that is, communion *[Verkehr]* with God) and the imperative for ethical conduct, or whether it emphasizes the theoretical understanding of relationships (speculation), one may speak of more religious or more philosophical formulations of the idea of salvation.

I need not discuss here the nature and dialectics of the religious relationship. Suffice it to say that in the experience of God—which can be hindered and interrupted by temptations, doubts, and skepticism—the experience of one's own incompleteness and imperfection, of one's own unworthiness in the face of the numinous *(numinoser Unwert)*, quite directly leads to the consciousness of one's own sinfulness, and with it, the sense of the distance between God and man. Salvation brought about by divine grace bridges this distance at the intercession of a mediator. Salvation then assumes the form of a state of grace that overcomes all alienation from God and eradicates inperfection. It becomes a blessed closeness or even union with God.

Philosophy, by contrast, when it does not fragment into specialized fields, such as epistemology, or into the purely formal collection of an encyclopedia, is led necessarily to the great problems of existence *(Dasein)* that disclose themselves in borderline situations. Both in the West and in the East, philosophy has sought—to speak in general terms—to solve these problems in two ways. In the first, philosophy takes over the basic presuppositions of the religions of salvation, with certain modifications, especially with regard to the world's and humanity's need for salvation. In doing so, philosophy emphasizes imperfection, error, and ignorance more than sin and guilt. But then philosophy solves the human predicament by means of human effort (Selbsterlösung) or, where it does not go quite so far, it seeks to overcome the human predicament by reinterpreting the religious mediator or savior in empirical terms. The idea of grace is dispensed with; human beings seek to overcome suffering by their own powers, by distancing themselves from the material world or liberating their souls. The philosophical ways and means of saving oneself are not so diverse as the ways and means of salvation in the religions of salvation, where the paths include various combinations of practical, theoretical, and emotional exercise. Philosophical solutions are limited to variations on the path of knowledge. In one variation, salvation comes through some specific intuition or knowledge, as in Schelling, Schopenhauer, Samkhya philosophy, and Gnosticism. Frequently this knowledge is associated with the teaching of the techniques and skills that constitute the path to salvation, as in Yoga, Buddhism, and Tantrism. This option tends to bridge the gap between philosophy and religion. In an alternate form of this variation, philosophy provides certain ethical precepts, such as work in and of itself, the control of the passions, or the performance of one's duty (Kant and Fichte). It is typical that the effort to save oneself is never pursued consistently when it is built on presuppositions borrowed from religions of salvation. Consider, for example, how the idea of grace infringes upon human effort in Vedanta philosophy or even in Schopenhauer's thought.

The second path that philosophers have followed in trying to solve the great problems of existence cannot be discussed at length here. As J. Burckhardt and W. Dilthey have shown, a new attitude toward life (Lebensgefühl) appeared in Europe at the time of the Renaissance, an attitude characterized by the ideas of self-sufficiency and of the power and beauty of humanity. In connection with this attitude, later periods, such as the Enlightenment, developed the notion of the autonomy of reason, and at the same time resurrected certain ancient attitudes and ideas. German classicism occupies a significant place in this development. It led eventually to a rejection of the belief that humanity is corrupt, sinful, and guilty, to a rejection of the idea of salvation, and to a transfiguration that left the cult of humanity (anthropocentrism) in its wake (Feuerbach and Nietzsche). Today, this view is widespread; it is the chief opponent of Christianity and the other religions of salvation.

In addition to the religious and philosophical conceptions of the idea of salvation, I must mention two other approaches that are not unrelated to the former: the social and artistic ideas of salvation. If the human need for salvation is understood not in terms of the depths of the soul and spirit but in terms of material needs, especially in a social sense, the idea of salvation assumes social and utopian form. In the modern social theories of Godwin, Fourier, Engels, and Marx, as in their ancient predecessors, the concern with salvation can be clearly seen. Consider, too, the modern German and Russian philosophies of religion. In all these views, salvation is understood as attaining a certain "just" order for distributing material goods. The theorists also expect that deeper happiness and satisfaction in the realm of soul and spirit will result (for example, in socialism, communism, and bolshevism).

The experience of being uplifted and the internal peace brought about by art is also frequently described as "salvation." Even in antiquity this was so (Plato and Plotinus), and more recent aestheticians, especially the Romantics, have developed similar theories. This view reached its climax with Schopenhauer's theory of art. In Schopenhauer's view, art provides us with a way of becoming free from "will" through the contemplation of ideas. It provides human beings with occasional flights from the world of appearances and its pressures— hence, a transitory salvation. The "salvific" effects of music have also often been praised.

HISTORY OF THE PHILOSOPHY OF SALVATION

From the role that the idea of salvation plays in the history of philosophy we can see most clearly that philosophy's roots lie in religion, regardless of how far philosophy may distance itself from particular religions. This is as true in the West as it is in the East; we see it better in the East only because there philosophy has not been so radically emancipated from religious thought. Among some of the older thinkers, the link between Greek philosophy and religion is quite apparent. Pythagoras is the first Western philosopher of salvation. Heraclitus belongs, if not for his thought at least for his attitude, to the line that leads to Plato, and the religious element in Plato's philosophy has been correctly noted. Plato sketched the first Western metaphysics of salvation in his dialogues, and that profound metaphysics has influenced even the latest of his followers. Plato's relatively loose connections with particular religions became closer in Neoplatonism. In response to the Neopythagoreans and to Ammonius, Plotinus developed an immense system of thought, perhaps the most powerful and extensive philosophy of salvation that the ancient West could produce. In the *Enneads,* everything is subordinated to the idea of salvation, which in Plotinus's view governed theoretical reflection as well as human conduct and aesthetic pleasure. Prior to Plotinus, however, the Jewish thinker Philo had allegorized the Torah in his daring philosophy of religion and had made salvation the highest goal of both the believer and the thinker. The religio-philosophical sketches and systems of numerous followers have set out in the direction that these two great minds pointed out. The best known of these followers were Iamblichus and the great systematician and schoolmaster Proclus. The latter marks the end of the Greek philosophy of salvation, a philosophy that had absorbed so much from Greek and Near Eastern religions.

Meanwhile, Christianity had begun to grow from a small religious community to a world-dominating power. At its center stood the idea of salvation, which it saw accomplished in the work of Christ. Every philosophy that emerged from this movement—and Christians began quite early to answer their opponents philosophically—was governed by the central idea of salvation: from Augustine's comprehensive philosophy of salvation and Anselm's theory of satisfaction to the culmination in Albert's and Thomas's scholasticism and the mysticism of Meister Eckhart. The Christian idea of salvation influenced many of the humanistic Platonists and natural philosophers of the Renaissance, but none more profoundly than Jacob Boehme. But since Descartes, modern European philosophy has preferred to examine epistemological problems and has preoccupied itself with analyzing human consciousness. As a result, the central existential problems of life and death have become more remote. Where skepticism has not led to radically new thought, the traditional Christian solution has generally been retained. It was only natural that the major work of a profound metaphysician like Spinoza would culminate in the idea of salvation. At the same time, the basic attitude of Leibniz, which with its unlimited optimism and unbounded confidence in the powers of the human mind prepared the way for the Enlightenment, allowed Enlightenment thinkers to deemphasize the human need for salvation and to withdraw from the possibility of salvation as expressed in Christian doctrine. Enlightenment thinkers, especially the French, often inveighed passionately against the soteriological side of religion and against the philosophy of religion associated with it. Kant revived the idea of salvation in his profound philosophy of religion, but at the same time he dissolved positive Christian doctrine, with which he by and large agreed, into an ethic or moral betterment and perfection. Hamann, Jacobi, and Herder philosophized about salvation more strictly on the basis of the Bible, and even Fichte, the first of Kant's great successors, found in the *Anweisung zum seeligen Leben* ("Instructions for the Spiritual Life") the Christian mystic's path to salvation. Schelling's restless mind circled in various ways about this central problem in the philosophy of religion, inspired by both ancient and modern philosophies of salvation. Prior to Schopenhauer, no one attempted to found philosophy more profoundly on metaphysics than Schelling. The early Romantic period fell in love with the idea of salvation. But only some later Christian followers penetrated it very deeply, and from the point of view of speculative philosophy, none more profoundly and sharp-sightedly than Kierkegaard. Even before Kierkegaard, Hegel's universal intellect had interpreted the idea of salvation speculatively and pointed the way for a great school in the philosophy of religion. Then came the speculative-historical J. J. Bachofen, the modern mythologist of salvation, and finally Schopenhauer, who created a comprehensive metaphysical doctrine of salvation. Once again philosophy's soteriological concern approached religion: the Indian religions of salvation deeply impressed Schopenhauer. The religious philosophy of Ed. von Hartmann continues the heritage of Schelling, Schopenhauer, and Hegel. It merges, as did Hegel's philosophy, into a religion of the spirit culminating in the idea of salvation. A. Drews and L. Ziegler began their thought from this point. Contemporary philosophy—not counting the Kantian and phenomenological schools—has become a philosophy of life heavily influenced by Nietzsche, the pupil of Feuerbach and critic of Hartmann. As such, its basic attitude is farther removed from the idea of salvation. Only where philosophical efforts associate more closely with the Christian or Eastern world of thought (neo-Buddhism, theosophy, anthroposophy) do they address the idea of salvation. Perhaps in the future this association will become more common.

Notes

Introduction

1. This introduction reproduces, in slightly revised form, Joseph M. Kitagawa, "*Verstehen* and *Erlösung:* Some Remarks on Joachim Wach's Work," *History of Religions* 11 (1971–1972):31–53.

2. This scheme provided the basis for Wach's article, "Universals in Religion," which was included in his *Types of Religious Experience: Christian and Non-Christian* (Chicago: University of Chicago Press, 1951), pp. 30–47.

' 3. *Religionswissenschaft: Prolegomena zu ihrer wissenschaftstheoretischen Grundlegung*, Veröffentlichungen des Forschungsinstituts für vergleichende Religionsgeschichte an der Universität Leipzig, no. 10 (Leipzig: J. C. Hinrichs, 1924), translated here in Part One.

4. *Das Verstehen: Grundzüge einer Geschichte der hermeneutischen Theorie im 19. Jahrhundert*, vol. 1 (1926), vol. 2 (1929), vol. 3 (1933) (Tübingen: J. C. B. Mohr–P. Siebeck).

5. *Einführung in die Religionssoziologie* (Tübingen: J. C. B. Mohr–P. Siebeck, 1931); *Typen religiöser Anthropologie: Ein Vergleich der Lehre vom Menschen im religionsphilosophischen Denken vom Orient und Okzident*, Philosophie und Geschichte, no. 40 (Tübingen: J. C. B. Mohr–P. Siebeck, 1932); and *Sociology of Religion* (Chicago: University of Chicago Press, 1944).

6. *Types of Religious Experience: Christian and Non-Christian* (Chicago: University of Chicago Press, 1951); and *The Comparative Study of Religions*, ed. Joseph M. Kitagawa (New York: Columbia University Press, 1958).

7. This concern led him to write his Ph.D. dissertation entitled "Grundzüge einer Phänomenologie des Erlösungsgedankens," which was published as *Der Erlösungsegedanke und seine Deutung*, Veröffentlichungen des Forschungsinstituts für vergleichende Religionsgeschichte an der Universität Leipzig, no. 8 (Leipzig: J. C. Hinrichs, 1922).

8. For a comprehensive study of Wach's Religionswissenschaft, see Richard W. Scheimann's unpublished Ph.D. thesis, "Wach's Theory of the Science of Religion," University of Chicago, 1963.

9. P. 95 below.

10. P. 99 below.

11. "Interpretation of Sacred Books," *Journal of Biblical Literature* 55 (1936):59.

12. See "Einleitung," in *Das Verstehen*, vol. 1.

13. Joachim Wach, "Verstehen," in *Religion in Geschichte und Gegenwart*, ed. H. Gunkel and L. Zscharnack, 2d ed. (1931), vol. 5, translated here in Part Two.

14. *Das Verstehen*, 1:181–82. For a fuller discussion of Boeckh's theories, see J. P. Pritchard, *A. Boeckh: On Interpretation and Criticism* (Norman: University of Oklahoma Press, 1968).

15. *Das Verstehen*, 1:178.

16. Ibid., p. 179.

17. Ibid., p. 180.

18. Ibid., pp. 182–83.

19. Ibid., p. 175.

20. Ibid., p. 186.

21. Ibid., p. 194.

22. Ibid., p. 185.

23. Ibid., p. 184.

24. P. 49 below.

25. P. 53 below.

26. P. 44 below.

27. P. 94 below.

28. Pp. 131–32 below.

29. "Typenlehre," in *Religion in Geschichte und Gegenwart,* vol. 5.

30. "Der Begriff des Klassischen in der Religionsgeschichte," in *Quantulacunque, in Honor of Kirsopp Lake* (London: Christophers, 1937), pp. 87–97.

31. P. 134 below.

32. P. 137 below.

33. P. 139 below.

34. P. 142 below.

35. Pp. 143–50 below.

36. "Religionssoziologie," in *Religion in Geschichte und Gegenwart,* 4:1929–34.

37. J. Wach, "Sociology of Religion," in *Twentieth Century Sociology,* ed. Georges Gurvitch and Wilbert E. Moore (New York: Philosophical Library, 1945), pp. 411–12.

38. J. Wach, *Sociology of Religion* (Chicago: University of Chicago Press, 1944), pp. 15–16. (My italics.) See also H. A. Hodges, *The Philosophy of Wilhelm Dilthey* (London: Routledge & Kegan Paul, 1952), pp. xiii–xxvi.

39. "Religionssoziologie," in *Religion in Geschichte und Gegenwart,* vol. 4.

40. *Sociology of Religion,* p. 3. (My italics.)

41. Ibid., p. 15. (My italics.)

42. H. Richard Niebuhr's review of Wach's *Sociology of Religion,* in *Theology Today,* vol. 2, no. 3 (October 1945).

43. Sociology of Religion, p. v. (My italics.)

44. Ibid., p. 5. (My italics.)

45. J. M. Kitagawa, ed. *Understanding and Believing* (New York: Harper, & Row, 1968).

46. Joachim Wach, *The Comparative Study of Religions,* ed. with introduction by J. M. Kitagawa (New York: Columbia University Press, 1958), p. 5.

47. Ibid., p. 6.

48. Ibid., p. 14.

49. Ibid., pp. 14–15.

50. "Erlösung. V. Religionsphilosophisch," in *Religion in Geschichte und Gegenwart* (1928), vol. 2, translated here in Part Two.

51. *Sociology of Religion*, p. 374.

52. *Types of Religious Experience*, p. 6.

53. *The Comparative Study of Religion*, p. 9.

54. *Types of Religious Experience*, p. 218.

55. Ibid., pp. 221–25.

56. Ibid., p. 226.

57. Ibid., pp. 221–22.

58. Ibid., p. 228.

59. Ibid., p. 229.

60. Ibid., p. 29.

61. Ibid., p. 14.

62. Ibid., p. 230. (My italics.)

63. Ibid., p. 229.

64. Ibid., p. 230.

65. *The Comparative Study of Religions*, p. 15.

66. Ibid., pp. 11–14.

67. Ibid., p. 17.

68. Ibid., p. 16.

69. Ibid., pp. 17–18.

70. Ibid., p. 18.

71. Cited in *Types of Religious Experience*, p. 231.

Chapter One

1. On the history of the term *"Religionswissenschaft,"* see Hardy's remarks in "Was ist Religionswissenschaft?" *Archiv für Religionswissenschaft* 1 (1898):10. Hardy finds that the term was first used by F. Max Müller in the preface to the German edition of his *Essays* [1st ed.: Leipzig, 1869], vol. 1, p. 10, in the sense of "comparative science of religions" *(vergleichende Wissenschaft von den Religionen)*. This discipline corresponds to an object that belongs neither to theology nor to the philosophy of religion. By contrast, H. Pinard de la Boullaye points out that Max Müller himself, in his *Introduction to the Science of Religion* (London, 1873), divides *Religionswissenschaft* into Comparative Theology and Theoretic Theology, "or, as it is sometimes called, the

Philosophy of Religion" (p. 21). Pinard continues: "If he believed that this science was new, that was less by reason of its object than by reason of the completely new material recently placed at its disposal and by reason of its method, which it was supposed to borrow from comparative linguistics" (*L'Etude comparée des religions, essai critique* [Paris, 1922], p. 504). Pinard himself demonstrates that a number of authors in the 1830s, 1840s, 1850s, and 1860s used the term *Religionswissenschaft ("science des religions").* Among these authors, however, the term was always used with some particular nuance or other.

On the history of the history of religions *[Religionswissenschaft]* a number of small volumes are already available. Recently Pinard de la Boullaye's study (see above) has described the discipline comprehensively and inventoried the entire literature with the utmost care. Pinard relies on a number of German works, of which I mention here only Edmund Hardy's essay, "Zur Geschichte der vergleichenden Religionsforschung," *Archiv für Religionswissenschaft* 4 (1901), and the article "Religionsgeschichte" in *Die Religion in Geschichte und Gegenwart* [1st ed.] (Tübingen, 1909–1913), vol. 4, cols. 2184ff. Fortunately, these fine studies make it possible to ignore Jean Reville's extraordinarily deficient book, *Phases successives de l'histoire des religions* (Paris, 1909).

2. Is the history of religions a human study *(Geisteswissenschaft)?* A positive answer to this question is one of the presuppositions that underlie my entire study. I am convinced that religions belong to the great complexes or systems of expression in which spirit *(Geist)* becomes conscious of itself, in which the religious subjectivity has objectified and continues to objectify itself. These objectifications also possess a structure; those who comprehend this subject come to understanding.—These last few sentences seem to me to provide the major presuppositions for constituting the history of religions as a human study. This entire work will have to set forth its shape; it will be up to future studies to clarify many other points.

Wilhelm Dilthey's important essay, "Das Problem der Religion" (*Gesammelte Schriften,* vol. 6 [Leipzig, 1924], pp. 288ff.), was, unfortunately, unknown to me until I had completed the present book, but it serves to confirm my observations. At this point, however, I cannot engage in a detailed discussion of Dilthey's essay.

3. There are signs today of new and energetic concern with the logical foundations of the human studies. In more recent times this concern began with the work of Dilthey. Initially, each individual discipline tried to answer its fundamental methodological questions for itself, and in general philosophy offered little of interest on these problems. Heinrich Rickert was the first to recognize the bearing and significance of the task, which must fall to philosophy, of formulating a logical and general foundation for the human studies. But his transcendental and subjective philosophical stance prevented him from doing justice to the nature of historical knowledge (cf. Ernst Troeltsch's decisive criticisms of Rickert's philosophy of history). Thus, although in the first decade of the twentieth century Rickert's influence on the individual human studies was extraordinary, one detects today a general abandonment of his theories. Wilhelm Wundt's logic and methodology have had relatively little influence. Once again we have returned to Dilthey. Both Erich Rothacker's *Einleitung in die Geisteswissenschaften* (Tübingen, 1920) and Troeltsch's investigations of historicism (*Der Historismus und seine Probleme* [Tübingen, 1922]) pave the way for this approach, and they are not alone. Today Dilthey has followers in every field. Compare Troeltsch's enumeration of Dilthey's followers in his portrayal of Dilthey's philosophy and in his bibliography (*Gesammelte Schriften*, vol. 3 [Tübingen, 1922], pp. 509–530).

   Since in this investigation I am including the history of religions within the system of the human studies, I am entirely justified both in continually noting constellations found in the other individual humanistic disciplines and in not shying away from somewhat lengthy digressions concerning these disciplines as the occasion arises.

4. A thinker of Feuerbach's inclination was probably driven by interests that were too narrowly philosophical to have given much attention to the creation of a scientific discipline to study religions. The *methodological* results of Max Müller and C. P. Tiele, who are, properly speaking, the theoreticians of the history of religions, are not satisfactory.

5. In France and England the need for methodological clarity has probably been perceived, for the history of religions is already much more firmly consolidated there, as it is in other lands outside Germany. But French and English works that seek to address this need are still not satisfactory. They do not have

the whole *(das Ganze)* sufficiently in view. Either they do not relate to concrete research or they are enslaved to a pet idea that destroys the whole (Foucart et al.). Still, we can learn much from the works of Albert Reville *(Prolegomènes de l'histoire des religions* [Paris, 1881]), F. B. Jevons *(An Introduction to the Study of Comparative Religion* [New York, 1908]), Georges Foucart *(Histoire des religions et méthode comparative* [Paris, 1912]), Goblet d'Alviella *(Croyances, rites, institutions,* 3 vols. [Paris, 1911]), and others, as well as from many works in the *Revue de l'histoire des religions,* the *Année sociologique,* and so on.

6. That was the intention of the so-called *religionsgeschichtliche Schule.* Especially Troeltsch, who is generally considered the dogmatician of this school, undertook this task; compare his *Gesammelte Schriften,* vol. 2, p. 738. On this topic, compare also Carl Clemen's *Die religionsgeschichtliche Methode in der Theologie* (Giessen, 1904), which builds upon the claims advanced by Tiele and Lagarde, and Max Reischle's very careful *Theologie und Religionsgeschichte* (Tübingen & Leipzig, 1904). On the Catholic side, see F. X. Kiefl's *Katholische Weltanschauung und modernes Denken* (Regensburg, 1922), chap. 18: "Die religionsgeschichtliche Forschung und ihre philosophische Voraussetzungen," and perhaps Gemmel's "Die Verheissungen der vergleichenden Religionswissenschaft," *Stimmen der Zeit* 101 (1921):380ff.

7. A similar terminological variation is still found today in the English-speaking world, but, of course, the terms in use are somewhat different: history of religion(s), comparative religion, religious studies, science of (or scientific study of) religion(s), and even interreligious dialogue. [Editors' note]

8. Max Weber, *Gesammelte Aufsätze zur Wissenschaftslehre* (Tübingen, 1922), pp. 215–16.

9. With regard to the history of religions there is always one difficulty in particular. In specific periods of human intellectual history, and consequently in individual scholars of religions as such, we may observe strong changes that affect work in the history of religions and exert decisive influences on its approach and its character. The situation is quite different, for example, in the study of art and of law, where evaluation remains relatively constant, regardless of whether conceptions about the nature of these subjects fluctuate in details. Even on these grounds the emancipation of the history of religions from the philosophy of

religion would be welcome. The development of that discipline would then be able to proceed more surely, more calmly, and more continuously.

Chapter Two

1. The other human studies divide up their tasks in a similar way: next to a historical branch, we always find a systematic branch. In addition to art history there is the systematic study of art *(Kunstwissenschaft)*; in addition to the history of laws, the systematic study of law *(systematische Rechtswissenschaft)*; in addition to literary history, the study of literature *(Literaturwissenschaft)*. These distinctions should not be confused with the dichotomy between empirical and historical disciplines, on the one hand, and normative disciplines on the other—the study of art and aesthetics, the study of law and the philosophy of law, the study of literature and poetics. Such confusion is, unfortunately, quite common, and its consequences have been especially unfortunate for the development of the history of religions, in particular, for the development of its systematic branch. The general history of religions—both historic and systematic studies—stands on one side, the philosophy of religion on the other.

2. I will devote an entire chapter to the systematic study of religion (see Chapter 5). Here I need only point out that my use of the term "systematic" does not coincide with that of the theologians when they speak of "systematic theology." As I use the term, "systematic" signifies—for the time being—a complement to the historical branch of the history of religions that, like it, is grounded in the empirical and that relies on a specific methodological procedure.

3. Cf. Troeltsch's numerous writings on the philosophy of religion and, further, the second volume of his *Gesammelte Schriften* (Tübingen, 1913), which contains his magnificent essay, "Wesen der Religion und der Religionswissenschaft."

4. Rudolf Otto's theology is quite typical of this approach; cf. especially his *Das Heilige* (Breslau, 1917) [translated as *The Idea of the Holy* [London, 1950]). His theology is quite significant for the history of religions, too. Characteristically, in the work

just mentioned Otto turns from the Kantian-Friesian subjectivism of his *Kant-Friesische Religionsphilosophie* (Tübingen, 1909) to the realm of the objective. Catholic theology and philosophy of religion have, of course, always opposed psychological subjectivism, but the thought of Max Scheler explicitly makes a turn similar to Otto's.

5. The question of the "autonomy" of religion is still debated, to some extent, in the field of "primitive religions" even today. In this area, ethnographers, theologians, and students of religion work side by side. Ever since the demise of animism, the most intense discussions have concerned the relations between religion and magic. The influence of these conceptions, which lead at times to the philosophy of religion, is occasionally reflected back upon discussions of the questions I am considering here: Otto has placed his theory of religion in the context of the investigation of "primitive" religion; Söderblom's *Das Werden des Gottesglaubens* (Leipzig, 1916) works out a conception similar to Otto's with material drawn from primitive religions; the "Anthropos" circle, represented by Wilhelm Schmidt, advocates a notion of the autonomy of religion that arose within Catholicism. Scholars who approach the question from the side of ethnology will hardly oppose the notion of religion's autonomy today. Only its precise boundaries are uncertain. The history of religions must speak the final word by treating systematically, reflecting on, and classifying the material that ethnology provides. For even when the autonomy of the history of religions has been carefully guarded, that discipline's material makes it stand in close relation to the philosophy of religion, and, as a result, it is ideally placed to mediate between the philosophy of religion and other disciplines.

6. Compare the distinction in (Lutheran) dogmatic theology between *notitia, assensus,* and *fiducia,* and especially the doctrines of the two forms of *assensus (specialis* and *generalis)* and of *fiducia* as an act of the will.

7. In another context, I intend to relate my theory of religio-historical knowledge to the doctrines of the essential nature of the Scriptures and of revelation developed by (old) Protestant dogmatics [i.e., Protestant dogmatics prior to Schleiermacher]: *auctoritas causativa* and *normativa, perspicuitas, efficacia,* and so on. One must also compare here the doctrine of the *ordo salutis.*

8. Our scientific logic cannot do justice to religious phenomena, to religious "thought." It should not always try to take religious thought to task. However different their results may be, studies such as Heinrich Maier's *Psychologie des emotionalen Denken* (Tübingen, 1908), esp. pp. 449ff.: "Das religöse Denken," Ernst Cassirer's *Begriffsform im mythischen Denken* (Leipzig, 1922), and Lucien Lévy-Bruhl's *Les fonctions mentales dans les sociétés inférieures* (Paris, 1910), raise significant questions, for they show us that rational thought as conceived by Western science is not the only sort of thought there is. Compare also Chapter 4 below.

9. "Religionsgeschichte und religionsgeschichtliche Methode," in *Die Religion in Geschichte und Gegenwart* (chap. 1, n. 1).

10. Compare also my essays, "Zur Methodologie der allegemeinen Religionswissenschaft" and "Bemerkungen zum Problem der 'externen' Würdigung der Religion," *Zeitschrift für Missionskunde und Religionswissenschaft* 38 (1923): 33–55 and 161–183.

11. Georg Wobbermin, *Systematische Theologie,* vol. 1 (Leipzig, 1913), p. 31.

12. Cf. esp. the essay mentioned in n. 3 above.

13. The psychological approach values especially the rise of self-consciousness and individual experience *(Erfahrung)*. Here belong such attempts at defining religion as Schleiermacher's, James's, Österreich's, Wobbermin's, and Scholz's, as well as Hauer's attempt to conceive the essential nature of religion as *Erlebnis.* On the danger of psychologism associated with this approach, see below. An example of the historical approach is Scholz's attempt to fill out "pregnant instances" through his introspective method. Before him, it was above all James and Höffding who set forth the historical approach explicitly.

14. See n. 3 above. See also his essay, "Was heisst Wesen des Christentums?" in *Gesammelte Schriften,* vol. 2, pp. 386ff., and his contribution to the *Festschrift* for Kuno Fischer, *Die Philosophie im Beginn des zwanzigsten Jahrhunderts,* ed. Wilhelm Windelband, 2nd ed. (Heidelberg, 1907), entitled "Religionsphilosophie."

15. Meanwhile, the pendulum has swung back in the other direction. Now we are sated with empiricism and look for the enlivening principle that holds the individual manifestations together. Scholars strive to conceive, for example, the "spirit"

of Gothic, the "spirit" of the nineteenth century, the "spirit" of the baroque. The ancestor of these attempts is Jakob Burckhardt. As a result, this approach became prominent in art history. There is probably no need to allude to the dangers connected with this search for the whole. Compare, among others, Konrad Burdach's typical protests against "Geschichtsmythologie und Geschichtsgnostik" in the foreword to his *Deutsche Renaissance* (Berlin, 1918).

16. Both Herder and Hegel still conceived the problem in religio-historical terms. To be sure, it was extremely important for them to determine the "principle of Christianity." But the world of non-Christian religions was not for them simply the background against which they set off their own religion favorably. Rather, the non-Christian religions possessed value in themselves, if only as stages. As a result, they took delight in studying these individuals intensely, and the reward for their labors was a magnificent characterization of foreign religions, in which Hegel surpassed Herder. In principle, the *religionsgeschichtliche Schule* has the same orientation. That school was, generally, the first to clarify these questions methodologically. But its chief accomplishments lay in the realm of the historical study of the religions of the Old and New Testaments. As a result, research undertaken by the *religionsgeschichtliche Schule* could advance the history of religions proper only a little in this regard.

17. See Troeltsch, "Was heisst . . .," p. 392.

18. Herder had used these expressions quite willingly in his characterizations, as had Hegel; cf. especially Herder's fine *Auch eine Philosophie der Geschichte der Menschheit* (1774). Later, the dispute over the *Volksgeist* and the *Volksseele* brought them into disrepute. The mistake of conceiving of the soul as something substantial was too tempting. The ethno-psychologists—Lazarus, Steinthal, Wundt—rightly pointed out that the composition and dispositions of collective individuals could be studied psychologically: Islam as the sum of all believers; "Hinduism" not as the notion of castes but as a designation for the psychological attitude of human beings who adhere to Hindu religions. In opposition to notions of the soul there stands what I call the "objective spirit" (see Chapter 5). The question of priority and primacy between these two—soul and objective spirit—already

forms a problem, because for religion it would be necessary to investigate exactly the extent to which one depends upon the other, and the extent to which one implicates the other (see, in general, Frankenberger, "Objektiver Geist und Völkerpsychologie," *Zeitschrift für Philosophie und philosophische Kritik* 154 [1914]).

19. As Jakob Burckhardt did in his history of Greek culture, which is methodologically significant in its own right. There, Burckhardt shows himself a true pupil of Boeckh, from whose *Methodologie* the student of religions, too, has infinitely much to learn.

20. An ambiguous phrase best left in the original. Troeltsch refers to a kind of abstraction peculiar to history in which historical phenomena are understood on the basis of the *Grundgedanken* or fundamental conceptions from which they result. [Translators' note].

21. Determining essential natures cannot be a critique for the historian of religions in the radical sense that Troeltsch demanded for theologians. Troeltsch thought, for example, that it was impossible for theologians to see the idea of Christianity in such movements as Catholicism and the sects. But instead of perceiving a profusion of "inversions and disruptions of the essential nature," the scholar of religions will include the formation of sects and schisms as part of the evolution of the whole that must be included in determining the essential nature (spirit and idea). Concepts such as "heresy" belong within theology; thus, they fall within our brackets. Sufism is a part of Islam, just as the Greek Church is a part of Christianity and Japanese Buddhism a part of Mahāyāna. The scholar's historical instinct must determine the extent to which an individual phenomenon realizes the idea that he claims for it. No exegetical technique—in both broader and more restricted senses—will mislead him. The scholar of religions will also formulate a "critique," in the process of working out decisive traits, but his critique is much more "immanent" than the critique that Troeltsch wants!

22. Johann Gottfried Herder, "Über Kulturgeschichte der Völker," *Werke*, vol. 8 (Berlin), p. 367.

23. For example, Ritschl and his school, especially Kaftan, explain the origin of religion with an eye particularly to Chrisianity.

24. For the student of religion, Max Müller's saying, "He who knows one religion, knows none," holds good. Harnack's inversion, to be taken with a grain of salt—"He who knows one, knows all"—holds good with regard to theologians, who may safely say with regard to their own religion that whoever does not know this religion, knows none. Still, of course, these statements do not deny that the historical study of religions is extremely useful and even necessary for theologians.

Chapter Three

1. The first thinker who opposed the principle of construction was Erasmus. "Erasmus sharpened the eye for historical critique, and that critique has become a prerequisite for shattering the preconceived notion of history that idealism brought along with it, the notion that history must follow the course that 'the Idea' demands" (Walther Köhler, *Idee und Persönlichkeit in der Kirchengeschichte* [Tübingen, 1910], p. 18). In general, it is possible to speak of the historical study of religions only beginning in the eighteenth century. Works such as those of J. Spencer, Calmet, and Ross are theological commentaries on the Old and New Testament or collections of curiosities. But the writings of Erasmus, followed by Sebastian Frank and above all by Arnold, were of decisive importance. Erasmus made it possible to treat the history of heresy and of heretics, and this made Göttinger's work possible, which in turn fostered the work of Mosheim, Meiners, and of the historical study of religions generally, that is, the historical study of non-Christian religions. A different line leads from the Socinians and Bodin to Dupuis and other Enlightenment figures.

2. Max Müller was profoundly influenced by Schelling, but he renounced grand attempts of a constructive nature.

3. Spengler, of course, renounces a unified construction of the entire course of religious history, but he searches nonetheless for the permeation of matter by idea.

4. The simple fact that various religions are juxtaposed makes it impossible for a synopsis to give an account of continuous evolution. Hegel was able to overcome this difficulty only through forced constructions. Tiele speaks of directions of

evolution: "A religious form is not always transformed completely into another single form. Rather, there arise from it several, different, contemporaneous new forms that evolve independently for centuries." Tiele calls this plurality of developing forms the "divergence of religious evolution" (C. P. Tiele, *Einleitung in die Religionswissenschaft* [Gotha, 1899–1901], p. 130).

5. Historians often deny that even philosophers of religion have a right to make such constructions; cf. Eduard Meyer, *Geschichte des Altertums*, vol. 2, part 1 (Stuttgart, 1921), p. 182. I, too, would attribute no special value to a construction of the whole that was to be drawn up within a philosophical frame.

6. Furthermore, historians of religions should not speak of "development" in the sense of "transformation." The "development" of something that is not religion into religion and of religion into something that is not religion lies outside the sphere of the history of religions proper. Cf. Tiele's remarks, vol. 1, pp. 26ff., and Otto's statements in chapter 14 of *Das Heilige* (chap. 2, n. 4), "Entwicklung," especially his comments on Wundt. With reference to the development of stages of the numinous, many questions remain unanswered.

7. On the idea of progress and the perfection of religion, see below. The philosopher may say, "Religions die, but not religion"; the scholar of religions has no right to make such claims.

8. Tiele, pp. 30–31.

9. Theological histories of religion, both Christian and Islamic, see the founding of their own religion as the climax of religious development. To that time in the future when everything will be complete they assign only secondary significance. Hegel or von Hartmann, however, locate the decisive point in the future; naturally, their notion of "the history of religions" *(Religionsgeschichte)* is modified as a result. In opposition to the "absolute relativism" of both these possibilities, "relative relativism" wishes not to renounce ordering principles nor to deny that ideas permeate matter but to avoid the forced character and the "perspectivism" of "absolute relativism." It is "centralistic" but at the same time "pluralistic."

10. In treating religions of primitive peoples and peoples at lower cultural levels, "history" is possible only in a limited sense.

Naturally, historical development can be studied, but it is difficult to conceive. See the introduction to R. M. Meyer, *Germanische Religionsgeschichte;* cf. Leo Frobenius's studies in the evolution of African religions. The historical study of Australian religions has had to work largely with theoretical constructions.

11. In Tiele's *Kompendium der Religionsgeschichte,* ed. Nathan Söderblom (Berlin, 1920), we read: "The historical study of religions, as distinct from an historical recounting of religions *(eine Geschichte der Religionen),* holds before its eyes the unity of the psychological phenomenon that has manifested itself in so many different ways among different tribes and peoples in the course of centuries. It seeks to track down the original cause *(Ursache)* of this variegated evolution" (p. 5). I must strongly protest against such a view of the historical study of religions. I object first of all to Tiele's psychologizing tendency. It is the task of the philosophy of religion to demonstrate the unity that Tiele, Söderblom, and Heiler postulate, more particularly, the task of the philosophy of the history of religion *(Geschichtsphilosophie der Religion).* In no case must such unity be considered a presupposition of religio-historical work.

12. Tiele succumbs to temptation when he says of the stages of religion, which he understands as "morphs" or "existential forms," that the higher form evolves from the lower (p. 49). Typically, Troeltsch thought that it was not necessary to renounce such an undertaking. In his treatment of the *Wesen* of religion and the history of religions, he expressly demands a philosophy of the history of religion. This philosophy must, in his view, undertake a "critical, evaluative gradation of the historical religious forms" ("Über . . ." [chap. 2, n. 3], p. 489). Such an evaluative gradation will assume different forms when done from the points of view of theology and of the philosophy of history, to say nothing of individual differences—a warning to the history of religions.

13. Herder, too, pledged his allegiance to searching for "monism" in the midst of "pluralistic" perceptions, although in his case the conflict was never fully resolved. His concept of evolution, however, clearly displays its origin in the Enlightenment: it is very uncertain and general, philosophically surmised rather than tested empirically and historically.

14. Like Tiele, Chantepie de la Saussaye distinguishes between genealogical and morphological classifications (see his *Lehrbuch der Religionsgeschichte*, vol. 1, section 2). Both sorts of classification presuppose that a unified, all-encompassing developmental process has been established for religion. Genealogical classification depends upon linguistic relationships, while morphological classification is grounded in value judgments. Chantepie refuses to include the former in the realm of scientific knowledge: "On the one hand, within the same linguistic families there are quite different sorts of religion; on the other, among the so-called lower races the various religions are so similar that a genealogical classification is wholly unfounded." But Chantepie does want to retain genealogical classification for historical treatment. He finds classification according to morphological principle objectionable because, in the course of its development, each historical religion runs through such different phases that one can assign it a firm place only rather dubiously and with little justification.

15. Tiele's classification, as presented in Chantepie's *Lehrbuch* (p. 12), runs as follows:
  I. Religions of Nature
    A. Polyzoic Naturalism (hypothetical)
    B. Polydaemonistic, magical religions dominated by animism (religions of savages)
    C. Refined or Organized Magical Religions
      a. unorganized
      b. organized
    D. The Veneration of Being in Human Form
  II. Ethical Religions (spiritualistic ethical religions of revelation)
    A. National nomistic (nomothetic) religious communities
    B. Universalistic Religious Communities

16. In practice, research concerned with the religions of late antiquity has been exemplary, and the discussions and investigations of ethnologists have, in general, been an exception to the general inattention to theory. Quite apart from their material benefits, ethnological discussions are important methodologically; they have been beneficial not only as applied to the religions of the so-called primitives but also as applied to religions of higher cultures and the place of religion in overall cultural life. I think here especially of the research of the "culture-circle" *(Kulturkreis)* school and its wonderful results. Cf., however, K. Th. Preuss, *Die geistige Kulture der Naturvölker* (Leipzig & Berlin, 1914) and A. Vierkandt, *Naturvölker und Kulturvölker* (Leipzig, 1896).

17. In France, scholars of religions and sociologists work more closely together than they do in Germany. Merely recall the work of Durkheim, Hubert, Mauss, and Lévy-Bruhl. Among German sociologists strictly speaking, Vierkandt and Scheler have especially pointed out these connections.

18. The question of the theoretical relationship between religion and economics—including the Marxists' *Überbau/Unterbau* formula—belongs to the philosophy of history. To assign to the question of the relationship between religion and economics a different place than one assigns to investigations of such relationships as those between religion and art or religion and law would be to make a prior judgment in favor of a certain philosophical point of view. Obviously, the sociology of religion, too, has to proceed in a manner that does not adopt any normative attitude; it must investigate without presuppositions the relations between religion and the state, classes, estates *(Stände)*, and vocations.

19. To reject psychological interpretation on principle is just as false as to make psychological interpretation the only interpretation possible (psychologism). Next to the psychological interpretation of an expression there stands a factual *(sachliche)* interpretation that does not ask about psychology. Cf. my remarks in Chapter 5, my *Erlösungsgedanken* (Leipzig, 1922), especially chapter 1, and, from the theological literature, works on hermeneutics, most recently, the works of Dilthey, Spranger, Freyer, and others.

20. In theology there are two opposing parties. Some wish to introduce religio-psychological questions into the methods of dogmatics and systematic theology; others believe that it is necessary to establish an autonomous branch of research for such questions. The radicals of the first group, such as Vorbrodt, go so far as to demand that the psychology of religion replace dogmatics. Others, such as Pfister, wish to cure dogmatics of its dominat intellectualism through psychologizing. Still others wish to expand boundaries that have been set too narrowly; in doing so, they assign to theology the most amazing

tasks, tasks that are anything but dogmatic. Some, such as Otto Ritschl, have even spoken of a psychological theology.

Chapter Four

1. On the widespread parallels along these lines in various disciplines, see especially the *Festschrift* for Kuno Fischer (chap. 2, n. 14), which was intended to be an introduction to the state of the various philosophical disciplines at the turn of the century.

2. Consider the effects of professionalized philosophy, especially the schools of Husserl, Windelband and Rickert, and Dilthey, on the individual humanistic studies. The effects of "professionalized" philosophy do not, however, in any way exhaust philosophical inclinations in the humanistic studies.

3. C. P. Tiele, *Einleitung* (chap. 3, n. 4), p. 13.

4. Ibid., p. 16.

5. C. P. Tiele, *Grundzüge der Religionswissenschaft* (Tübingen & Leipzig, 1904), pp. 1–2.

6. P. D. Chantepie de la Saussaye, *Lehrbuch der Religionsgeschichte*, p. 5.

7. Louis H. Jordan, *Comparative Religion: Its Genesis and Growth* (New York, 1905); see especially chapter 1.

8. Ernst Troeltsch, "Religionsphilosophie" (chap. 2, n. 14), pp. 492, 498, 427.

9. Ibid., pp. 423–424.

10. The Kantian schools, especially the school of Windelband and Rickert, dominated methodological discussion within the individual humanistic studies for a long time. Today, however, their influence is noticeably waning. Ernst Cassirer's change of mind is extremely typical of the modern era. Cassirer has felt it necessary to modify his standpoint in essentials, and it was no accident that he did so while considering problems significant to ethnology and the history of religions. See his *Die Begriffsform im mythologischen Denken* (chap. 2, n. 8) and *Philosophie der symbolischen Formen* (Berlin, 1923).

11. Ernst Troeltsch, "Wesen der Religion" (chap. 2, n. 3), pp. 460, 461.

12. Ibid., p. 462.

13. Ibid., pp. 468–469.

14. Heinrich Scholz, *Religionsphilosophie* (Berlin, 1921); for what follows, see especially the first chapter of Scholz's introduction.

15. In Scholz's sense, any religion is "experienceable" if it "still today may advance claims to truth or validity that can be seriously discussed" (ibid., p. 36). Whether a claim to truth can be discussed—obviously such a claim is met everywhere— is determined, in Scholz's view, by whether one can seriously consider it.

16. Cf. Wilhelm Dilthey, *Einleitung in die Geisteswissenschaften* (Leipzig, 1883) and *Der Aufbau der geschichtlichen Welt in die Geisteswissenschaften* (Berlin, 1910).

17. Even when this intention is not so prominent as it is among the older and newer Romantics, such as Creuzer, we still encounter the same attempts at "symbolic" interpretation wherever the study of religions attempts to plumb the depths. Consider the works of Bachofen, Nietzsche, Rohde, Klages, and Stucken. These attempts are always beset by the same dangers.

18. It is not without consequence that while my entire work seeks to raise the distinction between religio-historical and philosophical concerns to methodological consciousness, it employs philosophical categories in doing so. As a theory about knowledge in the history of religions, it is itself more an exercise in philosophy than the history of religions.

19. We must guard against a misunderstanding here. Someone may wish to object that all my distinctions are only theoretical, that in practice no one bothers with them. On this view, some philosophize in the midst of empirical work quite apart from such distinctions; they evaluate and speculate without having any clear idea of what they are doing. The rest would leave philosophizing alone even without my instructions, for they avoid such "encroachments" as a matter of principle. It is my opinion, however, that when scholars become clearly aware of methodology, everything that can be attained through the difficult intertwining of philosophy and the empirical will be attained. Those who speculate will recognize when and how they speculate; they will find themselves driven to more careful investigations. Extreme positivists will realize, for their part, that they are in fact more philosophical than they think.

20. The problem of understanding is one the most frequently discussed topics in the philosophy of the humanistic studies. In general, specialists prefer the works of Wilhelm Dilthey. On this question, Dilthey himself must be regarded as a student of Schleiermacher, whom he so greatly admired. Compare the literature cited in Spranger, *Der gegenwärtige Stand der Geisteswissenschaft* (Leipzig, 1922) and my *Erlösungsgedanken* (chap. 3, n. 19). I hope to contribute to the history of hermeneutical theory in another context.

21. In their totality, these disciplines constitute the history of culture *(Kulturgeschichte)*. Naturally, historiography in a narrower sense ("political" history) exhibits successful understanding. In contrast to the historical branches of the various humanistic disciplines, history has more to do with the activities of human beings, with events and developments, than with human objectifications. Naturally, different kinds of understanding are appropriate to these different sorts of scholarship.

22. In order to be critical—and I, too, have expressed similar sentiments ("Zur Methodologie" [chap. 2, n. 10])—scholars today very often go much too far. In formulating his methodology, Spengler actually forbids what he himself does with the greatest success every step of the way. Ernst Troeltsch, too, is so inconsistent that he will not allow European culture to be perceived from the outside, but in his own historical work he does not recognize such limits in theory or practice. Cf. his account of the tasks of the historical study of religions and his works in church history.

23. To have collaborated in such an undertaking was one of the grandest of Troeltsch's scholarly endeavors. In thinking about "cultural synthesis," however, he tries to infer from historical deliberation the inner goals toward which we work, and such thoughts we must leave to one side. We shall never learn from history what we should do; we learn that only from ourselves. Too close a fusion of ethics and the philosophy of history is always questionable. Nevertheless, few have been as aware of the problems and conditioned nature of our times as Troeltsch. Few have known the full complexity of both the questions that relate to culture and the attempts to solve them. Today we have advanced farther, but over and over again a gifted and able spirit will have to attempt to answer, profoundly and

comprehensively, questions about what we are and where we stand. Every more detailed work only makes sense in relation to that goal.

24. The term "relative a priori" derives from Simmel, who borrowed it from Steinthal, just as I have taken it from Frankenberger's essay on the ethno-psychologists (chap. 2, n. 18). Simmel himself deliberately psychologized this originally epistemological category.

25. Historians have already tried to conceive the relative a priori of specific periods and cultures in theoretical terms. Cf. Lamprecht's "diapason" and Spengler's "cultural soul" *(Kulturseele)*. Bernheim has pointed out the dangers, which include hypostasization and schematization. Investigations, however, must go so far as to study even individual differences, a task that is extremely difficult at present. Moreover, such investigations are necessary to clarify the question of understanding. Here belongs the theory of the formation of cultural worlds *(Bildungswelten)* that I demanded in my *Erlösungsgedanken.* Such a theory tries to differentiate and to define, with regard to the particular individual, collective and individual constituents so far as the individual's view of the world *(Weltanschauung)* is concerned. Cf. Ehrenreich's desire for insight into the worldview and conceptual framework of the primitive as preparation for the comparative study of mythology.

26. Examples of psychological types are the types of William James *(The Varieties of Religious Experience* [New York, 1902]) and Heinrich Scholz *(Religionsphilosophie,* vol. 2: *Lebensformen der Religion).* Spranger thinks that we always find the eternal type clothed in historical manifestations, whose particular forms are always determined by the surrounding cultural situation *(Geisteslage).* Nonetheless, such an "eternal" type is fictitious, as Spranger himself recognizes.

27. Troeltsch touches upon these questions when he discusses the relations of history and epistemology in his investigations into the philosophy of history. He wants to adopt a general scheme as the "a priori of the various categories for understanding the foreign." His transition, however, from this position to his basic metaphysical assumption—a doctrine of participation and mystical identity related to notions of Leibniz and Malebranche—is actually a "fatal leap." "This scheme," he writes,

"must ultimately derive from the subconscious or 'superconscious' essence *(Wesen)* of the Spirit common to all. As a result, it leads in the end to a ground common to all the individual spirits. . . ." The matter cannot be conceived so simply, even if Troeltsch's approach really might lead to a solution eventually.

28. The best remarks on this subject are found in Wilhelm von Humboldt's discussion of the tasks of the historiographer. He speaks of an " 'Assimilation' of the investigative power *(Kraft)* and the subject to be investigated."

29. In his theory of understanding, Spranger brings up the case in which the person who is understanding is actually linked in some way to the (earlier) epoch or person that he is trying to understand. In such a case, Spranger says, it is easy to overemphasize what is kindred in the earlier structures of the spirit, and as a result, objectivity is threatened. Here Spranger is already thinking of the actual process of interpretation, but I am still discussing its presuppositions. To my mind, the danger at which Spranger hints is relatively light when compared with the benefit that derives, even in practice, from an affinity between a scholar and the subject that he is studying.

30. It should be obvious that I am not speaking here about detailed work of a historical or systematic sort but of the conditions for a more profound sort of understanding in the history of religions.

31. It frequently happens in practice that internal sympathy entices scholars into subjectivism, but it is not *necessary* for them to be enticed. Just as it is possible to be aware of making value judgments and either to make such judgments or to refrain from doing so, the researcher will have to take accout of— and hold himself accountable for—the extent to which he may be credited with scientific objectivity.

32. Dilthey's teaching on the relation between experience *(Erlebnis)* and understanding *(Verstehen)* has often been misunderstood in this way. Even Simmel probably overestimates the "external experience *[Erfahrung]*."

33. "Poetic creation always begins from life-experience *[Lebenserfahrung]*, either personal experience *[Erlebnis]* or the understanding of other human beings, present as well as past, and the events in which they took part. Each of the countless

situations *[Lebenszustände]* through which a poet passes can be designated experience *[Erlebnis]* in a psychological sense. Only those moments of his existence *[Dasein]* that disclose to him one of life's characteristics possess a deeper relationship to his poetry" (Wilhelm Dilthey, *Das Erlebnis und die Dichtung* [Leipzig, 1913], p. 198).

34. I intend to return to these connections in another context. I have touched upon them here only in order to draw attention to them in a general sort of way.

35. I should emphasize once again that the procedure I describe here is not limited to treating "great" personalities, objects, and occurrences that are difficult to interpret, that is, to special phenomena in the subjective *(seelisch)* or objective world. All understanding and interpretation must be founded in this way, even the understanding and interpretation of the smallest individuality, of each particular trait of a cultural or psychological phenomenon.

36. I should note that, all differences in method aside—strictness and exactitude versus irregularity and restlessness—profound seriousness, without which such a condition and activity of the soul is unthinkable, is the best criterion for distinguishing the beginnings of scholarly inquiry from every form of aesthetic appreciation. Many undertake such an aesthetic approach to religions these days, in order to enjoy the ecstasy and fascination of the exotic. As Kierkegaard has shown, the aesthete is unable to see what is crucial in a religion—and not just in the Christian religion. Such a person is always content simply to taste the aesthetically beautiful.

37. By acquiring specific "points of orientation"—by observing the predominance of certain spheres (cult, ritual) and the preponderance of particular moments (laws of purification, service to the ancestors), by studying the attributes of the divinity, such as its relation to ethical and numinous predicates and its connection with and ordering in the given situation (the "valence" of individual moments)—it is possible to understand the structure of a religion and to approach its center. The scholar will thus be able to determine the specific "weight" that belongs to a particular set of expressions in the entire structure of a religion, a task that corresponds to organizing certain individual traits into an entire historical image. But each of these par-

ticular sets is also a world unto itself, with its own structure that must be understood; cultus, for example, consists of sacrifice, prayer, liturgical celebrations, and so on. And each of these activities possesses its own "meaning" *(Sinn)* that is to be ascertained by study and grasped from the spirit of the entire religion. What does this custom or that statement "mean"? In a specific form—for example, prayer—we can clearly perceive how an organization and classification presents itself to scholars in individual forms. The structure is contained in the fixed form, the formula, of the prayer. In individual instances (say, specific prayers), this structure is fitted out with specific meanings, almost with pluses and minuses of meaning, and religious forms exhibit the most varied possibilities of meaning.

38. Seen from the objective side, this is the "conflict" of all "culture." Simmel has seen fully the need to ground this fact in a metaphysic of life. In doing so, he pursues what had also been Hegel's intention. Cf. his *Lebensanschauung: Vier metaphysische Kapitel* (Munich & Leipzig, 1918), especially chapters 1 and 2.

Chapter Five

1. That does not mean, however, that we should introduce the unfortunate question of the "essential nature" *(Wesen)* of religion, which, as we have seen, has been the source of so much confusion. That question is inappropriate to the notion of systematization that I have in mind, because it can never be addressed by purely empirical means. Like the attempt to square the circle, it is condemned to fail from the very beginning, for it seeks to infer the normative from the empirical (history). Such an attempt would have no choice but to introduce nonempirical points of view into the history of religions. Within the bounds set for the history of religions, it is not possible to transcend the merely historical by introducing the question of the *Wesen* of religion.

2. The clearest account is still Scheler's; cf. his *Vom Ewigen im Menschen* (Leipzig, 1921), pp. 373–374. In discussing the required distinction, Scheler recalls the example of the jurists, who have long been accustomed sharply to distinguish dogmatic

and systematic studies from studies in the history of law. For a fundamental critique of Scheler's views on the philosophy of religion and his conception of the history of religions, see my essay, "Problem der 'externen' Würdigung" (chap. 2, n. 10). I have already emphasized the need for a fundamental separation of the history of religions and the historical study of religions in my *Erlösungsgedanken* (chap. 3, n. 19); see esp. p. 13, n. 6.

3. Edmund Hardy, "Was ist Religionswissenschaft?" (chap. 1, n. 1), pp. 9 & 17.

4. C. P. Tiele, *Einleitung* (chap. 4, n. 3), p. 15.

5. Ibid., p. 16.

6. Hardy, "Was ist Religionswissenschaft?", p. 11.

7. Friedrich Heiler, *Das Gebet*, 2nd ed. (Munich, 1920), pp. 16ff.

8. Ibid., p. 17.

9. Ibid., pp. 22ff.

10. Ibid, p. 23.

11. Cf. ibid., p. 24.

12. Heinrich Scholz, *Religionsphilosophie* (chap. 4, n. 14), pp. 41ff.

13. Ibid., p. 42.

14. Whether in Simmel's sense (cf. *Die Religion* [Frankfurt am Main, 1906]) or Cassirer's, whose large-scale attempt at a philosophy of symbolic forms, especially in relation to a declared phenomenology of mythical and religious thought, is of the greatest interest to the student of religion. However valuable Cassirer's work may be, it can never deny or escape the deleterious effects of starting from Kant's subjectivistic epistemology, despite every concession to "objectivism." Cassirer's "theory of the forms of spiritual expression" remains, as a result, an investigation "of the fundamental ways of understanding the world." It will never be able to understand the objective structure of the objectifications of the spirit, for there is no path that leads from the realm of the invesitgation of subjectivity to the "objective." When Cassirer's phenomenology of the linguistic form does manage to identify structures and the regularities that govern such structures, he has actually set aside his subjectivistic point of departure and worked in accordance with "realistic" presuppositions.

15. Rudolf Stammler, *Theorie der Rechtswissenschaft* (Halle, 1923); on what follows, cf. section 7 of the introduction.

16. See chapter 3 above. What is most important for the historian is the particular, not the typical. As we shall see, it is above all formal systematization that starts out from the typical.

17. There are many parallels to my conception of these tasks in the literature of sociology. See, for example, Georg Simmel, *Soziologie* (Leipzig, 1908) and Siegfried Kracauer, *Soziologie als Wissenschaft* (Dresden, 1922).

18. See Rudolf Otto, *Visnu-Narayana* (Jena, 1909).

19. Thus, Jordan writes: "Comparative Religion is that Science which compares the origin, structure, and characteristics of the various religions of the world, with the view of determining their genuine agreements and differences, the measure of relation in which they stand to one another, and their relative superiority or inferiority when regarded as types" (*Comparative Religion* [chap. 4, n. 7], p. 63).

20. Material systematization, therefore, designates a sort of mean between historical work and strictly systematic, that is, formal systematic, work. Formal systematization is totally alien to history *(Historie)*. Historical work will be altered by material systematization, but only to the extent that such systematization is a means of grasping the "flux" of historical development. Thus, the historian G. A. H. von Below, for example, in his *Die deutsche Geschichtsschreibung*, 2nd ed. (Munich & Breslau, 1924), does not wish to remain in the realm of the type but only to "use analogy to depict the particular in its own value" (pp. 150–151).

21. Both theology and ethnology (for example, Ratzel, Frobenius, Gräbner) have tended to focus upon questions of origin, diffusion, and migration. Without uncritically embracing notions about "elementary thoughts," one must emphasize in opposition to this theological and ethnological tendency the need for a strictly objective interpretive analysis in relation to questions of both "how" and "when" and a thorough psychological investigation. Philology, too—both classical and Indo-European philology—has a particularly bad record, and it needs to hear repeatedly that the historical study of language is not the historical study of religion and that the history of a word is not the history of its meaning *(Bedeutung)*. Philologists who study religion quite often fail to recognize the significance of changes in meaning *(Sinn)*.

22. A mere comparison of "form," a system that classified according to external similarities (analogies)—such as Ehrenreich ascribes to comparative mythology—would be of little value. As Ehrenreich demands, we need evidence of an internal relationship, evidence that can be obtained only through interpreting and explaining content.

23. Proponents of the "culture history method," in opposing the one-sided views that result from notions about "elementary thoughts," do not pay sufficient attention to the danger of taking recourse all too rashly to filiations and causal series. In other respects, the criteria and correctives that Gräbner advances for comparison as a methodological resource deserve careful attention (cf. Gräbner, *Methode der Ethnologie* [1911], esp. pp. 57ff.). He is quite correct in drawing attention to the phenomenon of convergence that has recently become a center of attention and that can explain the same sorts of phenomena as the notions of elementary thoughts and migratory hypotheses. Gräbner's emphasis on the environment as a determining factor also seems to me to be an important corrective to the overvaluation of the "criterion of form."

24. Obviously, comparison is not in any way limited to the totality of phenomena, that is, to the entire religion. The individual parts can themselves be compared. The only stipulation is that the immanent context must be preserved.

25. It is disputed, of course, whether one can come to know "monasticism" from a single example whose essential nature has been intuited by means of eidetic abstraction (Husserl), or whether several examples are necessary—so that the concept is enriched and completed by degrees—or whether such a notion can in general be obtained only as a generalized abstraction. It is necessary here to distinguish between the procedure of a systematization that is oriented toward concrete, empirical, and historical phenomena and philosophical systematization in a more specific sense. The latter is used not in the systematic study of religions but in the philosophy of religion.

26. But how remarkably naive and paltry Tiele's results are! Consider, for example, volume 1, chapter 10, of his *Einleitung* (chap. 4, n. 3), where Tiele claims to set forth the "chief law of religious evolution," and chapter 8, which discusses the "laws of evolution." This second chapter attempts to prove

two entirely different things: the evolution of religion is seen
as (1) the "necessary perfection of all human evolution" and
(2) "the consequence of the impulse that self-consciousness
receives through contact with another evolution, whether higher
or lower." Tiele's concern to work out "directions of evolution"
is more fruitful (chapters 6 & 7). In the time since Tiele made
his attempt, research has become extremely specialized. Work
in psychology has become much more subtle and thorough.
At the same time, the prospect has appeared of studying the
movement of the objective world. As a result, much that is
completely new must be taken into account.

Appendix

1. Cf. especially the chapter, "Probleme der Religion," in Scheler's *Vom Ewigen im Menschen* (chap. 5, n. 2), and his fundamental
   investigation of *Formalismus in der Ethik und die materiale Wert-
   ethik* (Halle, 1921).

2. Today it is above all Dilthey's school that, next to Rickert and
   his followers, considers these questions. In addition to the works
   of Dilthey and Troeltsch, I should mention those of Simmel,
   Spranger, and Littl. I am greatly indebted to H. Freyer, who
   has laid the foundations for such a philosophy of culture in
   his recent volume, *Theorie des objektiven Geistes* (Leipzig, 1923).

3. Cf. Frankenberger (chap. 2, n. 19).

4. Hermann Siebeck, *Zur Religionsphilosophie* (Tübingen, 1907), p.
   265.

5. Ibid., p. 266.

6. Ibid., p. 164.

7. Intellectualism and rationalism, too, for which especially Scheler
   and Pfister have rebuked Protestant theology. As Pfister demonstrates, intellectualism and rationalism have also dominated
   the questions posed by the history of religions. The strong
   overvaluation of all theoretical expressions also belongs here.

8. Especially characteristic of this is William James's philosophy
   and psychology of religion. James often explicitly advocates
   individualism even in theory. Wundt has correctly taken exception to this notion.

9. Hermann Usener, *Götternamen: Versuch einer Lehre von der religiösen Begriffsbildung* (Bonn, 1896).

10. One should also not forget the so-called literary-historical criticism of the Old and New Testaments as practiced by Gunkel, Dibelius, and Bultmann.

Index

INTRODUCTION
TO
THE HISTORY
OF RELIGIONS

lies behind objectifications. They must pursue regularities or types of religious experience—a task apart from which historical and systematic work is unthinkable. Penetrating the inner religious state is the concern of the psychology of religion. For some time, scholars thought of psychology as a key that could open every door. Today, we have come to recognize its uses and its limits.

Religion is not only and, from a genetic point of view, not originally a matter of the individual. At the very least, it is also a matter of the community, it is also social. Just as religion can unite a group of prople, it can itself also be conditioned by the character of the community. A special branch of study is devoted to these reciprocal relations: the sociology of religion.

In sum, we may say that the history of religions studies religion as an internal and external phenomenon, and it studies the latter in terms of theoretical (myth, doctrine, dogma), practical (cult, rite), and sociological forms (religious community, congregation).

Already in antiquity people were interested in foreign religions. Travelers, philosophers, and historians fostered and contributed to knowledge of such religions. Here the intellectual flexibility of the Greeks and their openness to the world had beneficial results. Scientific sensitivity first began to stir in the Greek world. In some areas of study, the value of information provided by ancient authors is still inestimable. In contrast to the Greek pursuit of knowledge for its own sake, the concern for foreign religions among early Christian writers was purposeful and oriented toward their own interests. It is true that we owe a considerable amount of important information to apologetic zeal. During the Middle Ages, three major movements of expansion added to knowledge of non-Christian religions: the crusades, missionary enterprises conducted by religious orders, and travels such as those of Marco Polo.

More recently, our knowledge of these religions has grown immensely. Discoveries, a new interest in antiquity (the Renaissance, humanism), and a new interest in matters of faith as a result of schisms within Christendom, have intensified both practical and scholarly interest in religion and religions.

The age of the "system of nature" (the Enlightenment) marked the dawn of a new day in the history of European concern with foreign religions. The Enlightenment distinguished between natural religion and positive religions, and it sought to probe natural religion philosophically. In addition, the amount of information about positive religions was growing steadily. But still, there was no single point of view that could unify studies motivated by philosophical, theological, philological, antiquarian, and exotic interests. Herder, a German driven not by clear systematic interests but by an anticipation of what was needed, full of enthusiasm and full of ideas, became the actual father of the modern history of religions. His extremely fascinating personality combined tendencies that would soon cause scholarship to fragment in many different directions: religious and aesthetic, philosophical and psychological, philological and archeological, historical and ethnological. After Herder, only Hegel and Schleiermacher displayed a similar universality. But these two men were, and wanted to be, primarily philosophers or theologians. They provided much stimulus for the history of religions, but they could not develop it into an independent discipline.

Schleiermacher's *Speeches* stand at the beginning of the nineteenth century. This century presents us with an immense amount of research, but research that is still quite diverse. The powerful development of philology, above all the study of Oriental languages and cultures, was of great significance for the study of religions, even though this study was not immune from the excesses of philologism. Ethnology has continually broadened our knowledge of primitive peoples; it has made an immense amount of material available for the study of religions. Archeology has unearthed monuments, and the study of prehistory has revealed previously unknown epochs. To all this, the nineteenth century added the work of the two

arises very late, if at all. More clearly than in a rationalistic philosophy of religion, a mystical philosophy of religion displays a distinctive attitude toward life *(Lebensgefühl)*, an attitude that is bound up with certain conceptions of God, the world, nature, and humanity. As long as mysticism remains within certain qualitative and quantitative bounds, it may be satisfied with the positive religion with which it is associated; but frequently mystical piety transcends these bounds, and then there are great conflicts between mystics and the religious community. Such conflicts are familiar from the histories of Christianity, Judaism, and Islam. The consequences of these conflicts can be devastating, because in contrast to the rationalistic philosophy of religion, a mystical philosophy of religion exercises a direct effect on practical life. In spite of the mystic's basic mistrust of reason, philosophically inclined mystics work by rational means. Paradoxically, mystical doctrine becomes developed into a full-fledged philosophy of religion. Mystics such as Eckhart, ibn Arabi, Shankara, and Ramanuja rank with the most outstanding thinkers in the history of human thought.

Of course, these two types of philosophy of religion—rationalistic and mystical—are not absolutely distinct from one another. Just as a mystical philosophy of religion often displays the influence of the rational, so the rationalistic approach is affected by mysticism. Consider Thomas Aquinas, al Ghazali, and Nagarjuna. But every philosophy of religion, whatever its stance toward the positive religion—interpretive, critical, or opposed—has an affect upon the positive religion from which it derives.

As I have discussed it so far, the philosophy of religion works on the whole to support and develop the truth contained in revelation. In no way does this activity exclude criticism of or opposition to dogma. This sort of philosophy of religion must elaborate and analyze religious knowledge (epistemology); it must formulate the view of nature and destiny contained in positive revelation (cosmology; philosophy of nature; philosophy of history); and it must formulate the implicit view of humanity, its nature and disposition (anthropology and ethics). As long as the philosophy of religion is concerned with elaborating dogma in the narrower sense, it simply continues the dogmatic task with other tools (philosophical tools). Where, however, the "expansion" of dogma leads to a systematically developed worldview, albeit a worldview derived from a particular revelation, criticism, discussion, and opposition will arise. This stage has been reached by Christianity, Judaism, Islam, Zoroastrianism, Buddhism, and Hinduism, and also in China. From this situation of conflict arises the need for polemics and apologetics; where a philosophy of religion rooted in revelation is put on the defensive, apologetics and polemics become decisively important religio-philosophical tasks.

Philosophical Consideration of Ultimate Questions Independently of a Positive Religion

The emancipation of philosophical reflection from concrete religions and from worldviews based on them has taken place, strictly speaking, only in the Western world. Of course, in East Asia, thought is in general less constrained than anywhere else in the Orient, and there we do encounter "autonomous" thought. In India, too, individual movements and persons have freed themselves from traditional speculations. But except for sporadic occurrences, such as mysticism, Greek influence on Judaism and Islam has led to no fundamental separation of philosophy from religion. In the West, by contrast, a unique "theoretical" and then a "scientific" attitude flourished first in Greece, and a radical separation of thought from the inherited faith was the result. Critique and opposition appeared alongside the defense, elaboration, and transformation of the religious view—that is, alongside interpretation. In addition to a philosophy of religion profoundly oriented toward revealed faith (both Greek and Near Eastern), then, late antiquity also knew autonomous speculation. In the East such independence has scarcely ever been achieved, even if we keep in mind that often in the East, especially in Islamic countries, the political situation has necessitated dissimulation, so that

Index

Godwin, William, 193
Goethe, J. W. von, 105
Goldziher, Ignacz, 65–66
Göttinger, 209n
Gräbner, Fritz, 222–23n
Grimme, Hubert, 66
Grünwedel, Albert, 74
Gunkel, Hermann, 225n
Guyau, Marie Jean, 90

Haas, Hans, 106, 167
Hamann, Johann Georg, 174, 195
Hardy, Edmund, 122–23, 124, 130, 200n, 201n, 221n
Harnack, Adolf von, 37, 55, 148, 209n
Hartmann, Eduard von, 55, 90, 147, 149, 175, 196, 210n
Hauer, Jakob Wilhelm, 206n
Hauser, J. W., 167
Hegel, G. W. F., xviii, xxii, 14, 24, 36, 40, 54, 58, 73, 82, 96, 138, 141, 144, 147, 149, 166, 167, 174, 177–78, 196, 207n, 209n, 210n, 220n
Hegelianism, 150
Heidegger, Martin, 175
Heiler, Friedrich, 124–26, 148, 167, 211n, 221n
Heraclitus, 194
Herbert of Cherbury, 173
Herder, J. G., 36, 43, 54, 59–60, 67, 138, 141, 144, 154, 166, 174, 177, 195, 207n, 208n, 211n
Hermeneutical circle (parts and whole), xv, 38–40, 156–57

Hermeneutics, history of, xv, 153–54
Herzfeld, Ernst E., 74
Hirt, H. E., 73
Historical study of religions (*Religionsgeschichte*), xix–xx, 4, 10, 12, 19, 53–71, 94–95, 209n, 211n
general, xx, 53–62
specialized, xx, 62–71
Historicism, xxvi, 100, 124
History, 8, 10, 16, 27, 30, 83, 101–102, 216n
History of religions (*Religionswissenschaft*)
amount of material for, 27–28
empirical character of, xiv, xix, xxvii, 4, 19, 37, 43, 46–47, 49–51, 82–83, 88, 94, 100, 128, 159, 204n, 220n
historical and systematic, xiv, xix, 19–20, 39, 53, 64–66, 76, 121–22, 123–24, 141–42, 164, 204n, 220–21n. *See also* Historical Study of Religions; Systematic Study of Religions
history of, xxv–xxvi, 7–8, 11–13, 161, 165, 167, 209n
institutional place of, 11–12, 43
presuppositions for studying, 100–116
tasks, 161–62, 164–65
terminology, 11, 94–95, 122–23, 159, 200–201n, 203n